MADRAS GOVERNMENT MUSEUM

Bulletin, Vol. II. No. 1.

ANTHROPOLOGY

MADRAS GOVERNMENT MUSEUM

Bulletin, Vol. II. No. 1.

ANTHROPOLOGY

**Badagas and Irulas of the Nilgiris;
Paniyans of Malabar; A Chinese-Tamil Cross;
A Cheruman Skull; Kuruba or Kurumba;
Summary of Results.**

With Seventeen Plates.

BY

EDGAR THURSTON,

SUPERINTENDENT, MADRAS GOVERNMENT MUSEUM.

GYAN

Published by

GYAN

Gyan Publishing House
5, Ansari Road
Daryaganj, New Delhi-110002
Phone: 011-47034999, 9811692060
E-mail: books@gyanbooks.com

Distribution Network
gyanbooks.com
India, USA, Canada, UK, Australia, France

ISBN : 978-81-212-3143-5 (PB)
First Published, 1897

2nd Impression 2020

Printed at: Gyan Press, Delhi.

Madras Government Museum
Author: Edgar Thurston

MADRAS GOVERNMENT MUSEUM.

Bulletin, Vol. II, No. 1.

ANTHROPOLOGY.

Badagas and Irulas of the Nilgiris;
Paniyans of Malabar; A Chinese-Tamil Cross;
A Cheruman Skull; Kuruba or Kúrumba;
Summary of Results.

With Seventeen Plates.

BY

EDGAR THURSTON,

SUPERINTENDENT, MADRAS GOVERNMENT MUSEUM.

MADRAS:

PRINTED BY THE SUPERINTENDENT, GOVERNMENT PRESS.

1897.

Madras Government Museum Bulletins.

BY EDGAR THURSTON.

Vol. I.

No. 1.—Pearl and Chank Fisheries of the Gulf of Manaar.

No. 2.—Note on Tours along the Malabar Coast.

No. 3.—Rámésvaram Island and Fauna of the Gulf of Manaar.

No. 4.—Anthropology of the Todas and Kotas of the Nilgiri Hills; and of the Bráhmans, Kammálans, Pallis and Pariahs of Madras City.

MADRAS GOVERNMENT MUSEUM.

Bulletin, Vol. II, No. 1.

ANTHROPOLOGY.

Badagas and Irulas of the Nīlgiris;
Paniyans of Malabar; A Chinese-Tamil Cross;
A Cheruman Skull; Kuruba or Kurumba;
Summary of Results.

With Seventeen Plates.

BY

EDGAR THURSTON,

SUPERINTENDENT, MADRAS GOVERNMENT MUSEUM.

MADRAS:

PRINTED BY THE SUPERINTENDENT, GOVERNMENT PRESS.

1897.

CONTENTS.

	PAGE
Badagas of the Nilgiris	1 – 7
Irulas of the Nilgiris	8 – 17
Paniyans of Malabar	18 – 30
A Chinese-Tamil Cross	31 – 32
A Cheruman Skull	33 – 37
Kuruba or Kurumba	38 – 43
Summary of Results	44 – 68

PL. I

GROUP OF BADAGAS

ANTHROPOLOGY.

THE BADAGAS OF THE NILGIRIS.

As the Todas are the pastoral, and the Kotas the artisan tribe of the Nílgiris, so the agricultural element on these hills is represented by the Badagas (or, as they are sometimes called, Burghers), whose number was returned as 29,613 at the Census 1891 against 24,130 at the previous Census. But, though the primary occupation of the Badagas is agriculture, there are, among their community, bricklayers, carpenters, tailors, sawyers, barbers, washermen, &c., and many work for Europeans as coolies on tea and coffee estates.

The name Badaga or Vadugan means 'northerner,' and the Badagas, who speak a language allied to Kanarese, are no doubt descended from Kanarese Hindu colonists from the Mysore country, who migrated, probably about three centuries ago, to the hills owing to famine, political turmoil, or local oppression in their own country. They have a tradition that five hundred years ago there were seven brothers living with their sister at a place called Badaghalli near Mysore. A Muhammadan Nawāb fell in love with, and asked the permission of the brothers to marry the girl, and they, being afraid of him, ran away and settled on the Nílgiri plateau.

Among the Badagas six distinct septs are recognised, viz.:—

Udaya (or Wodeyar).	Lingāyats ..	High caste.
Adhikāri	Do. ..	Do.
Kanaka	Do. ..	Do.
Hāruva	Saivites ..	Do.
Badaga	Do. ..	Do.
Toraya	Do. ..	Low caste.

The Hāruva, Adhikāri, Kanaka, and Badaga septs are permitted to intermarry one with the other, whereas the Udayas and Torayas may only marry into their own sept.

The Hāruvas wear the Brāhmanical thread, and it has been suggested by Mr. Natesa Sastri that they were originally poor Brāhman priests, who migrated with the Badagas to the Nílgiris. The Torayas are the lowest sept, and do menial work for the other septs, which regard them as sons or servants. Toraya women are distinguished by wearing bangles of glass and base metal round the left wrist. The Udaya, Hāruva, and Adhikāri septs are vegetarians, whereas the Kanakas, Badagas and Torayas are permitted to eat both animal and vegetable food. It is said that the vegetarian Adhikāri, if he marries into a flesh-eating caste, betakes himself to the new diet very readily—more readily, in fact, than an Englishman of my acquaintance, who had to abandon his carnivorous habits as a condition of acceptance by a vegetarian lady.

Living in extensive villages, generally on the summit of a low hillock, composed of rows of comfortable thatched or tiled houses, and surrounded by the fields which yield the crops of korāli (*Setaria italica*), sāmai (*Panicum miliare*), &c., the Badagas would seem, at first sight, to be a prosperous and thriving community as compared with the other tribes of the Nílgiris. A great newspaper discussion was recently carried on as to their condition, and whether they are a down-trodden race, bankrupt and impoverished to such a degree that it is only a short time before something must be done to ameliorate their condition, and save them from extermination by inducing them to emigrate to the Wynâd and the Vizagapatam district. After reading much, and hearing and seeing more of the Badagas, I am on the side of one who wrote to the effect that "so far from approaching ruin, the Badaga is in a far better condition than he was some years ago. The tiled houses, costing from Rs. 250 to Rs. 500, certainly point to their prosperity. They may frequently borrow from the Lubbay to enable them to build, but, as I do not know of a single case in which the Lubbay has ever seized the house and sold it, I believe this debt is soon discharged. The walled-in, terraced fields immediately around their villages, on which they grow their barley and other grains requiring rich cultivation, are well worked and regularly manured. The coats, good thick blankets, and gold ear-rings, which most Badagas now possess, can only, I think, point to their prosperity, while their constant feasts, and disinclination to work on Sundays, show that the loss of a few days' pay does not affect them."

PL. II

BADAGA MAN.

The Badaga ceremonies and rites have been so fully described by others[1] that I shall only touch lightly on this already well-trodden ground.

In his religion the Badaga is polytheistic and a demonolater, worshipping a select number of major, and thirty-three crores[2] of minor gods, and attributing fever contracted by being out after dark, and other ailments and mishaps, to the influence of devils. Worship is performed in all manner of edifices, from a small jungle or road-side shrine to the big temple with gopurams at Karamadai at the foot of the hills, whereat the Badaga worships in common with other Hindu sects and Todas. Their gods are represented by human images of gold and silver, stone bulls and roughly-hewn stones, to which oblations of milk are offered when a cow refuses to give milk in proper quantity. In omens, both good and bad, they believe implicitly. Among the former are reckoned two Brāhmans, a jackal, or a milk-pot in front, whereas a snake passing in front, a woman with her hair down her back, a widow, or a single Brāhman going before are harbingers of evil.

The investiture of youths of the Lingāyat sept with the badge of his religion, the linga or phallic emblem, which is tied round his neck, is the occasion of a solemn ceremonial, accompanied by payment of fees to the officiating priest, who acts as Grand Master of the Order, the pouring of an offering of the milk of cows and buffaloes into a rivulet, and a feast. When a Badaga lad has reached the youthful years at which he is expected to be of use to the community, he is instructed in the important duty of milking the cattle, and permitted to enter thenceforth within the milk-house (hāgōtu), wherein no female may set foot.

In the Udaya sept, according to Mr. Natesa Sastri, there is nothing in the nature of courtship, but the father settles the bride or bridegroom for his child. In the other septs a simple form of sexual selection takes place, and engagement, soon followed by marriage on an auspicious day, is announced as the result of a brief period of courtship, which affords some opportunity for testing compatibility or incompatibility. The marriage bond is not, however, really,

---

[1] S. M. Natesa Sastri, *Madras Christian College Magazine*, April and May 1892, Vol. IX, Nos. 10–11; Grigg, *Manual of the Nilagiri District*, 1880.

[2] A crore = 10,000,000.

sealed until the fifth month of the first pregnancy, when the relatives are invited to be present at the ceremony of kanni-kattēdu, or tying the marriage emblem round the neck of the woman. If, when he is performing this function, the husband gets the string entangled in his wife's hair, he is fined for carelessness. As a sign that a girl has reached puberty, and is available for matrimonial purposes, she is tattooed on the forehead with a needle dipped in the blacks collected from a cooking-pot and mixed with oil.

The funeral rites of the Badagas are carried out with a ceremonial very similar to that of the Kotas, which I have already described as an eye-witness (Bull: No. 4), and Kotas are engaged as musicians. In the course of these rites, an elder, standing by the corpse, offers up a prayer that the dead may not go to hell, that the sins committed on earth may be forgiven, and that the sins may be borne by a calf, which is let loose in the jungle, and used thenceforth for no manner of work. This Badaga custom of dedicating a scape-calf is of distinct interest, when compared with the Levitican dedication of a scape-goat. "But the goat on which the lot fell to be the scape-goat shall be presented alive before the Lord to make an atonement with him, and to let him go for a scape-goat in the wilderness, and the goat shall bear upon him all their iniquities unto a land not inhabited." (Lev. XVI, 10; 22).

A quarter of a century ago, a Badaga could be at once picked out from the other tribes of the Nílgiris by his wearing a turban. But, in the present advanced age, when 'manners and customs' are undergoing rapid modification owing to the influence of domestication and contact with Europeans, not only does the Toda occasionally appear in the national head-dress, but even Irulas and Kurumbas, who, only a short time ago, were buried in the jungles, living like pigs and bears on roots, honey, and other minor forest produce, turn up on Sundays in the Kotagiri bazār, clad in turban and coat of English cut. And, as the less civilised tribes don the turban, so the college student abandons this picturesque form of head-gear in favour of the less becoming, and less washable, pork-pie cap, while the Badaga glories in a knitted night-cap of flaring red or orange hue.

In colour the Badagas are lighter than the other hill-tribes, and the pallor of the skin is specially noticeable in the females, whom, with very few exceptions, I was only

PL. III.

BADAGA MAN.

able to study by surreptitious examination when we met on the roads. In physique the typical Badaga is below middle height, smooth-skinned, of slender build, with narrow chest and shoulders.

Like other Kanarese classes which I have investigated, the Badagas have, as shown in the subjoined tabular statement, a short span of the arms relative to the stature, when compared with many of the Tamil classes :—

		Span of arms relative to stature=100.
Kotas.	Kanarese?	103·3
Koramas.	Kanarese	103·2
Kurubas.	Do.	104·3
Badagas.	Do.	104·6
Kanarese Pariahs.	Kanarese	105·1
Tamil Pariahs.	Tamil	106·1
Tamil Brāhmans.	Do.	106·6
Kammālans.	Do.	107·1
Ambattans.	Do.	107·2
Vellālas.	Do.	107·2

The average distance from the tip of the middle finger to the top of the patella (knee-cap) in the position of 'attention' with the muscles of the thigh relaxed, is in the Badagas, as in two other Kanarese classes which I have examined (Kurubas and Koramas) considerable. But this character is discussed later on (p. 48).

The average height of the Badaga, according to my measurements, is 164·1 cm. One man (not included in the averages), whose father was still taller than himself, was 183·2 cm. high. The measurements of this man, as compared with the Badaga average, were as follows :—

	CM.	Badaga average. CM.
Height	183·2	164·1
,, sitting	92·8	84·5
,, kneeling	134	120·8
Span of arms	193·2	171·7
Shoulders	44·3	39·4
Cubit	50·6	46·2
Hand, length	19·5	17·7
Middle finger	13	11·5
Hips	30·1	26·6
Foot, length	28·1	25

The typical tribal costume of the Badaga men consists of langūti, white turban, and long body-cloth with red and blue stripes wrapped round them "so loosely that, as a man works in the fields, he is obliged to stop between every few strokes of his hoe, to gather up his cloth and throw one end over his shoulder." Male adornment with jewelry is limited to gold ear-rings, a silver bangle on the wrist, and silver, copper or brass rings.

As types of female attire, jewelry and tattooing, the following 'cases' may be cited :—

Girl, aged 13. Tattooed on forehead (pl. IV-A I). White cloth covering body, and white under-cloth tied round chest, tightly wrapped square across the breasts and reaching to knees. Gold ornament in left nostril, necklets of small glass beads, and of large glass beads with two silver ornaments.

Woman, aged 30. Body clothing the same as preceding. White cotton cap on head (pl. IV). Tattooed on forehead (pl. IV-A 1); spot on chin; double row of dots on each upper arm over deltoids (pl. IV-A 2); and pattern on right fore-arm (pl. IV-A 3). Gold ornament in left nostril. Gold ring in lobe of each ear. Necklets of small glass beads and of silver links with four-anna piece pendent. Silver armlet above right elbow. Four copper armlets above left elbow. Four silver, and seven composition bangles on left fore arm. Two silver rings on right ring-finger; two steel rings on left finger.

Woman, aged 45. Tattooed on forehead (pl. IV-A 4); single row of dots over right deltoid; pattern on left fore-arm (pl. IV-A 5); and three dots on back of left wrist.

Woman, aged 35. Tattooed on forehead (pl. IV-A 1); quadruple row of dots over right deltoid; and star on right forearm (pl. IV-A 6).

Woman, aged 30. Tattooed like the preceding on forehead and upper arm; spot on chin; elaborate device on right forearm (pl. IV-A 7); and star on back of right hand.

Woman, aged 35. Tattooed like the two preceding on forehead and upper arm; double row of dots and star on right forearm (pl. IV-A 8).

Woman, aged 40. Tattooed like the three preceding on forehead and upper arm; elaborate device on right forearm (pl. IV-A 3); triple row of dots on back and front of left wrist; and double row of dots with circle surrounded by dots across chest (pl. IV-A 9).

PL. IV.

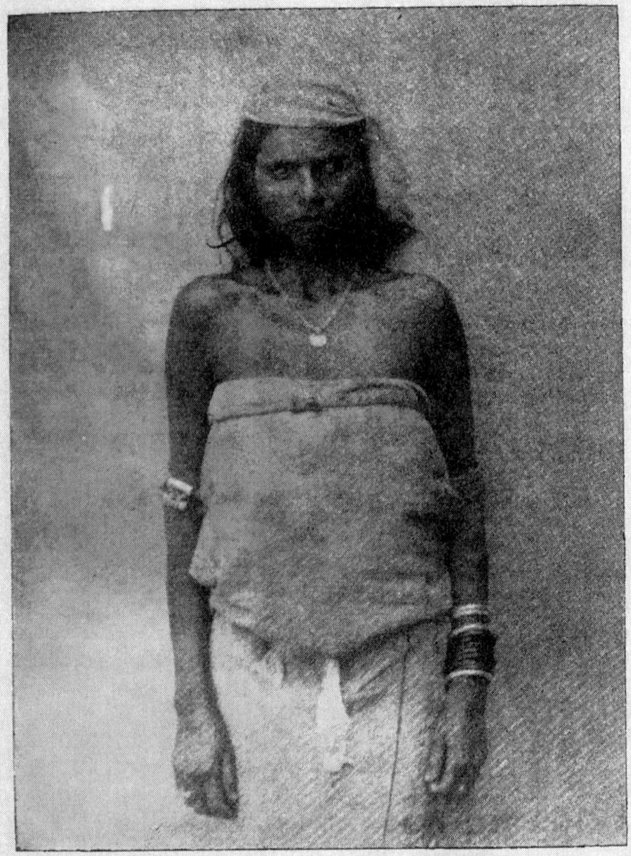

BADAGA WOMAN.

TABLE I.

SUMMARY OF MEASUREMENTS.

BADAGAS.

	Max.	Min.	Average.	Mean above.	Mean below.
Weight	125	90	105	115	98
Height	180·2	154	164·1	169·4	159·9
Height, sitting	89·2	80·7	84·5	87·3	82·4
Height, kneeling	130·5	114·3	120·8	124·1	117·2
Height to gladiolus	138	116	123·7	128	119·9
Span of arms	191	158·4	171·7	176·8	166·7
Chest	87	73	80·4	8·3	77·7
Middle finger to patella ...	17·4	7·8	12·2	14·5	10·6
Shoulders	43·8	36·2	39·4	40·7	38·3
Cubit	49·7	42·6	46·2	47·5	44·9
Hand, length	19·2	16	17·7	18·2	17·2
Hand, breadth	8·7	7·5	8·1	8·3	7·9
Middle finger	12·3	10·7	11·5	11·9	11·2
Hips	29·4	24·3	26·6	27·5	25·5
Foot, length	27·2	23·2	25	25·7	24·2
Foot, breadth	9·6	7·8	8·6	8·9	8·3
Cephalic length	20·2	18	18·9	19·4	18·4
Cephalic breadth	14·5	12·8	13·6	13·9	13·3
Cephalic index	77·5	66·1	71·7	73·9	69·5
Bigoniac	10·2	8·6	9·7	10	9·3
Bizygomatic	13·5	12	12·7	13	12·4
Maxillo-zygomatic index ...	83·6	67·2	76·9	79·4	73·9
Nasal height	5·1	4·1	4·6	4·8	4·4
Nasal breadth	3·9	3·2	3·4	3·6	3·3
Nasal index	88·4	62·7	75·6	80	71·4
Vertex to tragus	14·6	12·7	13·6	14	13·2
Vertex to chin	22·6	19·7	21·2	21·8	20·7
Facial angle	77	67	71	73	68

Note.—The results are based on the measurement of forty subjects.

In this and the following tables, the weight is recorded in pounds; the measurements are in centimetres.

THE IRULAS OF THE NILGIRIS.

For the purpose of comparing the characteristics of the five tribes which inhabit the Nilgiri hills, no better hunting ground can be selected than the Kotagiri bazār. There on market day (Sunday) may be seen gathered together Todas from the distant Kodanād mand, Kotas from the adjacent Kota village, Badagas from the surrounding villages, and, in fewer numbers, Irulas and Kurumbas, who have walked up from their homes on the lower slopes to purchase the weekly supplies, laden with which they tramp cheerfully back in the afternoon. In distinguishing a Toda, Kota, or Badaga, no difficulty is experienced even on very slight acquaintance with them, but to decide between Irula and Kurumba is not nearly so easy; and, when I have seen both together on a coffee estate, I have several times committed an error of diagnosis. The manager of an estate, after several years acquaintance with them, said he could always, without fail, distinguish a Kurumba from an Irula, although unable to explain exactly how he did so. He thought the difference was mainly in the more prominent cheek-bones and shorter and flatter noses of the Irulas.[3] In the Manual of the Nilgiri District, 1880, Mr. H. B. Grigg states that "the Irulas belong to a still more primitive race than the Kurumbas, namely, the Bedas or hunters of the forests of the peninsula. The opinion that the Nilgiri Irulas are allied to these Bēdas receives confirmation from the fact that they, like the Mysore Bedas, are worshippers generally of Vishnu, a remarkable circumstance considering the almost universal Sivaism of the aboriginal tribes of South India." It was suggested, on the other hand, by Colonel Ross King[4] that the Irulas and Kurumbas were originally one, and that the slight physical differences between them may have resulted from the nature of their respective situations and consequent modes of life. At the present day both Irulas and Kurumbas are occasionally found living in the same hamlet (or *motta*).

The hill Kurumbas (or Kurumans) it may be noted, *en passant*, are sub-divided by the Census Commissioner, 1891, into Mulla Kurumans, Vetta Kurumans, Ūrāli Kurumans, Tēn Kurumans, and Tac'chanādan Muppan. Of these five sub-divisions my persuasive powers have so far permitted of my measuring only four Ūrāli Kurumans—a meagre result

---

[3] Breeks' Primitive Tribes of the Nilgiris.
[4] Aboriginal Tribes of the Nilgiri hills.

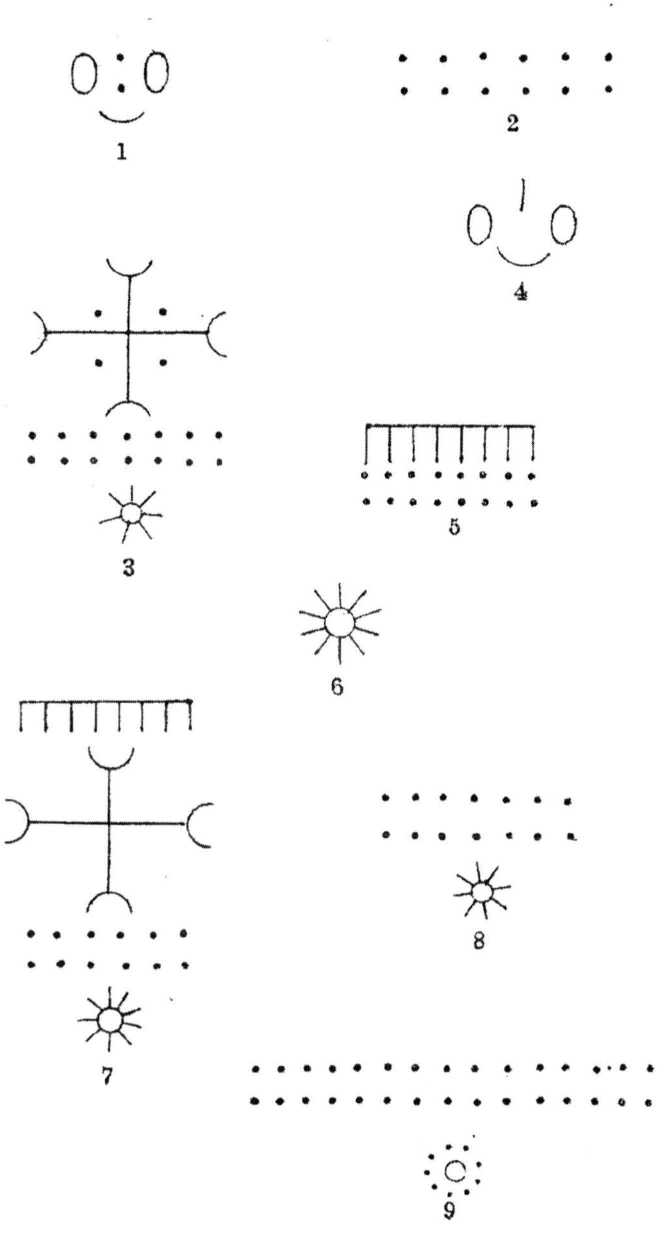

Badaga Tattoo Marks

for a long march. There is, however, a further sub-division calling themselves Pāla Kurumans, who, like the Irulas, live on coffee estates or in the jungles of the eastern slopes of the Nilgiris, and of these, with great difficulty, I succeeded in measuring eleven male individuals. Comparing their principal measurements, though the number is confessedly very few, with those of twenty-five Irulas, and, as a 'control,' with those of the short, broad-nosed Paniyans of the Wynâd, the results pan out (to use a mining phrase) as follows :—

	Irula.	Kurumba.	Paniyan.
Height	159·8	158	157·4
Span of arms	169·8	168·9	165·2
Span of arms relative to statnre = 100	106·3	106·9	105
Middle finger to patella	10·7	10·7	7·3
Middle finger to patella relative to stature=100	6·7	6·8	4·6
Cubit	45·8	45·5	45·3
Hand, length	17·5	17·5	18·5
Foot, length	24·9	24·9	25
Hips	25·4	25·3	24·3
Cephalic length	18	18	18·4
Cephalic breadth	13·7	13·7	13·6
Bigoniac	9·7	9·6	10
Bizygomatic	12·7	13	12·6
Nasal height	4·4	4·3	4
Nasal breadth	3·7	3·8	3·8
Nasal index	84·9	88·7	95·1
Vertex to chin	20·7	20·6	19·8

Further investigation of the Pāla Kurumbas is, of course, necessary (though experience leads me to anticipate no marked variation from the averages obtained), but the figures afford, I think, evidence of a close affinity between the Irulas and Kurumbas.

In my hunt after Irulas it was necessary to invoke the assistance and proverbial hospitality of various planters, without which my researches would have been barren. On one occasion news reached me that a party of Irula men, women, and children, collected for my benefit under a promise of substantial remuneration, had arrived at a planter's bungalow, whither I proceeded. The party included a man who had been 'wanted' for some time in connection with the shooting of an elephant on forbidden ground. He, suspecting me of base designs, refused absolutely to be measured on the plea that he was afraid the height-measuring standard was the gallows. Nor would he let me take his photograph, doubtless fearing (though he had never heard of Bertillonage) lest it should be used for the purpose of criminal identification.

As the Badagas are the fairest, so the Irulas are the darkest-skinned of the Nílgiri tribes. The name Irula, in fact, as has often been pointed out, means darkness or blackness (Tamil *irul*), whether in reference to the dark jungles in which the Irulas, who have not become domesticated by working as contractors or coolies on planter's estates, dwell, or to the great darkness of their skin, is doubtful. Though the typical Irula is dark-skinned, with broad nose and high nasal index, I have noted some who possessed skins of markedly paler hue and narrow noses. The nasal index of those who were examined ranged between 70 and 80 in seven, between 80 and 90 in eleven, and between 90 and 100 in seven cases; the height of the nose ranging between 4·8 and 3·9 cm. and the breadth between 4·3 and 3·2 cm.

The language of the Irulas is a corrupt form of Tamil. In their religion, they are worshippers of Vishnu under the name of Rangaswāmi, to whom they do puja at their own rude shrines, or at the Hindu temple at Karamadai, where Brāhman priests officiate. In his 'Primitive Tribes of the Nilgiris' Breeks says that, "an Irula pujāri lives near the temples, and rings a bell when he performs puja to the gods. He wears the Vishnu mark on his forehead. His office is hereditary, and he is remunerated by offerings of fruit and milk from Irula worshippers. Each Irula village pays about

PL. V.

IRULA WOMAN.

two annas to the pujāri in May or June. They say that there is also a temple at Kallampalla in the Sattiyamangalam taluk, north of Rangaswāmi's peak. This is a Siva temple, at which sheep are sacrificed: the pujāri wears the Siva mark. They don't know the difference between Siva and Vishnu. At Kallampalla temple is a thatched building containing a stone called Mariamma, a form of Durga, the well-known goddess of small-pox, worshipped in this capacity by the Irulas. A sheep is led also to this temple, and those who offer the sacrifice sprinkle water over it, and cut its throat. The pujāri sits by, but takes no part in the ceremony. The body is cut up, and distributed among the Irulas present including the pujāri."

A village on a coffee estate, which I inspected, was, at the time of my visit, in the possession of pariah dogs and nude children, the elder children and adults being away at work on the estate. The village was protected against nocturnal feline and other feral marauders by a rude fence, and consisted of rows of single-storied dwelling houses, with verandah in front, made of split bamboo and thatched, detached huts, and an abundance of fowl-houses, and cucurbitaceous plants twining up rough stages. Surrounding the village were a dense grove of plantain trees, castor-oil bushes, and cattle-pens.

When not engaged in work on estates, the Irulas cultivate, for their own consumption, rāgi (*Eleusine Coracana*), sāmai (*Panicum miliare*), tenai (*Setaria italica*), tovarai (*Cajanus indicus*), maize, plantains, &c. They will not attend to cultivation on Saturday or Monday. At the season of sowing Badagas bring cocoanuts, plantains, milk and ghī, and give them to the Irulas, who, after offering them before their swāmi, return them to the Badagas.

The Irulas will (so they say) not eat the flesh of buffaloes or cattle, but will eat sheep and goat, fowls, deer and pig (which they shoot), hares (which they snare with skilfully made nets), jungle-fowl, pigeons, and quail (which they knock over with stones).

The Irulas, as a rule, have one wife. A young man of marriageable age selects a girl for himself, and gives her parents a present of money, varying from thirteen to twenty-five rupees, as a dowry. There is no marriage tāli. At the marriage feast, which is of a very simple nature, a sheep is killed, and the guests make a present of four to eight annas to the bridegroom, who ties up the money in a cloth and goes to the bride's house to conduct her to her future home. Widows are permitted to re-marry. If a woman is barren, her husband may marry a second wife, but has to support the first.

When an Irula dies, two Kurumbas come to the village, and one shaves the head of the other. The shorn man is fed and presented with a cloth, which he wraps round his head. This quaint ceremonial is supposed, in some way, to bring good luck to the departed. Outside the house of the deceased, in which the corpse is kept till the time of the funeral, men and women dance to the music of the Irula band. The dead are buried in a sitting posture with the legs crossed tailorwise. Each village has its own burial ground. A circular pit is dug, from the lower end of which a chamber is excavated, in which the corpse, clad in its own clothes, jewelry, and a new cloth, is placed with a lamp and grain. The pit is then filled in, and the position of the grave marked by a stone. The following description of an annual memorial service was given to me. A lamp and oil are purchased, and rice is cooked in the village. They are then taken to the shrine at the burial ground, offered upon stones on which some of the oil is poured, and puja done. At the shrine a pujāri, with three white marks on the forehead when on duty, officiates. Like the Badaga dēvadāri, the Irula pujāri at times becomes inspired by the god.

The leading characteristics of the Irulas, the system of tattooing, and personal adornment, are summed up in the following cases :—

1. Man, aged 30. Sometimes works on a coffee estate. At present engaged in the cultivation of various grains, pumpkins, jack-fruit, and plantains. Goes to the bazār at Mettupálaiyam to purchase rice, salt, chillies, oil, &c. Acquires agricultural implements from Kotas at Kotagiri, to whom he pays annual tribute in grain or money. Wears brass ear-rings acquired from Kotas in exchange for vegetables and fruit. Wears turban and plain loin-cloth, wrapped round body and reaching below the knees. Bag containing tobacco and betel slung over shoulder inside cloth. Skin very dark. Moustache and slight beard. Hair cut short in front, long and tied in a knot behind. Hair feebly developed on body and limbs. Bushy eye-brows,

PL. VI

GROUP OF IRULAS.

small, twinkling eyes. Ears outstanding. Prominent cheek bones. Lips thin, not everted.

Height	.. .. ..	158·6 cm.
Weight	.. .. ..	100 lb.
Chest	.. .. ..	79·5 cm.
Shoulders	.. .. ..	37·8 ,,
Span of arms	.. ..	168 ,,
Cubit	.. .. ..	44·3 ,,
Hand, length	.. ..	16·6 ,,
Foot, length	.. ..	23·7 ,,
Cephalic length	.. ..	18 ,,
Cephalic breadth	.. ..	13·5 ,,
Bigoniac	.. .. ..	9·8 ,,
Bizygomatic	.. ..	12·8 ,,
Nasal height	.. ..	4·4 ,,
Nasal breadth	.. ..	3·2 ,,
Nasal index	.. ..	72·7
Facial angle (of Cuvier)	..	69

2. Man. Body cloth as No. 1 supplemented by coloured print cloth with brass buttons, and plain loin-cloth. Hair of head not shaved or cut, straggling and tied in a knot behind. Moustache, untrimmed whiskers, and billy-goat beard. Prominent cheek-bones and zygomatic arches. Silver bangle on right wrist.

3. Man. Conjunctivæ pigmented. Slight moustache. Bridge of nose broad. Hair rising in very stiff curls all over head.

4. Man. Pale by contrast with surrounding men. Hair when undone reaches in wavy locks to middle of back. Ornamental brass ear-rings in each lobe. Brass and glass bead ornaments in each helix. Steel ring on left little finger.

5. Man. Wears turban, body-cloth with red and blue stripes, and loin-cloth. Hair curly with no parting, tied in a knot on top. Brass ear-ring in each lobe. Two brass rings on left little finger.

6. Man. Head shaved on top *á la Hindu*, and tied in a knot behind.

7. Man. Two brass rings in lobe of each ear. Silver bangle on right wrist.

8. Man. Brass ear-ring in lobe of each ear. Brass bangle on right wrist. Greenish-yellow irides. Brown moustache.

9. Thin brass ring in helix of each ear. Brass link necklace.

10. Man. Brass ear-ring of Badaga pattern in right lobe. Brass and glass ornament in left lobe. Brass ring on left little finger. Grass necklace.

11. Man. Plug of wood in lobe and helix of each ear. One brass ring and two steel rings on left little finger.

12. Man. Facial angle 60° (very low as compared with the average).

13. Man suffering from leucoderma. Skin of face black with pink patch on forehead. Skin of body and extremities pink and white with dark and light brown patches. Growing bald. Only recognisable as an Irula by very dark face and broad nose.

14. Boy, æt. 10. String round neck and right wrist to drive away sickness.

15. Woman, æt. 30. Height 144·8 cm. Hair curly, without parting, tied in a bunch behind round black cotton swab. Wears a plain waist-cloth and print cotton body-cloth, worn square across breasts and reaching below knees. Tattooed on forehead. A mass of glass bead necklaces. Gold ornament in left nostril. Brass ornament in lobe of each ear. Eight brass bangles on right wrist; two brass and six glass bangles on left wrist. Five brass rings on right first finger; four brass and one tin ring on right ring-finger.

16. Woman, æt. 25. Height 153·3 cm. Hair parted in middle, wavy, tied in a bunch behind. Bushy eyebrows. Red cajan roll in dilated lobes of ears. Brass and glass bead ornament in helix of right ear. Brass ornament in left nostril. A number of bead necklets, one with young cowry shells pendent, another consisting of a heavy roll of black beads. The latter is very characteristic of Irula female adornment (pl. VII). One steel bangle, eight brass bangles, and one chank-shell bangle on right wrist; three lead, six glass bangles, and one glass bead bangle on left wrist; one steel and one brass ring on left little finger.

17. Woman, æt. 35. Wears loin-cloth only. Breasts fully exposed. Cap of Badaga pattern on head. Massive brass ornament in lobe of each ear. Brass ornament in left nostril. Thirteen brass and two lacquer bangles on right forearm. Four brass rings on right thumb. Four brass

IRULA GIRL.

rings on right second finger. Five brass rings on right ring finger. Six brass rings on right little finger. Five brass rings on left thumb. Four brass rings on left first finger. Four brass rings on left second finger. Seven brass rings on left ring finger. Seven brass rings on left little finger.

Brass ring on second, third and fourth toe of each foot.

18. Woman, æt. 30. Elaborately tattooed across forehead. Red cajan plug in lobe of each ear. Brass and glass bead ornament in each helix. Silver ornament in left nostril. Brass link and glass bead necklaces, one with young cowry shells pendent. A black thread necklet with thread tassel pendent. Ten brass bangles, one chank, and one bead bangle on right wrist. Two silver, three lead, seven glass, and three composition bangles on left wrist. Two silver rings on left little finger. Two brass rings on right second toe.

19. Girl, æt. 16. Red cajan rolls in lobe of each ear. A number of bead necklets. Three steel armlets on right forearm. Nine brass bangles and one chank bangle on right wrist. One chank, two brass, and seven glass bangles on left wrist. Four brass rings on right little finger; three brass rings on left first finger; one brass and one steel ring on left ring-finger.

20. Girl, æt. 14. Height 146·4 cm. Length of foot 23·7 cm. (=16·2 relative to height=100). Very fair in contrast with the surrounding men. Bridge of nose broad and flat (a common type). Body-cloth of striped cotton, worn straight across breasts, and reaching below knees. Print cotton cloth thrown over shoulders and tied in knot in front. Wooden plug in left nostril. Mass of glass bead necklets. Four glass bangles on left wrist. One brass ring on left ring-finger.. Two base metal rings on right second toe; a single base metal ring on left second toe.

21. Girl, æt 15. Tattooed on forehead. Pleasant expression of countenance. Hair without parting, long, wavy. Mass of glass bead necklets. Gold ornament in lobe of each ear. Five glass bangles and one brass bangle on right wrist; four glass bangles, and one brass bangle on left wrist.

22. Girl, æt. 8. Tattooed on forehead. Lobe of each ear being dilated by a number of wooden sticks like matches. Two glass bead necklets, and a necklet consisting of a

heavy roll of black beads. Left nostril pierced. Hair cut short, except a long lock carried over top of head and behind left ear.

23. Girl, æt. 8. Hair parted in middle, long, wavy. Bushy eyebrows. Long, fine hairs on forehead merging into hair of head. (The same hairy growth on the forehead I have noticed as being very prevalent among the Cheruman women of Malabar.) Gold ornaments in left nostril and in lobe of each ear. One brass and eight glass bangles on right wrist; one glass bead and six glass bangles on left wrist.

24. Girl, æt. 9. Tattooed on forehead. Wooden plug in left nostril. Mass of glass bead necklets, one with pendent beads and cowries. Nine brass bangles on right wrist; four brass bangles on left wrist.

25. Baby in arms. Brass ring in lobe of each ear. Steel bangle on left ankle.

TABLE II.

TABLE OF MEASUREMENTS.

IRULAS.

	Max.	Min.	Aver-age.	Mean above.	Mean below.
Weight	140	90	101	125	94
Height	168	152	159·8	162·9	156·8
Height, sitting	86·8	78·7	82	83·6	80·4
Height, kneeling	124·2	111	117·5	119·9	115·6
Height to gladiolus ...	124·6	115·6	118·7	121·5	116·9
Span of arms	179·6	160	169·8	174·2	165·2
Chest	89	73	79·4	82·5	76·5
Middle finger to patella ...	14·6	7	10·7	12·9	9·4
Shoulders	42	35·8	38·5	40	37·7
Cubit	49	42·5	45·8	47·2	44·4
Hand, length	19·1	16·3	17·5	18·1	16·7
Hand, breadth	8·6	7·3	8·1	8·4	7·8
Middle finger	12·3	10·5	11·3	11·7	10·9
Hips	26·9	24·1	25·4	26·1	24·8
Foot, length	26·2	23	24·9	25·5	24·1
Foot, breadth	9·4	7·8	8·7	9	8·3
Cephalic length	19·1	17	18	18·4	17·6
Cephalic breadth	14·3	13·1	13·7	14	13·3
Cephalic index	80·9	70·8	75·8	78	73·8
Bigoniac	11·1	9·1	9·7	10·1	9·3
Bizygomatic	13·4	11·9	12·7	13·1	12·3
Maxillo-zygomatic index ...	84·6	71·9	75·7	78·5	72·7
Nasal height	4·8	3·9	4·4	4·6	4·2
Nasal breadth	4·3	3·2	3·7	3·9	3·5
Nasal index	100	72·3	84·9	93·2	78·4
Vertex to tragus	14·5	11·6	13·5	13·9	13·1
Vertex to chin	22·4	19·2	20·7	21·4	20
Facial angle	72	60	68	70	64

Note.—The results are based on the measurement of twenty-five subjects.

THE PANIYANS OF MALABAR.

The Paniyans are a dark-skinned tribe, short in stature, with broad noses and curly hair, inhabiting the Wynâd and those portions of the Ernâd, Calicut, Kurumbranâd, and Kottayam taluks of Malabar which skirt the base of the ghâts, and the Mudanâd, Cherangôd, and Namblakôd amshams of the Nīlgiri district.

A common belief, based on their general appearance, prevails among the European planting community that the Paniyans are of African origin, and descended from ancestors who were wrecked on the Malabar coast. This theory, however, breaks down on investigation. Of their origin nothing definite is known. The Nair Janmis say that, when surprised in the act of some mischief or alarmed, the Paniyan calls out 'Ippi'! 'Ippi'! as he runs away, and they believe this to have been the name of the country whence they came originally; but they are ignorant as to where Ippimala, as they call it, is situated. Kapiri (Africa or the Cape ?) is also sometimes suggested as their original habitat, but only by those who have had the remarks of Europeans communicated to them. The Paniyan himself, though he occasionally puts forward one or other of the above places as the home of his fore-fathers, has no fixed tradition bearing on their arrival in Malabar, beyond one to the effect that they were brought from a far-country, where they were found living by a Rāja, who captured them, and carried them off in such a miserable condition that a man and his wife only possessed one cloth between them, and were so timid that it was only by means of hunting nets that they were captured.

The number of Paniyans, returned at the Census 1891, was 33,282, and nine sub-divisions were registered; but, as Mr. H. A. Stuart, the Census Commissioner, observes:—"Most of these are not real, and none has been returned by any considerable number of persons." Their position is said to be very little removed from that of a slave, for every Paniyan is some landlord's 'man'; and, though he is, of course, free to leave his master, he is at once traced, and good care is taken that he does not get employment elsewhere.

In the fifties, when planters first began to settle in the Wynâd, they purchased the land with the Paniyans living on it, who were practically slaves of the land-owners. The Paniyans used formerly to be employed by rich receivers as

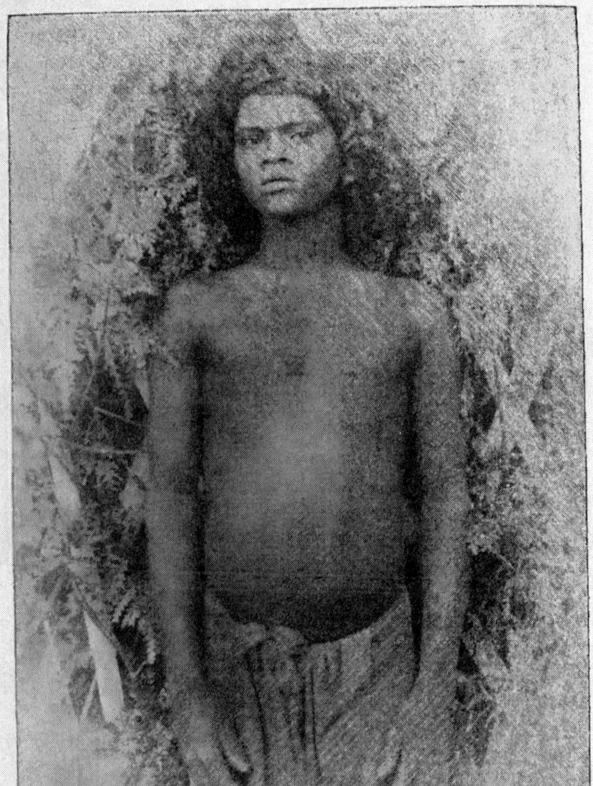

PANIYAN MAN.

professional coffee thieves, going out by night to strip the bushes of their berries, which were delivered to the receiver before morning. Unlike the Badagas of the Nilgiris, who are also coffee thieves, and are afraid to be out after dark, the Paniyans are not afraid of bogies by night, and would not hesitate to commit nocturnal depredations. My friend, Mr. G. Romilly, on whose estate my investigation of the Paniyans was mainly carried out, assures me that, according to his experience, the domesticated Paniyan, if well paid, is honest, and fit to be entrusted with the responsible duties of night watchman.

In some localities, where the Janmis have sold the bulk of their land, and have consequently ceased to find regular employment for them, the Paniyans have taken kindly to working on coffee estates, but comparatively few are thus employed. The word Paniyan means labourer, and they believe that their original occupation was agriculture, as it is, for the most part, at the present day. Those, however, who earn their livelihood on estates, only cultivate rice and rāgi (*Eleusine coracana*) for their own cultivation; and women and children may be seen digging up jungle roots, or gathering pot-herbs for food. They will not eat the flesh of jackals, snakes, vultures, lizards, rats, or other vermin. But I am told that they eat land-crabs, in lieu of expensive lotions, to prevent baldness and grey hairs. They have a distinct partiality for alcohol, and those who came to be measured by me were made more than happy by a present of a two-anna piece, a cheroot, and a liberal allowance of undiluted fiery brandy from the Meppādi bazār. The women are naturally of a shy disposition, and used formerly to run away and hide at the sight of a European. They were at first afraid to come and see me, but confidence was subsequently established, and all the women came to visit me, some to go through the ordeal of measurement, others to laugh at and make derisive comments on those who were undergoing the operation.

Practically the whole of the rice cultivation in the Wynâd is carried out by the Paniyans attached to the edoms (houses or places) or dévasoms (temple property) of the great Nair landlords; and Chettiyars and Moplahs also frequently have a few Paniyans, whom they have bought or hired by the year at from four to eight rupees per family from a Jenmi. When planting paddy or herding cattle, the Paniyan is seldom seen without the kontay or basket-work protection from the rain. This curious, but most effective substitute for the umbrella-hat of the Malabar coast, is made of split reeds interwoven with arrow-root leaves, and shaped something like a huge inverted coal-scoop turned on end, and gives to the individual wearing it the appearance of a gigantic mushroom. From the nature of his daily occupation the Paniyan is often brought in contact with wild animals, and is generally a bold, and, if excited, as he usually is on an occasion such as the netting of a tiger, a reckless fellow. The young men of the villages vie with each other in the zeal which they display in carrying out the really dangerous work of cutting back the jungle to within a couple of spear-lengths of the place where the quarry lies hidden, and often make a show of their indifference by turning and conversing with their friends outside the net.

Years ago it was not unusual for people to come long distances for the purpose of engaging Wynâd Paniyans to help them in carrying out some more than usually desperate robbery or murder. Their mode of procedure, when engaged in an enterprise of this sort, is evidenced by two cases, which had in them a strong element of savagery. On both these occasions the thatched homesteads were surrounded at dead of night by gangs of Paniyans carrying large bundles of rice straw. After carefully piling up the straw on all sides of the building marked for destruction, torches were, at a given signal, applied, and those of the wretched inmates who attempted to escape were knocked on the head with clubs, and thrust into the fiery furnace.

The Paniyans settle down happily on estates, living in a settlement consisting of rows of huts and detached huts, single or double storied, built of bamboo and thatched. During the hot weather, in the unhealthy months which precede the advent of the south-west monsoon, they shift their quarters to live near streams, or in other cool, shady spots, returning to their head-quarters when the rains set in.

They catch fish either by means of big flat bamboo mats, or, in a less orthodox manner, by damming a stream, and poisoning the water with herbs, bark, and fruit, which are beaten to a pulp and thrown into the water. The fish, becoming stupified, float on the surface, and fall an easy and unfairly earned prey.

The Paniyan language is a debased Malayalam patois, spoken in a curious nasal sing-song, difficult to imitate; but most of the Paniyans employed on estates can also converse in Kanarese.

Wholly uneducated and associating with no other tribes, the Paniyans have only very crude ideas of religion. Believing in devils of all sorts and sizes, and professing to worship the Hindu divinities, they reverence especially the god of the jungles, Kād Bagavādi, or according to another version, a deity called Kūli, a malignant and terrible being of neither sex, whose shrines take the form of a stone placed under a tree, or sometimes a cairn of stones. At their rude shrines they contribute as offerings to the swāmi rice boiled in the husk, roasted and pounded, half-a-cocoanut, and small coins. The banyan and a lofty tree, apparently of the fig tribe, are reverenced by them, inasmuch as evil spirits are reputed to haunt them at times. Trees so haunted must not be touched, and, if the Paniyans attempt to cut them, they fall sick.

Some Paniyans are believed to be gifted with the power of changing themselves into animals; and there is a belief among the Paniyan dwellers in the plains that, if they wish to secure a woman whom they lust after, one of the men gifted with this special power, goes to her house at night with a hollow bamboo, and encircles the house three times. The woman then comes out, and the man, changing himself into a bull or dog, works his wicked will. The woman, it is believed, dies in the course of two or three days.

Monogamy appears to be the general rule among the Paniyans, but there is no obstacle to a man taking unto himself as many wives as he can afford to support.

Apparently the bride is selected for a young man by his parents, and, in the same way that a wealthy European sometimes sends his betrothed a daily present of a bouquet, the more humble Paniyan bridegroom-elect has to take a bundle of firewood to the house of his fiancée every day for six months. The marriage ceremony (and the marriage knot does not appear to be very binding) is of a very simple nature. The ceremony is conducted by a Paniyan Chemi (a corruption of Janmi). A present of sixteen fanams (coins) and some new cloths is given by the bridegroom to the Chemi, who hands them over to the parents of the bride. A feast is prepared, at which the Paniyan women (Panichis) dance to the music of drum and pipe. The tāli (or marriage badge) is tied round the neck of the bride by the female relations of the bridegroom, who also invest the bride with such crude jewelry as they may be able to afford. The Chemi seals the contract by pouring water over the head and feet of the young couple. A man may, I was told, not have two sisters as wives; nor may he marry his deceased wife's sister. Re-marriage of widows is permitted. Adultery and other forms of vice are adjudicated on by a panchāyat (or council) of headmen, who settle disputes and decide on the fine or punishment to be inflicted on the guilty. At nearly every considerable Paniyan village there is a headman called Kuttan, who has been appointed by the Nair Janmi to look after his interests, and be responsible to him for the other inhabitants of the village. The investiture of the Kuttan with the powers of office is celebrated with a feast and dance, at which a bangle is presented to the Kuttan as a badge of authority. Next in rank to the Kuttan is the Mudali or head of the family, and they usually constitute the panchāyat. Both Kuttan and Mudali are called Moopenmar or headman. In a case of proved adultery a fine of sixteen fanams (the amount of the marriage fee), and a sum equal to the expenses of the wedding, including the present to the parents of the bride, is the usual form of punishment.

No ceremony takes places in celebration of the birth of children. One of the old women of the village acts as midwife, and receives a small present in return for her services. As soon as a child is old enough to be of use, it accompanies its parents to their work, or on their fishing and hunting expeditions, and is initiated into the various ways of adding to the stock of provisions for the household.

The dead are buried in the following manner:—A trench, four or five feet deep, and large enough to receive the body to be interred, is dug, due north and south, on a hill near the village. At the bottom of this excavation the earth is scooped out from the western side on a level with the floor throughout the length of the grave, so as to form a receptacle for the corpse, which, placed on a mat, is laid therein upon its left side with the head pointing to the south and the feet to the north. After a little cooked rice has been put into the grave for the use of the departed spirit, the mat, which has been made broad enough for the purpose, is

PL. IX

GROUP OF PANIYANS

folded up and tucked in under the roof of the cavity, and the trench filled up. It has probably been found by experience that the corpse, when thus protected, is safe from the ravages of scavenger jackals and pariah dogs. For seven days after death a little rice gruel is placed at distance of from fifty to a hundred yards from the grave by the Chemi, who claps his hands as a signal to the evil spirits in the vicinity, who, in the shape of a pair of crows, are supposed to partake of the food, which is hence called kāka conji or crow's rice.

The noombu or mourning ceremonies are the tī polay, seven days after death; the kāka polay or karuvelli held for three years in succession in the month of Magaram (January-February); and the matham polay held once in every three or four years, when possible, as a memorial service in honour of those who are specially respected. On all these occasions the Chemi presides, and acts as a sort of master of the ceremonies. As the ceremonial carried out differs only in degree, an account of the kāka polay will do for all.

In the month of Magaram the noombu karrans or mourners (who have lost relatives) begin to cook and eat in a pandal or shed set apart from the rest of the village, but otherwise go about their business as usual. They wash and eat twice a day, but abstain from eating meat or fish. On the last day of the month, arrangements are made, under the supervision of the Chemi, for the ceremony which brings the period of mourning to a close. The mourners, who have fasted since daybreak, take up their position in the pandal, and the Chemi, holding on his crossed arms two winnowing sieves, each containing a seer or two of rice, walks round three times, and finally deposits the sieves in the centre of the pandal. If, among the male relatives of the deceased, one is to be found sufficiently hysterical, or actor enough, to simulate possession and perform the functions of an oracle, well and good; but should they all be of a stolid temperament, there is always at hand a professional corresponding to the Komaran or Villichipād of other Hindus. This individual is called the Patalykaran. With a new cloth (mundu) on his head, and smeared on the body and arms with a paste made of rice flour and ghī (clarified butter), he enters on the scene with his legs girt with bells, the music of which is supposed to drive away the attendant evil spirits (payan mar). Advancing with short steps and rolling his eyes, he staggers to and fro, sawing the air with two small sticks which he holds in either hand, and works himself up into a frenzied state of inspiration, while the mourners cry out and ask why the dead have been taken away from them. Presently a convulsive shiver attacks the performer, who staggers more violently and falls prostrate on the ground, or seeks the support of one of the posts of the pandal, while he gasps out disjointed sentences, which are taken to be the words of the god. The mourners now make obeisance, and are marked on the forehead with the paste of rice flour and ghī. This done, a mat is spread for the accommodation of the headmen and Chemi; and the Patalykaran, from whose legs the bells have been removed and put with the rice in the sieves, takes these in his hands, and, shaking them as he speaks, commences a funeral chant, which lasts till dawn. Meanwhile food has been prepared for all present except the mourners, and when this has been partaken of, dancing is kept up round the central group till daybreak, when the pandal is pulled down and the kāka polay is over. Those who have been precluded from eating make up for lost time, and relatives, who have allowed their hair to grow long, shave. The ordinary Paniyan does not profess to know the meaning of the funeral orations, but contents himself with a belief that it is known to those who are initiated.

The women attend the ceremony, but do not take part in the dance. In fact, the nearest approach to a dance that they ever attempt (and this only on festive occasions) resembles the ordinary occupation of planting rice, carried out in dumb show to the music of a drum. The bodies of the performers stoop and move in time with the music, and the arms are swung from side to side as in the act of placing the rice seedlings in their rows. To see a long line of Paniyan women, up to their knees in the mud of a rice field, bobbing up and down and putting on the pace as the music grows quicker and quicker, and to hear the wild yells of Hou! Hou! like a chorus of hungry dogs, which form the vocal accompaniment as they dab the green bunches in from side to side, is highly amusing.

The foregoing account of the Paniyan death ceremonies was supplied by Mr. Colin Mackenzie, to whom, as also to Mr. Fred. Fawcett, Mr. George Romilly, and Mr. Martelli.

PL. X

PANIYAN WOMAN.

I am indebted for many of the facts recorded in the present note. From Mr. Fawcett the following account of a further ceremony was obtained :—

At a Paniyan village, on a coffee estate where the annual ceremony was being celebrated, men and boys were dancing round a wooden upright to the music of a small drum hanging at the left hip. Some of the dancers had bells round the leg below the knee. Close to the upright a man was seated, playing a pipe, which emitted sounds like those of a bagpipe. In dancing, the dancers went round against the sun. At some little distance a crowd of females indulged in a dance by themselves. A characteristic of the dance, specially noticeable among the women, was stooping and waving of the arms in front. The dancers perspired freely, and kept up the dance for many hours to rhythmic music, the tune of which changed from time to time. There were three chief dancers, of whom one represented the goddess, the others her ministers. They were smeared with streaks on the chest, abdomen, arms and legs, had bells on the legs, and carried a short stick about two feet in length in each hand. The sticks were held over the head, while the performers quivered as if in a religious frenzy. Now and again the sticks were waved or beaten together. The Paniyans believe that, when the goddess first appeared to them, she carried two sticks in her hands. The mock goddess and her attendants, holding the sticks above the head and shivering, went to each male elder, and apparently received his blessing, the elder placing his hand on their faces as a form of salutation and then applying his hand to his own face. The villagers partook of a light meal in the early morning, and would not eat again until the end of the ceremony, which concluded by the man-goddess seating himself on the upright and addressing the crowd on behalf of the goddess concerning their conduct and morality.

Games.—A long strip of cane is suspended from the branch of a tree, and a cross-bar fixed to its lower end. On the bar a boy sits and swings himself in all directions. In another game a bar, twelve to fourteen feet in length, is balanced by means of a point in a socket on an upright reaching about four feet and-a-half above the ground. Over the end of the horizontal bar a boy hangs, and, touching the ground with the feet, spins himself round.

The Paniyans are, as already stated, of low stature, dark-skinned, with curly hair and broad noses. The great breadth relative to the height of the nose is brought out by the following table of nasal indices, which ranged between 83·7 and 108·6 in the men, and between 82·5 and 119·4 in the women :—

NASAL INDEX.

Men.	No.	Women.	No.
80–90	6	80–90	6
90–100	9	90–100	2
100–110	10	100–110	3
		110–120	1
	25		12

The average height of the men, according to my observations, is 157·4 cm., and of the women 146 cm. The men have very long hands and feet. The average length of the latter (25 cm.), in fact, exceeds the average breadth of the hips (24·3 cm.) by ·7 cm.—a difference in favour of the foot greater than in any of the other tribes which I have as yet investigated. The average distance from the middle finger to the patella is (in men) only 4·6 cm. relative to stature = 100, and approximates very closely to the recorded results of measurement of long-limbed African Negroes.

The leading characteristics of the Paniyans, and their decoration with cheap jewelry, are summed up in the following descriptive cases :—

1. Mau, æt. 30. Of sturdy build and muscular. Skin very dark. Hair of head clipped short in front so as to form a fringe. Long, wavy curls reaching down to shoulders. Long tail of matted hair worn as a vow, hanging down back. Thread tied round right wrist as a charm to drive away fever, from which he suffers. Hair of body only well developed in axillæ and over pubic region. Conjunctivæ injected and pigmented. Iris very dark. Large, pendulous lobes to ears, which are pierced. Five brass rings in right ear, four in left. Nose as broad as high. Lips thick, everted. Not prognathous. Three copper, three brass rings, and a single steel ring on right ring-finger. Clothing consists of a plain loin-cloth reaching below knees, langūti, and belt of European design round loins.

Height	154·6 cm
Weight	94 lb.
Chest	84 cm.
Shoulders	36·4 ,,
Span of arms	160·4 ,,
Cubit	44 ,,
Hand, length	17·5 ,,
Foot, length	24·6 ,,
Cephalic length	18·4 ,,
Cephalic breadth	14 ,,
Bigoniac	10 ,,
Bizygomatic	12·4 ,,
Nasal height	3·8 ,,
Nasal breadth	3·8 ,,
Nasal index	100
Facial angle (of Cuvier) ..	66°

2. Man, æt. 25. Hair of head a dense mass of short curls with no parting. Lower lip much everted. Lobes of ears large and pendulous. Conjunctivæ injected. Square face. Nasal index 108·6. Twelve brass rings, removed from fingers while he is at work, tied up in loin-cloth. Thread round right wrist to ward off fever.

3. Man, æt. 40–45. Hair exceptionally well developed on chest, abdomen, legs, and back. Bald on top of head. Seven steel rings on little finger.

4. Man, æt. 25. Mass of tufted curly hair standing out like a mop. Pot-bellied.

5. Man. Steel bangle on right forearm. Three brass rings on each ring-finger; two brass rings on each little finger. Three brass rings in each ear.

6. Man. Two brass rings on right little finger; one copper and one steel ring on left little finger.

7. Man. Short, thin, matted tail, and long, broad, matted tail of hair hanging down back, worn as a vow.

8. Man. Thread round left ankle as a charm against sickness.

9. Man. Chunam (lime) smeared over throat to cure cough.

10. Boy, æt. 8. Long, curly hair parted in middle line. Brass ear-rings. Steel bangle on right wrist.

11. Woman, æt. 20-25. Fat, squat, and uncomely. Skin very dark. Hair of head a dense mass of short curls

without parting, reaching behind to nape of neck. Nose considerably broader than long. Lips thick and everted. Lobes of ears enormously dilated by cajan ornaments. Iris very dark. Square face. Tattooed with a circle between eye brows. Two brass bangles on left wrist. Brass ring on left little finger. Outer clothing consists of a plain dirty cloth covering the body and tied in front in a knot.

Height	144·8 cm.
Weight	92 lb.
Shoulders	34·2 cm.
Cubit	40·1 ,,
Hand, length	17 ,,
Foot, length	23·4 ,,
Cephalic length	18 ,,
Cephalic breadth	13·7 ,,
Bigoniac	10 ,,
Bizygomatic	12 ,,
Nasal height	3·1 ,,
Nasal breadth	3·7 ,,
Nasal index	119·4
Facial angle	66°

12. Woman, æt. 25-30. Long, curly hair reaching below shoulders. Lobes of ears completely torn across as the result of dilatation by cajan ornaments. Long, brass link ear-rings in helix of ears. Steel bangle on left wrist.

13. Woman. Thirty-one brass and steel rings tied up in her cloth. Left nostril pierced and plugged with wood.

14. Woman. Wears string round neck as charm to cure sores.

15. Woman. Hair of head cut short all over as a sign of mourning for her dead husband. Four brass bangles on left forearm. Glass bead necklet.

16. Girl, æt. 8. Hair in long, wavy curls; cut in front so as to form a fringe. Left nostril pierced and plugged with wood. Brass ear-rings in helix of each ear. Lobes of ears being gradually dilated by cajan-roll ornaments.

TABLE III.

SUMMARY OF MEASUREMENTS.

PANIYAN MEN.

	Max.	Min.	Average.	Mean above.	Mean below.
Weight	120	89	99·6	104	94
Height	171·6	152	157·4	161·4	153·6
Height, sitting	87	77·6	81·3	83·4	79·4
Height, kneeling	125·6	111·7	115·9	118·5	113·9
Height to gladiolus	130·8	111·4	117·1	120·1	114·7
Span of arms	180·2	148·4	165·2	170	160·7
Chest	86·5	77·5	81·5	83·4	79·6
Middle finger to patella ...	10·2	4·2	7·3	8·5	5·8
Shoulders	38·5	34·2	35·9	36·9	34·9
Cubit	49·4	40	45·3	46·9	44
Hand, length...	20	15	18·5	19·1	17·7
Hand, breadth	8·6	7	7·8	8·2	7·5
Middle finger	12·1	10·1	11·4	11·8	11·1
Hips	26·2	23	24·3	25·1	23·7
Foot, length	26·7	22·5	25	26	24·2
Foot, breadth	9	7·7	8·2	8·5	8
Cephalic length	19·3	17·5	18·4	18·7	18
Cephalic breadth	14·9	13	13·6	14·1	13·3
Cephalic index	81·1	69·4	74	76·3	72
Bigoniac	11·1	9·1	10	10·4	9·5
Bizygomatic	13·4	11·8	12·6	13	12·4
Maxillo-zygomatic index ...	86·6	72·7	78·9	80·9	75·3
Nasal height	4·8	3·3	4	4·2	3·7
Nasal breadth	4·2	3·2	3·8	4	3·6
Nasal index	108·6	83·7	95·1	100·9	88·2
Vertex to tragus	12·8	11·6	12·3	12·6	12
Vertex to chin	21	18·5	19·8	20·1	19·3
Facial angle	71	65	67	69	66

Note.—The results are based on the measurements of twenty-five subjects.

TABLE IV.

SUMMARY OF MEASUREMENTS.

PANIYAN WOMEN.

	Max.	Min.	Average.	Mean above.	Mean below.
Weight	101	72	84·8	92	78·3
Height	155	134·1	146	150·9	141·2
Height, sitting	80·8	71·6	75·1	78·3	72·9
Height, kneeling	114·6	100	107·9	111·4	104·4
Span of arms	161·2	138·8	152	156·9	146·4
Shoulders	36·8	31·5	33·2	34·4	32·4
Cubit	43·8	37·8	43·3	43·5	40·7
Hand, length	18·8	15·5	17·1	18	16·5
Hand, breadth	7·6	6·8	7·2	7·5	7
Middle finger	11·7	9·8	10·8	11·3	10·4
Foot, length	24·2	20·7	22·8	23·6	21·9
Foot, breadth	8·1	7·1	7·6	7·8	7·3
Cephalic length	18·5	17	17·5	18·1	17·2
Cephalic breadth	13·7	12·2	13·1	13·4	12·8
Cephalic index	80·6	70·8	74·9	77·3	72·6
Bigoniac	10	9	9·5	9·7	9·3
Bizygomatic	12·9	11·7	12·1	12·5	11·9
Maxillo-zygomatic index ...	83·3	73·2	78·5	81	76·2
Nasal height	4·3	3·1	3·6	4	3·4
Nasal breadth	3·7	3	3·4	3·6	3·2
Nasal index	119·4	82·5	94·3	105·7	87·5
Vertex to tragus	12·5	11·4	11·9	12·3	11·7
Vertex to chin	19·8	17·7	18·5	19·1	18
Facial angle	72	64	67	69	65

Note.—The results are based on the measurements of twelve subjects.

ON A CHINESE-TAMIL CROSS.

Halting in the course of a recent anthropological expedition on the western side of the Nilgiri plateau, in the midst of the Government Cinchona plantations, I came across a small settlement of Chinese, who have squatted for some years on the slopes of the hills between Naduvatam and Gudalūr, and developed, as the result of 'marriage' with Tamil pariah women, into a colony, earning an honest livelihood by growing vegetables, cultivating coffee on a small scale, and adding to their income from these sources by the economic products of the cow. An ambassador was sent to this miniature Chinese Court with a suggestion that the men should, in return for monies, present themselves before me with a view to their measurements being recorded. The reply which came back was in its way racially characteristic as between Hindus and Chinese. In the case of the former, permission to make use of their bodies for the purposes of research depends essentially on a pecuniary transaction, on a scale varying from two to eight annas. The Chinese, on the other hand, though poor, sent a courteous message to the effect that they did not require payment in money, but would be perfectly happy if I would give them, as a memento, copies of their photographs.

The measurements of a single family, excepting a widowed daughter whom I was not permitted to see, and an infant in arms, who was pacified with cake while I investigated its mother, are recorded in the following table :

TABLE V.

		Cephalic length.	Cephalic breadth.	Cephalic index.	Nasal height.	Nasal breadth.	Nasal index.
Tamil Pariah ...	Mother of children.	18·1	13·9	76·8	4·7	3·7	78·7
Chinese	Father of children.	18·6	14·6	78·5	5·3	3·8	71·7
Chinese-Tamil ...	Girl, aged 16 ...	17·6	14·1	80·1	4·7	3·2	68·1
Chinese-Tamil ...	Boy, aged 10 ...	18·1	14·3	79	4·6	3·3	71·7
Chinese-Tamil ...	Boy, aged 9 ...	17	14	82·4	4·4	3·3	72·7
Chinese-Tamil ...	Boy, aged 5 ...	17·1	13·7	80·1	4·1	2·8	68·3

The father was a typical Chinaman, whose only grievance was that, in the process of conversion to Christianity, he had been obliged to 'cut him tail off.' The mother was a typical Tamil Pariah of dusky hue. The colour of the children was more closely allied to the yellowish tint of the father than to the dark tint of the mother; and the semi-mongol parentage was betrayed in the slant eyes, flat nose, and (in one case) conspicuously prominent cheek-bones.

To have recorded the entire series of measurements of the children would have been useless for the purpose of comparison with those of the parents, and I selected from my repertoire the length and breadth of the head and nose, which plainly indicate the paternal influence on the external anatomy of the offspring. The figures given in the table bring out very clearly the great breadth, as compared with the length of the heads of all the children, and the resultant high cephalic index. In other words, in one case a mesaticephalic (79), and, in the remaining three cases, a sub-brachycephalic head (80·1; 80·1; 82·4) has resulted from the union of a mesaticephalic Chinaman (78·5) with a sub-dolichocephalic Tamil Pariah (76·8). How great is the breadth of the head in the children may be emphasised by noting that the average head-breadth of the adult Tamil Pariah man is only 13·7 cm., whereas that of the three boys, aged ten, nine, and five only, was 14·3, 14, and 13·7 cm. respectively.

Quite as strongly marked is the effect of paternal influence on the character of the nose; the nasal index, in the case of each child (68·1; 71·7; 72·7; 68·3), bearing a much closer relation to that of the long nosed father (71·7) than to the typical Pariah nasal index of the broad-nosed mother (78·7).

It will be interesting to note, hereafter, what is the future of the younger members of this quaint little colony, and to observe the physical characters, temperament, improvement or deterioration, fecundity, and other points relating to the cross-breed resulting from the union of Chinese and Tamil.

NOTE ON A CHERUMAN SKULL.

The Cherumans are a large caste, of low stature, very dark-skinned, and platyrrhinian (with wide nasal skeleton), inhabiting Malabar, where they were formerly agrestic slaves, and now work for the most part as field labourers.

The skull, which forms the subject of the present note, is that of an old man without the lower jaw.

Alveolar process of superior maxilla absorbed. Superciliary ridges feebly developed. Serrations of coronal suture between frontal and parietal bones not developed for about 3·6 cm. on each side of the median line ; lateral serrations fine. Serrations of sagittal and lambdoid sutures coarse. Parietal eminences very prominent, the skull narrowing gradually from a breadth of 13·1 cm. across these eminences to a maximum breadth of 10·6 cm. across the lateral surfaces of the frontal bone. A small wormian bone, 1·5 cm. long and 1 cm. maximum breadth, in the position of the anterior fontanelle at the junction of the coronal and sagittal sutures. A large wormian bone, 2 cm. long and 3 cm. maximum breadth, in the position of the posterior fontanelle at the junction of the sagittal and lambdoid sutures. Axes of orbits nearly horizontal.

Profile of nasal bones concave. Nasal spine large. Antero-posterior arch elevated in parietal region. Horizontal arch prominent in parietal region. Transverse arch somewhat pointed in parietal region.

Max : length from glabella						17·5 cm.
Max : transverse breadth						13·1 ,,
Cephalic index						74·9
Min : frontal breadth						9·1 cm.
Horizontal circumference						50 ,,
Ant-posterior curve (nasion to basion) :—						
Frontal	Tape	12·3 cm.	Callipers			10·5 cm.
Parietal[5]	Do.	14·7 ,,	Do.			12·2 ,,
Occipital	Do.	14 ,,	Do.			10·5 ,,
Basio-nasal length						9·4 cm.
Basio-alveolar length						8·2 ,,
Bizygomatic breadth						12·3 ,,
Nasio-alveolar length						5·1 ,,
Nasal height						4·6 ,,
Nasal breadth						2·4 ,,
Nasal index						54·3
Orbital breadth						3·9 cm.
Orbital height						2·8 ,,

[5] Including wormian bones.

The following averages of the head-measurements of twenty-five living Cheruman men are recorded for comparison, so far as is possible, with those of the single skull :—

	Living subject. CM.	Skull. CM.
Cephalic length	18·3	17·5
Cephalic breadth	13·5	13·1
Cephalic index	73·9	74·9
Bigoniac	9·9	..
Bizygomatic	12·6	12·3
Maxillo-zygomatic index ..	79·6	..
Nasal height	4·4	4·6
Nasal breadth	3·4	2·4
Nasal index	78·1	54·3

A character, with which I am very familiar, when measuring all sorts and conditions of Natives of Southern India, and is well marked in the Cheruman skull and skulls of Pariahs, ' Hindus,' ' Telugus ' and a Brâhman in my possession, is the absence of convexity of the segment formed by the posterior portion of the united parietal bones. The result of this absence of convexity is that the back of the head, instead of forming a curve gradually increasing from the top of the head towards the occipital region, as in the European skull figured in plate xi. 1, forms a flattened area of considerable length almost at right angles to the base of the skull as in the ' Hindu ' skull represented in plate xi. 2. And to the existence of this character is due, in large measure, the short length of head in Irulas, Kongas and Koramans, which is referred to hereafter (p. 50).

Some time ago, when passing through the Museum library, I found a student busily engaged in copying extracts from one of my publications, and sympathetically asked him with what object he was so doing. The uncomplimentary, but innocent, reply came forth : " Unfortunately for us it is one of our text-books." The same fate is presumably destined for the present bulletin, which will, I fear, have to be studied by candidates for the M.A. degree of the Madras University in history, which includes ethnology with special reference to the Indian Peninsula. It is, therefore, not out of place to record (*vide* Tables vi and vii) as a lesson in comparative craniometry, the more important measurements of a series of skulls, the property of the Madras Medical College, which constitute a loan-collection in the anthropological section of the Museum, where they are available

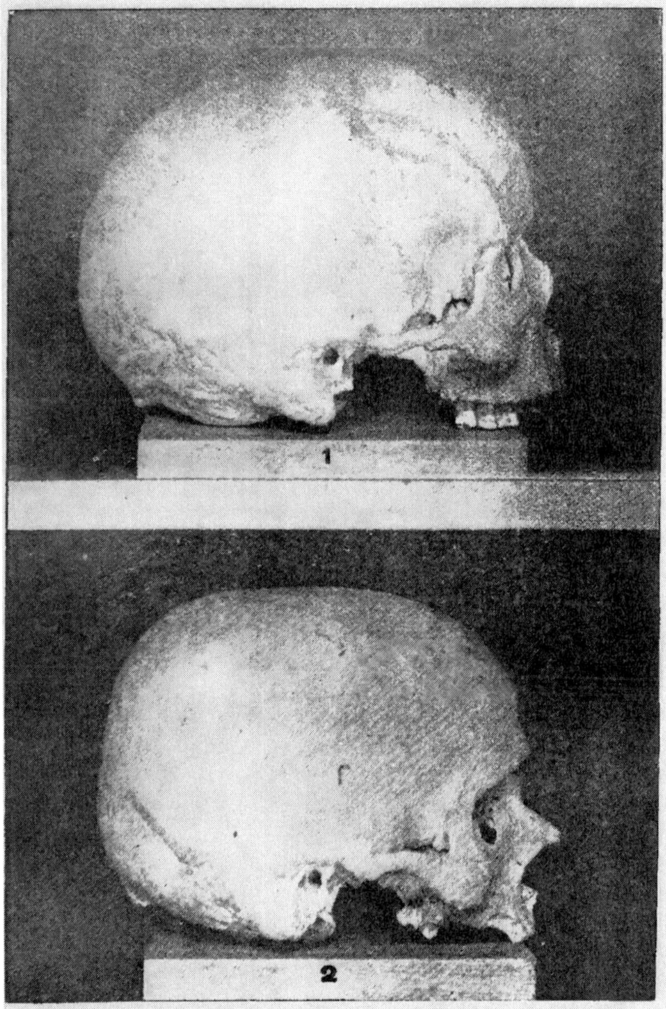

SKULLS OF EUROPEAN AND HINDU.

for study. The number of the skulls is confessedly small for the purpose of generalisation, but analysis of the measurements, combined with examination of the skulls, will nevertheless not be labour lost. As a guide to the main points which should be observed, the following summary may be of use :—

(*a*) The greater maximum length and horizontal circumference of the skulls of the Europeans and Jew, as compared with the others.

(*b*) The brachycephalic character, and consequent high cephalic index of the Mongolian, Andamanese, Cinghalese, and Burmese skulls.

(*c*) The prevailing narrow frontal region of the skulls of the four South Indian classes, Muhammadans, Hindus, Brāhman, and Cheruman.

(*d*) The difference between the nasal skeletons of the platyrrhine (broad-nosed) Negro, with high nasal index, and the leptorrhine (narrow-nosed) European.

(*e*) The marked prognathism of the skulls of Negroes.

TABLE VI.

COMPARISON OF MEASUREMENTS OF SKULLS.

	Maximum length from glabella.	Maximum transverse breadth.	Cephalic index.	Minimum frontal breadth.	Horizontal circumference.	Nasal height.	Nasal breadth.	Nasal index.
European	19	14·2	74·7	9·9	55	4·7	2·5	53·2
European	18·6	14·6	78·5	9·7	53·5	5·6	2·1	37·5
Jew	19·3	14·9	74·1	10·8	56·3	5·8	2·6	44·8
Muhammadan ...	18·2	13	71·4	9·2	51·6	5·2	2·6	50
Muhammadan ...	17·2	13·6	79·1	9·2	49·5	4·8	2·4	50
Muhammadan ...	17·6	13·5	76·7	8·7	50·2	4·3	2·1	48·8
Muhammadan ...	17·5	12·6	72	9·1	49·7	4·4	2·5	56·8
Tamil Hindu ...	17·5	13·5	77·1	9·3	51	4·7	2	42·6
Tamil Hindu ...	17·5	13·1	74·9	9·1	49·8	5·4	2·5	46·3
Tamil Hindu ...	17·3	12·9	74·6	9·1	50	4·8	2·5	52·1
Tamil Hindu ...	18	13·4	74·4	10	51·5	4·5	2·6	57·8
Tamil Hindu ...	18·4	13·9	75·5	9·5	52·8	4·8	2·1	43·8
Tamil Hindu ...	17·4	13	74·7	9·6	50	5	2·5	50
Tamil Hindu ...	18	13·4	74·4	9·1	51·8	4·9	2·5	51
Brāhman	17·7	13·3	75·1	9·1	49·7	4·5	2·5	55·6
Cheruman	17·5	13·1	74·9	9·1	50	4·6	2·4	52·2
Negro	17·1	12·9	75·4	9	49·6	4·5	2·4	53·3
Negro	17·8	12·9	72·5	9·9	51	4·6	2·8	60·9
Mongolian	17·6	14·3	81·2	9·5	52·1	4·8	2·6	54·2
Mongolian	17·8	14·5	81·5	9·2	52·8	5·2	2·6	50
Andamanese ...	16·1	13·4	83·2	8·5	48	4	2·2	55
Cinghalese	17·4	14·8	85·1	9·9	53	5·2	2·5	48·1
Burmese	16·4	14·2	86·6	9·8	51·3	5·4	2·5	46·3

TABLE VII.

AVERAGES OF MEASUREMENTS OF SKULLS.

	Maximum length from glabella.	Maximum transverse breadth.	Cephalic index.	Minimum frontal breadth.	Horizontal circumference.	Nasal height.	Nasal breadth.	Nasal index.
2 Europeans ...	18·8	14·4	76·6	9·8	54·3	5·2	2·3	45·4
1 Jew	19·3	14·9	74·1	10·8	56·3	5·8	2·6	44·8
4 Muhammadans ...	17·6	13·2	74·8	9·1	50·3	4·7	2·4	51·4
7 Hindus	17·7	13·3	75	9·4	50·1	4·9	2·4	49·1
1 Brâhman	17·7	13·3	75	9·1	49·7	4·5	2·5	55·6
1 Cheruman ...	17·5	13·1	74·9	9·1	50	4·6	2·4	54·3
2 Negroes	17·5	12·9	74	9·5	50·3	4·6	2·6	57·2
2 Mongolians ...	17·7	14·4	81·4	9·4	52·5	5	2·6	52·1
1 Andamanese ...	16·1	13·4	83·2	8·5	48	4	2·2	55
1 Cinghalese ...	17·4	14·8	85·1	9·9	53	5·2	2·5	48·1
1 Burmese	16·4	14·2	86·6	9·8	51·3	5·4	2·5	46·3

KURUBA OR KURUMBA?

As an introduction to the study of this intricate question, it will be best to commence by quoting the opinions of various writers, who have entered superficially into it.

Madras Census Report, 1891.—" The Kurumbas or Kurubas are numerous in Kurnool, Cuddapah, Bellary, Anantapur, North Arcot, South Arcot, Salem, Coimbatore, Trichinopoly and Madura. They are the modern representatives of the ancient Kurumbas or Pallavas, who were once so powerful throughout Southern India, but very little trace of their greatness now remains. In the seventh century the power of the Pallava Kings seems to have been at its zenith; but shortly after this, the Kongu, Chóla and Chálúkya chiefs succeeded in winning several victories over them. The final overthrow of the Kurumba sovereignty was effected by the Chóla king Ádondai about the seventh or eighth century A.D., and the Kurumbas were scattered far and wide. Many fled to the hills, and in the Nilgiris and the Wynaad, in Coorg and Mysore, representatives of this ancient race are now found as wild and uncivilised tribes. Elsewhere the Kurumbas are more advanced, and are usually shepherds and weavers of coarse woollen blankets."

" Kuruman.—This caste is found in the Nilgiris and the Wynaad, with a slight shrinkling in the Nilambúr and Attapádi hills in Malabar. Their principal occupations are wood-cutting and the collection of forest produce. The name is merely another form of Kurumban, but, as they differ considerably from the ordinary Kurumbas, it seemed better to show them separately. I think, however, that they were originally identical with the shepherd Kurumbans, and their present separation is merely the result of their isolation in the fastnesses of the Western Ghâts, to which their ancestors fled or gradually retreated after the downfall of the Kurumba dynasty. The name Kurumbranád, a sub-division of Malabar, still bears testimony to their once powerful position."—H. A. Stuart.

Mysore Census Report, 1891—Kádu Kuruba or Kurumba. —" The tribal name of Kuruba has been traced to the primeval occupation of the race, *viz.*, the tending of sheep, perhaphs when pre-historic man rose to the pastoral stage. The civilised Úor ru Kurubas, who are genuine tillers of the soil, and who are dotted over the country in populous and thriving communities, and many of whom have under the present ' Pax Britannica ' further developed into enterprising trades-

PL. XII.

KURUBA MAN.

men and withal lettered Government officials, are the very antipodes of the Kádu or wild Kurubas or Kurumbás. The latter, like the Iruligás and Sóligás, are the denizens of the south and south-western backwoods of the country, and have been correctly classed under the aboriginal population."—V. N. Narasimaiyengar.

Oppert: Original inhabitants of India—Kurubas or Kurumbas.—" However separated from each other and scattered among the Dravidian clans with whom they have dwelt, and however distant from one another they still live, there is hardly a province in the whole of Bharatavarasha which cannot produce, if not some living remnants of this race, at least some remains of past times which prove their presence. Indeed the Kurumbas must be regarded as very old inhabitants of this land, who can contest with their Dravidian kinsmen the priority of occupation of the Indian soil."

"The terms Kuruba and Kurumba are originally identical, though the one form is in different places employed for the other, and has thus occasionally assumed a special local meaning. Mr. H. B. Grigg appears to contradict himself when, while speaking of the Kurumbas, he says that 'in the low country they are called Kurubas or Cúrubáru, and are divided into numerous families, such as the Áné or elephant, náya or dog, Málé or hill Kurumbas.'[6] Such a distinction between mountain-Kurumbas and plain-Kurubas cannot be established. The Rev. G. Richter will find it difficult to prove that the Kurubas of Mysore are only called so as shepherds, and that no connection exists between these Kurubas and the Kurumbas. Mr. Lewis Rice calls the wild tribes as well as the shepherds Kurubas, but seems to overlook the fact that both terms are identical, and refer only to the ethnological distinction.

"The stunted growth of animals and plants in cold, wet, and high elevations is a well-known natural law, to which the human species has also to submit. In consequence of their loneliness and comparative physical weakness, the small mountaineers, when they meet their taller but less clever neighbours of the plains, display often a spiteful distrust, use poisoned arrows, and frighten them by their mysterious proceedings into abject superstition. This is the reason why the Kurumbas of the Nilgiri hills are so shunned."

---

[6] Manual of the Nilgiri District, 1880.

KING : Aboriginal Tribes of the Nilgiri Hills—Kurumbas. —"This tribe is of another race from the shepherd Kurumbas, described by Sir Walter Elliot as having a distinct priesthood, and worshipping the god Bhyra. The Nilgiri tribe have neither cattle nor sheep, and, in language, dress, and customs, have no affinity whatever with their namesakes."

The above extracts amply suffice for the purpose of showing that the distinction between Kuruba and Kurumba, and their relationship towards each other, call for a 'permanent settlement' by the application of scientific methods; and the problem, which is no easy one, appears to depend essentially on anthropometric observations and a study of physical characters for its solution. This research, which must be carried out among the Kurumbas or Kurubas of the plains of Southern India, the Kurubas of the Mysore plateau, and the Kurumbas who inhabit the jungles, must of necessity be prolonged; and I am at present unable to undertake it in its entirety. As a basis for future operations, I may, however, place on record the results of my investigations, so far as the jungle Kurumbas of the eastern slopes of the Nīlgiris and the more highly civilised Úru Kurubas of the Mysore province are concerned.

The picture, which is drawn by King[7] of the Nīlgiri Kurumbas, is not a pleasant one. "Their chief food," he says, "is wild roots and berries, or grains soaked in water, with occasional porcupines or polecats. Their dwellings are nothing more than a few branches piled up together like heaps of dead brushwood, in a plantation, often simply holes or clefts among the rocks. Their clothing is, with the males, a small dirty cloth round the loins; and, with the females, a rag thrown on any way that its condition and size render most available. The appearance of these rude people is wretched, and even disagreeable. Low in stature, they are also ill-made; the complexion is of an unhealthy hue, and their heads are thinly covered with mangy-looking hair. They have bleared eyes, a rather wide mouth, and often projecting teeth. Spare to leanness, there is also a total absence of any apparent muscle, and the arms and legs are as much like black sticks as human limbs. No such ceremony as marriage exists among these people, who live together like the brute creation." A quarter of a century has elapsed since this description was written, and the *fin de siècle*

---

[7] Aboriginal tribes of the Nilgiris, 1870.

PL. XIII.

KURUMBA MAN.

Kurumba, who works for regular wages on planters' estates, is more domesticated, better fed, better nourished, and better clothed. But by no stretch of the imagination, can the dark-skinned, broad-nosed Kurumba, whose portrait appears on plate xiii be regarded as an example of a high type of civilisation. Nor would the light-skinned Úru Kuruba, with sharp-cut features, and aquiline nose, whose portrait is reproduced on plate xii, appreciate being linked in the bonds of common ancestry with the Kurumba.

The average measurements of the Nilgiri Kurumbas and the Úru Kurumbas of Shimoga in the Mysore Province (some of whom are traders, or in the service of Government) are given in table VIII. I would, however, invite more special attention to the subjoined tabular statement, wherein the averages, and maxima and minima of the more important measurements, from a comparative point of view, are recorded with the object of bringing out the main points of difference between Kuruba and Kurumba.

	Kuruba.			Kurumba.		
	Maxima.	Minima.	Average.	Maxima.	Minima.	Average.
Height	CM. 176·4	CM. 155	CM. 163·9	CM. 163·6	CM. 149·6	CM. 157·5
Span of arms	184·4	155·2	171	173·4	156·6	167·5
Do. rel. to stature=100 ...	...	...	104·3	...	...	106·3
Middle finger to patella ...	16·2	9	12·3	12·6	6	9·8
Do. rel. to stature=100.	...	...	7·5	...	...	6·2
Hips	...	...	26·3	...	...	24·5
Foot, length	...	...	25·1	...	...	24·6
Cephalic length ...	19·6	17	18·3	18·7	16·9	17·9
Cephalic breadth	15	13·1	13·9	14·5	13	13·7
Cephalic index	82·1	71·6	75·8	83·3	71·8	77
Nasal height	5·3	4·2	4·7	4·4	3·6	4·2
Nasal breadth	3·9	3·1	3·4	4·2	3·4	3·8
Nasal index	85·9	62·3	73·2	111·1	79·1	88·8

Standing first in importance as distinguishing characters are stature and nose measurements. Coming under the heading 'below middle height' (163·9 cm.), with a maximum recorded height of 176·4 cm. (very tall), the Kuruba is clearly differentiated from the Kurumba of low stature (157·5 c.m.), whose maximum recorded height does not even reach the Kuruba average. More important, however, than stature, is the relation of height to breadth of nose; and it is obvious that there is a very wide distinction between the Kurubas with an index (average 73·2) ranging between 85·9 and 62·3, and the Kurumbas, whose index (average 88·8) ranges between 111·1 and 79·1. And, to take extreme cases, a light-skinned, leptorrhine Kuruba, with long, narrow nose, 5·3 × 3·3 cm. (index 62·3) cannot reasonably be linked together with a dark-skinned platyrrhine Kurumba with short, broad nose, 3·6 × 4 cm. (index 111·1).

Relatively to stature, the span of the arms is greater in the semi-domesticated Kurumba than in the more civilised Kuruba. And, in consequence of the greater length of the upper extremity relative to stature, the hand reaches nearer to the knee in the former than in the latter. In the Kurumbas the breadth of the hips across the iliac spines and the length of the foot are approximately the same, whereas, in the Kuruba, the breadth of the hips is considerably (1·2 cm.) greater than the foot length. In length and breadth of head, as might be expected, the Kuruba is in advance of the Kurumba, and the maxima recorded in the former are considerably in excess of those recorded in the latter.

PL. XIV.

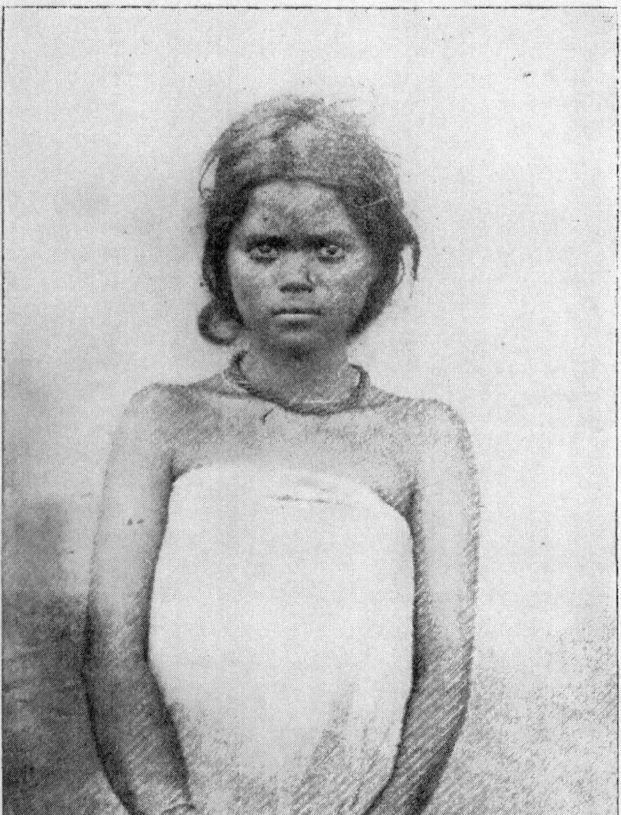

KURUMBA GIRL.

TABLE VIII.

COMPARISON OF MEASUREMENTS. KURUBAS AND KURUMBAS.

	Kurubas.	Kurumbas.
Height	163·9	157·5
Height, sitting	84	80·5
Height, kneeling	120·5	115·4
Height to gladiolus	123·3	116·4
Span of arms	171	167·5
Span of arms rel. to stature=100	104·3	106·3
Chest	83·8	79·3
Middle finger to patella	12·3	9·8
Middle finger to patella rel. to stature=100 ...	7·5	6·2
Shoulders	39·5	37·5
Cubit	45·7	45·2
Hand, length	18·3	17·8
Hand, breadth	8	7·9
Middle finger	11·5	10·7
Hips	26·3	24·5
Foot, length	25·1	24·6
Foot, breadth	8·6	8·2
Cephalic length	18·3	17·9
Cephalic breadth	13·9	13·7
Cephalic index	75·8	77
Bigoniac	10·1	9·8
Bizygomatic	12·9	12·9
Maxillo-zygomatic index	77·7	76
Nasal height	4·7	4·2
Nasal breadth	3·4	3·8
Nasal index	73·2	88·8
Vertex to tragus	14·1	13·3
Vertex to chin	21·2	20·4

SUMMARY OF RESULTS.

When, as sometimes happens, I am, owing to fear or superstitious objection on the part of the members of a tribe to undergo the entire course of treatment at my hands, reduced to the necessity of selecting a few only out of the series of twenty-one measurements, which I am in the habit of recording, I select, as being most useful for the purposes of classification and correlation, the stature, length and breadth of head, and height and breadth of nose. With these data to work on, it is comparatively easy to fit any community approximately into its proper place in the South Indian anthropological puzzle.

Some of the measurements, *e.g.*, chest girth and breadth of shoulders (*vide* tables xiv and xv), though useful as a guide to physical development, possess no racial value. Others, though important for comparison between the inhabitants of Southern India and other parts of the world, have little or no value as factors in differentiating between the various castes, tribes, etc., of Southern India. The facial angle, for example, though of great importance in separating prognathous from so-called orthognathous races, is of little use as an aid to comparison and classification of the different communities of Southern India, in whom the average of the angle of Cuvier (with its vertex at the edge of the incisor teeth) ranges, in the people examined by me, between 67° and 71°, as shown in the subjoined statement.

Badagas	71
Kotas	70
Kammālans	70
Brāhmans (Madras City)	69
Pallis	69
Vellālas	69
Tiyyans	69
Muppas	69
Pāl Kurumbas	69
Kongas	69
Todas	68
Pattar Brāhmans	68
Malaiālis	68
Tamil Pariahs	68
Kanarese Pariahs	68
Irulas	68
Sheik Muhammadans	67
Paniyans	67

In tables ix to xiii I have brought together, for the purpose of comparison, statistical evidence relating to the average stature, head, and nose measurements of the different classes which I have so far investigated. The most troublesome heads to measure were those of my hairy Toda friends, whose dense locks constituted an effective obstacle to easy shifting of the callipers, while the desired maximum was being groped for in the dark; the easiest were those of men with heads clean shaved in observance of some religious or domestic rite.

An examination of the section of the Madras Census Report, 1891, devoted to 'caste, tribe, and race,' will show how hopeless, to a worker with only one collaborateur, must be the prospect of making even a semblance of an approach to a complete anthropological survey of the multifarious tribes and castes inhabiting the vast tract of country comprising Southern India, which is included in my beat. All I can hope to do, amid other duties of a manifold nature, is to examine the more important communities when at head-quarters in Madras, and to make periodical roving expeditions with a view to carrying on the research in selected tribe-hunting grounds. In this way the material summarised in tables ix to xv has been brought together during the last two years; and including, as it does, examples of dwellers in the plains, on the hill tops, in the jungles at the bases of the hills, and on the Mysore plateau, it may, I think, be taken as fairly representative, and used for the purpose of generalisation. The nature and extent of the material collected up to the present time, and utilised in the following summaries of results, is shown by the subjoined tabular statement :—

Class.	Habitat.	Number measured.	
		Male.	Female.
Todas	Plateau of the Nīlgiri hills.	25	25
Kotas	Plateau of the Nīlgiri hills.	25	20
Badagas	Plateau of the Nīlgiri hills.	40	..

Class.	Habitat.	Number measured.	
		Male.	Female.
Irulas	Lower slopes of the Nīlgiri hills.	25	..
Kurumbas	Lower slopes of the Nīlgiri hills.	15	..
Sholigas	Base of Mysore hills ..	3	..
Malaialis	Shevaroy hills	36	..
Paniyans	Wynâd, Malabar ..	25	12
Muppas	Do. ..	24	..
Tiyyans	Calicut, South Malabar.	25	25
Cherumans ..	Do. do.	25	25
Pattar Brāhmans ..	Do. do.	25	..
Kongas	Coimbatore District ..	20	..
Tamil Brāhmans (poorer classes).	Madras City	40	..
Tamil Pariahs ..	Do.	40	..
Kammālans ..	Do.	40	..
Pallis	Do.	40	..
Vellalas	Do.	40	..
Muhammadans ..	Do.	75	..
Kanarese Pariahs ..	Mysore Province ..	33	..
Kurubas.. ..	Do. ..	25	..
Koramas	Do. ..	25	..
Lambādis (nomad).	Do. ..	40	40
	Total ..	711	147

1. STATURE.

The tallest men whom I have come across are a Toda (185 cm.) and Badaga (183·2 cm.); the shortest a Muppa (144·6 cm.), Cheruman (145·8 cm.), Kammālan (146·4 cm.) and Tamil Pariah (149·4 cm.).

The following table shows the average heights of the classes investigated :—

Very tall 170 cm. and upwards.

.. ..

Above middle height 170 to 165 cm.

Todas .. .. .. 169·6

Below middle height 165 to 160 cm.

Sheik Muhammadans ..	164·5
Lambādis	164·3
Pattar Brāhmans ..	164·3
Badagas	164·1
Kurubas	163·9
Malaiālis	163·9
Tiyyans	163·7
Kotas	162·9
Brāhmans (Madras city)	162·5
Pallis	162·5
Vellālas	162·4
Tamil Pariahs	161·9
Kanarese Pariahs ..	161·8

Low stature below 160 cm.

Irulas	159·8
Kammālans	159·7
Koramas	159·3
Kongas	159
Muppas	157·7
Cherumans	157·5
Urāli Kurumbas ..	157·5
Pāl Kurumbas	157·5
Paniyans	157·4

In Keane's 'Ethnology,' Hindus *and* Dravidians are (after Topinard) aggregated together, in an anthropological conglomerate, as possessing an average height of 164·5 cm., which I take to be rather exaggerated. In the foregoing table a very large majority of Hindu-Dravidians are undoubtedly included, but the aberrant Todas alone reach this average. The Todas, according to my estimate, possess approximately the same stature as the Irish (169·7 cm.), and just miss the dignity of being included with the English among the very tall races of the world. The hairy Ainu of Japan, it may be noted, is placed by Keane, in company with the Toda, in a siding on the family tree of Homo Caucasicus. The average height of the stalwart, black-haired Toda (5 feet 7½ inches) is, according to Mr. Savage Landor's measurement[8] of five typical examples, conspicuously in excess of that of the short, sometimes red-haired Ainu (5 feet 2½ inches).

Between the Todas and the next tallest class, the Sheik Muhammadans, there is a well-defined gap of 5·1 cm. But

[8] Alone with the hairy Ainu.

from Sheiks to Pariahs there is a gradual decrease in height, with a break of 2 cm. between the lowest representatives of middle stature and the tallest of low stature. Among the classes of middle height, the uniformity of the height of Brāhmans, Pallis, and Vellālas, and of Tamil and Kanarese Pariahs is noteworthy. So also is the presence of the Kammālans among the classes of low stature, amid the humble environment of Irulas, Koramas, and Kongas.

The length of the upper extremities, in the classes under consideration, relative to stature, as estimated by the determination of the distance from the tip of the middle finger to the top of the knee-cap (patella), when the subject is at attention with the extensor muscles of the thigh relaxed, is shown by the following table :—

	Average.	Average relative to stature=100.
Koramas	13·3	8·3
Kurubas	12·3	7·5
Badagas	12·2	7·4
Lambādis	11·7	7·1
Pattar Brāhmans	11·3	6·9
Irulas	10·7	6·7
Kotas	10·7	6·6
Malaiālis	10·8	6·6
Sheik Muhammadans	10·7	6·5
Tiyyans	10·6	6·5
Vellālas	10·4	6·4
Kongas	9·9	6·2
Tamil Brāhmans	10·1	6·2
Kanarese Pariahs	9·8	6·1
Tamil Pariahs	9·4	5·8
Pallis	9·5	5·8
Kammālans	8·4	5·3
Todas	·9	5·3
Muppas	8·2	5·3
Cherumans	7·8	4·6
Paniyans	7·3	4·4

The more the distance diminishes, the greater is the length of the upper extremities. The arm then is shortest in the Kanarese Koramas, Kurubas, and Badagas, and longest in the short, broad-nosed Paniyans, who approach the Negro average (4·37).

As examples of inordinately long upper extremities (not included in the averages), which brought to mind the

Hindu ideal of the long-armed Ráma, "whose hands reach to the knees," the two following cases are worthy of being placed on record. The one was a venerable, white-haired Kuruba; the other a Tamil Pariah, who is referred to later on in connection with his nose.

	Kuruba. CM.	Pariah. CM.
Height	177·8	160·8
Span of arms	199·2	183·8
Difference between span and height.	21	23
Cubit	53	
Middle finger to patella	5·7	6·4
Middle finger to patella relative to stature=100.	3·2	4

2. HEAD MEASUREMENTS.

For the benefit of my amateur readers, to whom the meaning of the term 'cephalic index' may not be clear, it may be stated that this index, which expresses the ratio of the length to the breadth of the head, is estimated by multiplying the maximum breadth by 100, and dividing the product by the maximum length.

Examples.

Toda { cephalic length 20 cm.
cephalic breadth 14 cm.

$$\frac{14 \times 100}{20} = 70 = \text{cephalic index.}$$

Brāhman { cephalic length 18·2 cm.
cephalic breadth 15 cm.

$$\frac{15 \times 100}{18{\cdot}2} = 82{\cdot}4 = \text{cephalic index.}$$

The terms used in the headings of the columns in table ix, in which the nomenclature of Broca is followed, have the following significance:—

Dolichocephalic	Index	75 and under.
Sub-dolichocephalic	,,	75·01 to 77·77.
Mesaticephalic	,,	77·78 to 80.
Sub-brachycephalic	,,	80·01 to 83·33.
Brachycephalic	,,	83·34 and upwards.

Turning now to table ix. Conspicuous by its almost complete absence is the brachycephalic head, which, were I dealing with the Burmese instead of the inhabitants of Southern India, would be very largely represented, with a corresponding decrease in the numbers of dolicho-and sub-dolichocephalic heads. The columns in table ix would, in fact, have been inverted. The solitary heads, which prevent the brachycephalic column from being a perfect and absolute blank, were the property of a Kanarese Koraman, and a Tamil Brāhman guru (religious instructor) who shares with a Toda the honour of possessing the maximum head-breadth (15·2 cm.) recorded in my notes. But the length of the Toda's head was 19·6 cm. against the Brāhman's 18·1 cm. The only other brachycephalic heads, which I have met with during the examination of nine hundred subjects, belonged to two broad-headed Lambadi lassies, whose cephalic indices were 83·9 and 85·5 respectively.

It is worthy of notice that the tribes, which stand first and second in the list, so far as head length is concerned, are the Todas and Kotas—the two oldest existing tribes of the Nīlgiri plateau—in whom alone the average head length exceeds 19 cm. The maximum head lengths recorded, in the classes under review, reached, or slightly exceeded 20 cm. only in the Todas, Kotas, and Badagas of the Nīlgiri plateau, and in the Tiyyans and Pattar Brāhmans of Malabar. In the other classes investigated, the maximum head-length ranged between 19·9 cm. in the Brāhmans of Madras city (belonging to the poorer classes) and 19·1 in the Irulas and Kongas, whose mental development is of a very low order. The Irulas, it may be mentioned, *en passant*, are an uncultivated jungle tribe, who have only in recent years been brought by the European planting community under the influence of civilisation; and the Kongas are a degraded sub-division of the Vellālas, who occupy a low position in the Vellāla community. "No other Vellāla," it is said,[9] "would take his meals with them because they employ Uppiliyans and other low caste people as cooks for their marriages, &c."

The average head-length ranges between 19·4 cm. in the Todas and 17·8 cm. in the Kongas and Koramas. The latter are inhabitants of the Mysore plateau, very dark-skinned and short of stature, "with crime and vice writ

[9] Madras Census Report, 1891.

large on their physiognomy," who combine professional burgling, and animal and bird-snaring with ingenious contrivances, with the more orthodox occupation of basket making. Only under marked protest, and with the assistance of the police, did the Koramas permit me to use them for the purposes of anthropometry, and my recollection of my sojourn among them is far from a happy one.

The coincidence of the head length in four out of the five Hindu classes examined in Madras City—Brāhmans, Vellālas, Pallis, and Pariahs—appears to me suggestive. In the fifth class, the Kammālans, the head-length was slightly less.

As in length, so in breadth of head, the Todas and Kotas of the Nīlgiris stand out conspicuously in the first rank, but, in this case, bracketed equal with the Brāhmans of Madras city (14·2 cm.), who are close followed by the Pattar Brāhmans of Malabar, descended from Tamil Brāhmans who migrated to Malabar from the east coast, and have, I imagine, become modified as regards physical characters by alliances contracted in the home of their adoption (*vide* table xvi). In the remaining classes, the average head-breadth ranges between 13·8 cm. and 13·5 cm. and calls for no special remark, except that breadth of head exceeding 15 cm. occurred only among the Todas (15·2), Kotas (15·1), Brāhmans of Madras City (15·2), and Pattar Brāhmans (15·1).

Arranging the classes under review in sequence, according to the cephalic index, the results are as follows:—

Dolichocephalic.

Badagas	71·7
Muppas	72·3
Tiyyans	72·7
Pallis	73
Todas	73·1
Tamil Pariahs	73·6
Cherumans	73·9
Paniyans	74
Kotas	74·1
Vellālas	74·1
Malaiālis	74·4
Pattar Brāhmans	74·5
Kammālans	75

Sub-dolichocephalic.

Lambādis	75·4
Kurubas	75·8
Sheik Muhammadans	76·2
Brāhmans (Madras city)	76·5
Kanarese Pariahs	76·8
Kongas	77
Koramas	77·5

Only, as shown in table ix, in the Todas, Badagas, and Muppas, was the head confined to the dolichocephalic and sub-dolichocephalic types; the remaining classes possessing a greater or less proportion of mesaticephalic (intermediate) and sub-brachycephalic heads. In the majority of the classes examined, the head was dolichocephalic in more than half the cases; and it is clear from the foregoing statistics that the dolichocephalic head is the prevailing type, so far as Southern India is concerned. The classes, in which the head was dolichocephalic in less than half the cases, were the Brāhmans and Sheik Muhammadans of Madras City, Irulas, Kongas, Kurubas, Kanarese Pariahs, and Koramas. A glance at table ix shows at once the high proportion of sub-dolichocephalic heads in the Brāhmans and Kurubas, and mesaticephalic heads in the Koramas. I have already (Bulletin No. 4) dealt with the great breadth of the Brāhman head in comparison with that of the other classes examined in Madras. The Lambādis, Kurubas and Sheik Muhammadans come intermediate between the Brāhmans and a group composed of Kanarese Pariahs, Irulas, Koramas, and Kongas, all people of low origin, whose high cephalic index is explained, not as in the case of the Brāhmans, by the great breadth of the head in proportion to its length, but, as shown in the following summary, by the shortness of its length in relation to its breadth:—

	Length.	Breadth.
	cm.	cm.
Brāhmans	18·6	14·2
Lambādis	18·4	13·9
Kurubas	18·3	13·9
Sheik Muhammadans ..	18·2	13·8
Kanarese Pariahs	18	13·8
Irulas	18	13·7
Koramas	17·8	13·9
Kongas	17·8	13·7

PL. XV.

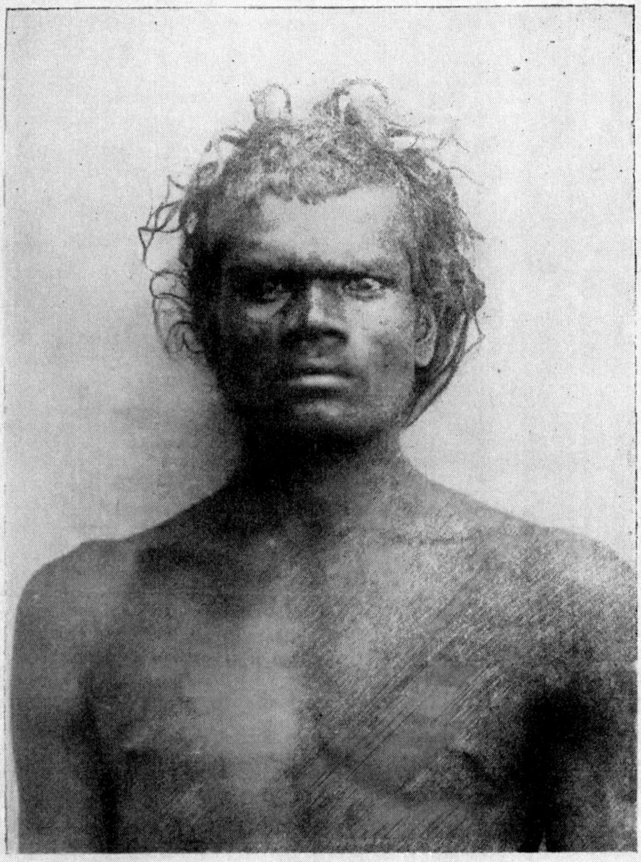

TAMIL PARIAH.

3. THE NOSE.

Readers of Marryat's novels will doubtless remember that Japhet, in search of his father, borrowed from Mr. Cophagus a book containing a dissertation upon the human frame, sympathies, antipathies, and those features and peculiarities most likely to descend from one generation to another, wherein it was asserted that the nose was the facial feature most likely to be transmitted. The nose I regard as an all-important element, so far as the people in whom I am interested are concerned, as a basis of classification, and as an aid to the elucidation of the ancestry of caste and tribe. Not, however, the shape of the nose, but the relation of its height to its breadth (nasal index), is that to which a prominent place must be assigned in a study of the comparative anthropography of the people of Southern India. "Le plus important des caractéres cephalométriques," says Topinard,[10] "est l'indice nasal. C'est le seul caractére se mesurant qui partage tous les types de l'humanité en trois groupes fondamentaux répondant à la division classique de Cuvier en races blanches (leptorrhiniennes, nez long, et étroit), races jaunes (mésorrhiniennes, nez large et bas). Cet indice varie, dans les moyennes, de 63 dans une série de 100 Francais dolichocéphales et blondes mesurés par le docteur Collignon a 109 dans une série de Tasmaniens mesurés pour nous sur leurs moulages; et dans les cas particuliers, de 50 et moins chez des Européens a 153 chez un Australien."

A photograph (pl. xv), which I regard with some affection, has been challenged on the ground that it must have been deformed. It may, therefore, be stated that noses disfigured by small-pox and other diseases, or pugilistic encounters, are invariably rejected.

Once more, for the amateur, it may be explained that the nasal index expresses the relation of the height of the nose, measured from the under surface (not the tip), to the breadth measured across the widest part of the nostrils when at rest. This index is, like the cephalic index, estimated by multiplying the breadth by 100, and dividing the product by the height.

---

[10] L'Homme dans la Nature.

Examples.—

Brāhman { nasal height 5·5 cm.
nasal breadth 3·4 cm.

$$\frac{3{\cdot}4 \times 100}{5{\cdot}5} = 61{\cdot}8 = \text{nasal index.}$$

Kurumba { nasal height 4 cm.
nasal breadth 4 cm.

$$\frac{4 \times 100}{4} = 100 = \text{nasal index.}$$

Paniyan { nasal height 3·5 cm.
nasal breadth 3·8 cm.

$$\frac{3{\cdot}8 \times 100}{3{\cdot}5} = 108{\cdot}6 = \text{nasal index.}$$

These examples, taken from my case-book, show (1) that the greater the height in proportion to the breadth, the lower is the index; (2) that, when the height is exactly equal to the breadth, the index is 100; (3) that, when the breadth is greater than the height, the index exceeds 100.

Turning now to tables xi–xiii, it will be seen that the average nasal index of the people investigated ranges from 69·1 in the tall, light-skinned, and long narrow-nosed Lambādis (who speak an Aryan language), to 95·1 in the short, dark-skinned, and short, broad-nosed Paniyans; and that the indices recorded range between a minimum of 59·2 in a Lambādi and a maximum of 108·6 in a Paniyan. The maximum index, however, which I have met with, was in the case of a Paniyan woman, who possessed a nose 3·1 cm. in height and 3·7 cm. in breadth, and a nasal index of 119·4.

In table xii the noses are arranged according to their height. But the actual sequence of nasal indices is recorded in table xi, which shows, in each case, the maxima and minima observed, the average, and the range. In the same table, the noses are further classified according as the average index is from 60–70, 70–80, 80–90, or 90–100; and the main interest, to my mind, lies in the connection which exists between the noses in the earlier and later series. Assistance in tracing this connection will, I think, be found in table xiii, in which statistics relating to twenty to twenty-five members of the various classes examined are given, showing the frequency of noses with indices of 50–60 60–70, 70–80, 80–90, 90–100, and 100–110.

Only in one case—the Lambādis—do noses occur with an index below 60. The most popular columns, so far as number of entries is concerned, are those containing noses ranging between 70 and 80 and between 80 and 90, which contain respectively 236 and 146 out of 515 noses examined. Occupying a very prominent position in the column of noses between 80 and 90 are the Tamil Pariahs, Irulas, and Muppas, all of whom get into double figures. In the column containing noses with indices from 90 to 100, the Paniyans and Irulas hold a high place, and the same two classes monopolise, in the proportion of 10 : 1, the final column, which contains those wondrous noses, of which the breadth exceeds the height. In this column the Kurumbas and Sholigas would figure largely, but the material at my disposal is too scanty for record in the table.

On a coffee estate in the Ouchterlony valley, I was introduced to a Sholiga dwarf, the son and brother of dwarfs with hereditary polydactyly, who was very angry at my measuring operations, and kept on muttering that such a thing would not have been permitted when Mr. Ouchterlony was alive. The big but normal nose of this little man, measuring 4×4·1cm., with nasal index of 102·5, presented an irresistably comical appearance, but he failed to appreciate my lively interest in it.

In the subjoined tabular statement the various castes and tribes are classified according to the range of their nasal indices, *i.e.*, the difference between the maximum and minimum recorded in each case.

10—20.	
Badagas	15·7
Todas	17·9
Kotas	18·9
20—30.	
Tiyyans	21·8
Muppas	21·8
Kurubas	23·6
Lambādis	24·5
Paniyans	24·9
Sheik Muhammadans ..	25·1
Kanarese Pariahs	26·6
Kammālans	27·6
Irulas	27·7
Koramas	28·2
Kongas	28·7
Cherumans	29·3

30—40.		
Pattar Brāhmans	.. ..	30·1
Vellālas	.. .. ..	30·7
Malaiālis	.. .. ..	34·2
Pallis	.. ..	34·3
Brāhmans (Madras City)	..	35·1
Tamil Pariahs	.. ..	39

It is noteworthy that the tribes, whose nasal indices have the least variation, are the three which inhabit the plateau of the Nīlgiri hills, where they lived an isolated existence until the settlement of the English on these hills in recent times; and that the owners of the greatest variation (exceeding 30) constitute a group of Tamil classes made up of Brāhmans, Vellālas, Pallis, and Pariahs of Madras city, the Malaiālis of the Shevaroy hills, (descended, it is said, from Vellālas of Conjeveram), and the Pattar Brāhmans descended from east-coast Tamil Brāhmans.

Very suggestive are the following measurements of a very dark-skinned Tamil Pariah cooly, whom I met by chance when changing camp in the course of a recent wandering, and detained, much against his will, until the measuring instruments came up.

Height ..	.. ..	160·8	cm.
Nasal height	.. ..	4	,,
Nasal breadth	.. ..	4·2	,,
Nasal index	.. ..	105	,,

Looking at the portrait of this man (pl. xv), there is an irresistable impulse to connect him, in the ties of ethnical relationship, with the jungle tribes; and I regard this man, and other Pariahs of a kindred nature, whom I have come across, as important witnesses in support of my belief that the constantly recurring high nasal index among existing Aryo-Dravidians and Dravidians must be traced to the influence of a platyrrhine (broad-nosed) ancestor.

The Sheik, Pathān, and Saiyad Muhammadans of Madras claim to be descendants of immigrants from the north, and to be distinct from the converted Dravidians, the Máppilas and Labbais. Their claim is no doubt justified; but well-marked signs of admixture of Dravidian blood are conspicuous in some members of their communities, whose dark skin and high nasal index betray their non-Aryan ancestry.

PLATE XVI

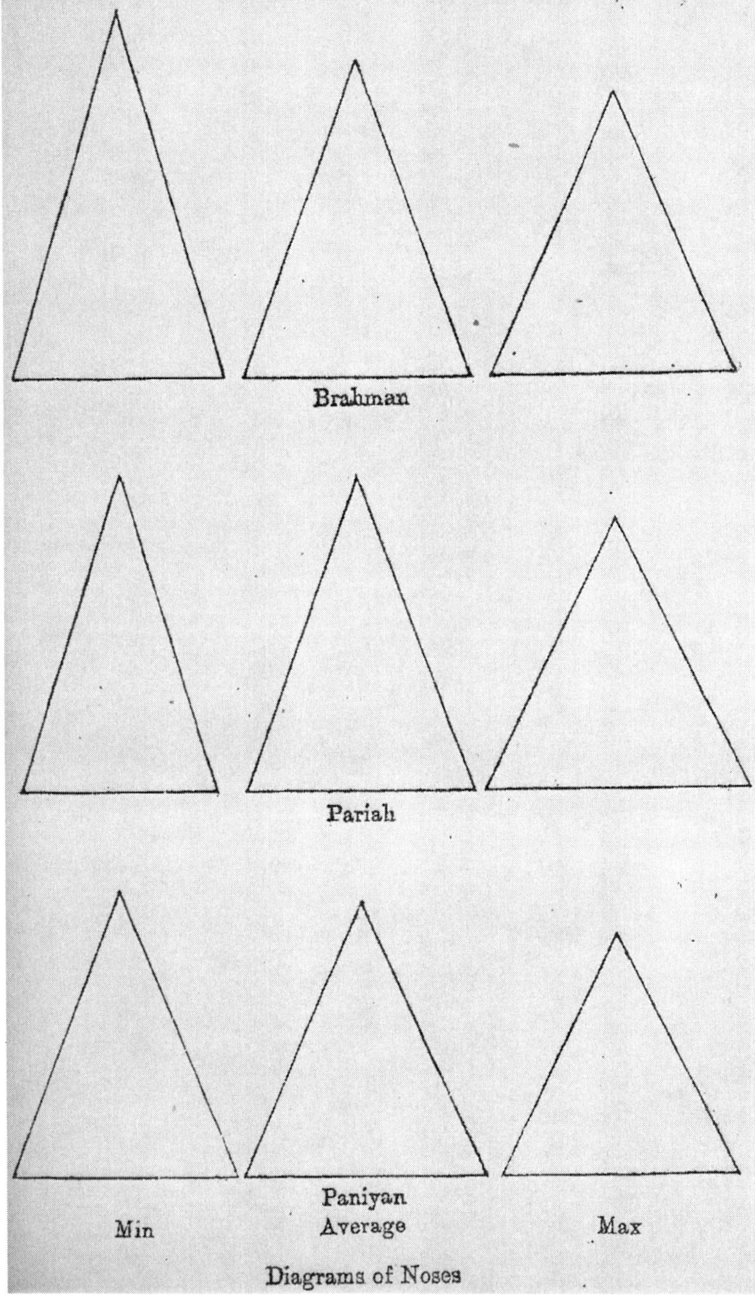

Diagrams of Noses

In plate xvi are figured a series of triangles representing (natural size) the maxima, minima, and average nasal indices of Brāhmans of Madras city (belonging to the poorer classes) Tamil Pariahs, and Paniyans. There is obviously far less connection between the Brāhman minimum and the Paniyan maximum than between the Brāhman and Pariah maxima and the Paniyan average; and the frequent occurrence of high nasal indices, resulting from short, broad noses, not only in Brāhmans and Pariahs, but also in Cherumans, Muppas, Kongas, and others, has to be accounted for.

Sir. A. Lyall somewhere refers to the gradual Brāhmanising of the aboriginal Non-Aryan, or casteless tribes. "They pass," he says, "into Brāhmanists by a natural upward transition, which leads them to adopt the religion of the castes immediately above them in the social scale of the composite population, among which they settle down; and we may reasonably guess that this process has been working for centuries." In the Madras Census report, 1891, the Census Commissioner, Mr. H. A. Stuart, states that "it has often been asserted, and is now the general belief, that the Brāhmans of the south are not pure Aryans, but are a mixed Aryan and Dravidian race. In the earliest times the caste division was much less rigid than now, and a person of another caste could become a Brāhman by attaining the Brāhmanical standard of knowledge, and assuming Brāhmanical functions. And when we see the Nambudiri Brāhmans, even at the present day, contracting alliances, informal though they be, with the women of the country, it is not difficult to believe that, on their first arrival, such unions were even more common, and that the children born of them would be recognised as Brāhmans, though perhaps regarded as an inferior class. However, those Brāhmans, in whose veins mixed blood is supposed to run, are even to this day regarded as lower in the social scale, and are not allowed to mix freely with the pure Brāhman community."

Between a Brāhman of high culture, with fair complexion, and long, narrow nose on the one hand, and a less highly-civilised Brāhman with dark skin and short, broad nose on the other, there is a vast difference, which can only be reasonably explained on the assumption of admixture of races. And it is no insult to the higher members of the Brāhman community to trace, in their more lowly brethren, the result of crossing with a dark-skinned, broad-nosed race of short stature. Whether the jungle tribes—Irulas, Kurumbas, Sholigas, and others—are the existing microscopic remnant of a pre-Dravidian people, or of Dravidians driven by a conquering race to the seclusion of the jungles, it is to the lasting influence of some such broad-nosed ancestor that the high nasal index and short stature of many of the inhabitants of Southern India must, it seems to me, be attributed. Viewed in the light of this remark, the connection between the following mixed collection of individuals, all of very dark colour, short of stature, and with nasal index exceeding 90, calls for no explanation: —

—	Stature.	Nasal height.	Nasal breadth.	Nasal index.
	CM.	CM.	CM.	
Kammālan	154·4	4·4	4	90·9
Korama	159·8	4·6	4·2	91·3
Saiyad Muhammadan ..	160	4·4	4	90·9
Vellāla	154·8	4·7	4·3	91·6
Muppa	151·2	3·7	3·4	91·9
Malaiāli	158·8	4	3·7	92·5
Konga	157	4·1	3·8	92·7
Pattar Brāhman ..	157·6	4·2	3·9	92·9
Kurumba	159·6	4·4	4·1	93·2
Smārta Brāhman ..	159	4·1	3·9	95·1
Palli	157·8	4·1	3·9	95·1
Irula	155·4	4·1	3·9	95·1
Paniyan	157·8	4·1	3·9	95·1
Irula	158·6	4·3	4·3	100
Tamil Pariah	160	4	4·2	105
Paniyan	158·8	3·8	4	105·3

Though the present chapter is entitled 'Summary of Results,' it aims at no finality, but must be regarded in the light of a preliminary summary based on the evidence collected up to date. Absence from India will create a breach of continuity in my work in connection with the anthropological survey of Southern India, which I hope to resume, with renewed vigour, in 1898.

"The more remote and unknown the race or tribe," it has been said, "the more valuable is the evidence afforded by the study of its institutions, from the probability of their being less mixed with those of European origin." Tribes which, only a few years ago, were living in a wild state, clad in a cool and simple garb of forest leaves, and buried away in the depths of the jungle, have now come under the domesticating, and sometimes detrimental, influence of contact with Europeans, with a resulting modification of their conditions of life, morality, and even language. The Paniyans of the Wynâd, and the Irulas who inhabit the slopes of the Nīlgiris, now work regularly for daily wage on planters' estates; and I was lately shocked by seeing a Toda boy studying for the third standard in Tamil, instead of tending the buffaloes of his mand. The Todas, whose natural drink is milk, now delight in bottled beer, and mixture of port wine and gin, which they purchase in the Ootacamund bazár. On one occasion, I am told, a planter met two stalwart Todas returning from a funeral ceremony, and carrying across their shoulders a bundle, which, on examination, resolved itself into a Toda woman in a very advanced stage of intoxication.

"The rapid extermination of savages at the present time, and the rapidity with which they are being reduced to the standard of European manners, renders it of urgent importance to correct these sources of error as soon as possible." Ample proof can be adduced in support of the fact that European influence, import trade with other countries, and the struggle for existence, are bringing about a rapid change (said from an ethnographic standpoint) among the native inhabitants of Southern India, both civilised and uncivilised. The employment of tiles and kerosine tins in lieu of primitive thatch; the import of cotton piece goods, which represents roughly 40 per cent. of the total import trade, and of umbrellas to the value of over 40,00,000 rupees annually; cooly trade and migration by sea to Assam, Burma and Ceylon; the decline of the national turban in favour of the less becoming porkpie cap or knitted night cap of gaudy hue; the replacement of peasant jewelry of indigenous manufacture by the importation of beads and imitation jewelry made in Europe, and accurately copied, in many instances, from specimens sent to exhibitions, and purchased by the agents of the manufacturers; the abandonment of the use of indigenous vegetable dyes in favour of the cheaper and more rapidly operating anilin and alizarin dyes; the use of lucifer matches by 'aboriginal' tribes, who formerly made fire by friction; the supply of new forms of food, and of beer and spirits, in the bazaars; the influence of the Government in suppressing thuggi, sutti, the human (meriah) sacrifices of the Khonds, and Toda infanticide; the administration of justice; the spread of education; religious teaching:—these and many other factors are the causes, or signs of, a radical change in the ethnographic conditions of the country.

A Toda lassie curling her ringlets with the assistance of a cheap looking-class; a Toda man smeared with Hindu sect marks, doing púja, and praying for male offspring at a Hindu shrine; a Bengali babu with close-cropped hair and bare head, clad in patent leather boots, white socks, dhuti, and conspicuous unstarched shirt of English device; a Hindu or Parsi cricket eleven engaged against a European team; the increasing struggle for small-paid appointments under Government:—these are a few examples of changes resulting from the refinement of modern civilization.

It has recently been said that "there will be plenty of money and people available for anthropological research, when there are no more aborigines"; and it behoves our museums to waste no time in completing their anthropological collections.

TABLE IX.

CLASSIFICATION OF HEADS.

	Dolichocephalic.	Sub-dolichocephalic.	Mesaticephalic.	Sub-brachycephalic.	Brachycephalic.
Todas	22	3	...	...	...
Badagas	21	4	...	...	...
Pallis	20	2	3	...	...
Tiyyans	20	2	2	1	...
Muppas	19	5	...	...	...
Vellālas	19	5	1	...	...
Tamil Pariahs	18	6	1	...	...
Kotas	17	6	2	...	...
Cherumans	17	5	2	1	...
Malaiālis	17	3	4	1	...
Paniyans	15	8	1	1	...
Kammālans	14	6	3	2	...
Pattar Brāhmans	14	6	3	2	...
Lambādis	13	7	2	3	...
Irulas	11	8	5	1	...
Sheik Muhammadans	10	7	6	2	...
Kanarese Pariahs	8	7	5	5	...
Tamil Brāhmins	7	12	3	2	1
Kurubas	7	13	4	2	...
Kongas	6	8	9	2	...
Koramas	6	3	13	1	2

TABLE X.

AVERAGES.

CEPHALIC LENGTH, BREADTH, AND INDEX.

	Length.	Breadth.	Index.
	cm.	cm.	—
Todas	19·4	14·2	73·3
Kotas	19·2	14·2	74·1
Badagas	18·9	13·6	71·7
Tiyyans	18·9	13·7	72·7
Pattar Brâhmans	18·8	14	74·5
Tamil Brâhmans	18·6	14·2	76·5
Tamil Pariahs	18·6	13·7	73·6
Vellâlas	18·6	13·8	74·1
Pallis	18·6	13·6	73
Muppas	18·5	13·4	72·3
Lambâdis	18·4	13·9	75·4
Kammâlans	18·4	13·7	75
Paniyans	18·4	13·6	74
Kurubas	18·3	13·9	75·8
Malaiâlis	18·3	13·7	74·4
Cherumans	18·3	13·5	73·9
Sheik Muhammadans	18·2	13·8	76·2
Kanarese Pariahs	18	13·8	76·8
Irulas	18	13·7	75·8
Kongas...	17·8	13·7	77
Koramas	17·8	13·9	77·5

TABLE XI.

NASAL INDEX.

	Max.	Min.	Average.	Range.
	60–70.			
Lambâdis	83·7	59·2	69·1	24·5
Sheik Muhammadans	85·1	60	70	25·1
	70–80.			
Vellâlas	91·5	60·8	73·1	30·7
Kurubas	85·9	62·3	73·2	23·6
Todas	89·1	61·2	74·9	17·9
Tiyyans	83·3	61·5	75	21·8
Kotas	92·9	64	75·5	18·9
Badagas	88·4	62·7	75·6	15·7
Koramas	90·9	62·7	75·7	28·2
Kanarese Pariahs	88·1	61·5	75·9	26·6
Pattar Brâhmans	95·3	64·7	76·5	30·1
Brâhmans (Madras city)	95·1	60	76·7	35·1
Kammalans	90·9	63·3	77·3	27·6
Malaiâlis	100	63·8	77·8	34·2
Pallis	95·1	60·8	77·9	34·3
Cherumans	88·9	69·6	78·1	29·3
Kongas	92·7	64	79·9	28·7
	80–90.			
Tamil Pariahs	10·5	66	80	39
Muppas	92·3	70·5	81·5	21·8
Irulas	100·	72·3	84·9	27·7
Pâl Kurumbas	...	...	87	...
	90–100.			
Urâli Kurumbas	...	...	93·4	...
Sholigas	...	...	94·4	...
Paniyans	108·6	83·7	95·1	24·9

TABLE XII.

AVERAGES OF NASAL HEIGHT, BREADTH, AND INDEX.

	Height.	Breadth.	Index.
Lambâdis	4·9	3·4	69·1
Sheik Muhammadans	4·9	3·4	70
Vellâlas	4·7	3·4	73·1
Kurubas	4·7	3·4	73·2
Tiyyans	4·7	3·5	75
Todas	4·7	3·6	74·9
Pattar, Brâhmans	4·7	3·6	76·5
Brâhmans (Madras city)	4·7	3·6	76·7
Kanarese, Pariahs	4·7	3·6	75·9
Badagas	4·6	3·4	75·6
Koramas	4·6	3·4	75·7
Malaiâlis	4·6	3·5	77·8
Kammâlans	4·6	3·6	77·3
Pallis	4·6	3·6	77·9
Kotas	4·5	3·5	77·2
Kongas	4·5	3·5	79·9
Tamil Pariahs	4·5	3·6	80
Cherumans	4·4	3·4	78·1
Irulas	4·4	3·7	84·9
Pâl Kurumbas	4·3	3·7	87
Sholigas	4·2	3·9	94·4
Muppas	4·1	3·3	81·5
Urâli Kurumbas	4·1	3·8	93·4
Paniyans	4	3·8	95·1

TABLE XIII.

COMPARISON OF NASAL INDICES OF 20-25 MEMBERS OF VARIOUS CLASSES.

	50-60	60-70	70-80	80-90	90-100	100-110
Lambādis	2	13	6	4	...	...
Sheik Muhammadans ...	...	13	11	1	...	...
Vellālas	...	9	13	3	...	...
Kurubas	...	8	14	3	...	...
Koramas	...	6	12	4	1	...
Kanarese Pariahs	...	6	10	9	...	...
Tiyyans	...	5	13	7	...	...
Todas...	...	4	13	8	...	...
Kotas	...	4	11	8	1	...
Brāhmans (Madras city) ...	...	4	12	8	1	...
Pattar Brāhmans	...	4	15	4	2	...
Badagas	...	3	14	8	...	...
Malaiālis	...	3	12	9	1	...
Kammālans	...	2	16	6	1	...
Kongas	...	2	7	8	3	...
Pallis	...	1	14	7	3	...
Tamil Pariahs	...	1	9	14	1	...
Cherumans	...	1	16	8	...	...
Muppas	...	...	11	11	2	...
Irulas	...	...	7	11	6	1
Paniyans	...	...	...	5	9	10

TABLE XIV.

CHEST GIRTH.

	Average.	Average relative to stature = 100.
	CM.	
Paniyans	81·5	51·8
Kurubas	83·8	51·1
Kotas	83	51
Pāl Kurumbas	79·2	50·3
Lambādis	82·5	50·2
Kanarese Pariahs	81·3	50·2
Tiyyans	82	50·1
Brāhmans (Madras city)	81	49·8
Koramas	79·4	49·8
Kongas	79·2	49·8
Irulas	79·4	49·7
Muppas	77·4	49·1
Cherumans	78·4	49·1
Vellālas	79·8	49·1
Badagas	80·4	49
Todas	83	48·9
Tamil Pariahs	79·3	48·9
Kammālans	78	48·8
Malaiālis	80	48·8
Pallis	79·2	48·7

The measurements were taken round the nipples, the arms being above the head, and hands joined.

The English average = 93·9, *i.e.*, 54 relative to stature = 100 (Topinard).

TABLE XV.

BREADTH OF SHOULDERS.

	Average.	Average relative to stature = 100.
	CM	
Tiyyans	40·3	24·6
Kammālans	39·2	24·5
Vellālas	39·7	24·4
Tamil Pariahs	39·4	24·3
Kongas	38·7	24·3
Brāhmans (Madras city)	39·3	24·2
Pallis	39·4	24·2
Kurubas	39·5	24·1
Irulas	38·5	24·1
Badagas	39·4	24
Kanarese Pariahs	38·8	24
Lambādis	39·5	24
Pāl Kurumbas	37·8	24
Malaiālis	38·8	23·7
Koramas	37·7	23·7
Cherumans	37	23·5
Todas	39·3	23·2
Kotas	37·7	23·1
Paniyans	35·9	22·8
Muppas	35·3	22·4

TABLE XVI.

SUMMARY OF MEASUREMENTS OF BRÁHMANS OF MADRAS CITY AND PATTAR BRÁHMANS OF MALABAR.

	Madras.	Pattar.
Weight	115 lb.	112 lb.
Height	162·5 cm.	164·3 cm.
Height, sitting	85·4	85·6
Height, kneeling	119·2	121·3
Height to gladiolus	122·1	122·7
Span of arms	173·3	173
Chest	81	83·9
Middle finger to patella	10·1	11·3
Shoulders	39·3	41
Cubit	46	46·2
Hand, length	18·3	18·6
Hand, breadth	8	8·2
Middle finger	11·6	11·8
Hips	26	27·1
Foot, length	25·9	25·8
Foot, breadth	8·7	8·9
Cephalic length	18·6	18·8
Cephalic breadth	14·2	14
Cephalic index	76·5	74·5
Bigoniac	10	10·1
Bizygomatic	12·9	12·9
Maxilio-zygomatic index	77·7	78·4
Nasal height	4·7	4·7
Nasal breadth	3·6	3·6
Nasal index	76·7	76·5
Facial angle	69	68

MADRAS GOVERNMENT MUSEUM.

Bulletin, Vol. II, No. 2.

ANTHROPOLOGY.

Eurasians of Madras and Malabar;
Note on Tattooing; Malagasy-Nias-Dravidians;
Toda Petition.

With Ten Plates.

BY

EDGAR THURSTON,

SUPERINTENDENT, MADRAS GOVERNMENT MUSEUM.

MADRAS:

PRINTED BY THE SUPERINTENDENT, GOVERNMENT PRESS.

1898.

Madras Government Museum Bulletins.

BY EDGAR THURSTON.

Vol. I.

No. 1.—Pearl and Chank Fisheries of the Gulf of Manaar.

No. 2.—Note on Tours along the Malabar Coast.

No. 3.—Rámésvaram Island and Fauna of the Gulf of Manaar.

No. 4.—Anthropology of the Todas and Kotas of the Nilgiri Hills; and of the Bráhmans, Kammálans, Pallis and Pariahs of Madras City.

Vol. II.

No. 1.—Anthropology of the Badagas and Irulas of the Nīlgiris; Paniyans of Malabar; Chinese-Tamil Cross; Cheruman Skull; Kuruba or Kurumba; Summary of Results.

MADRAS GOVERNMENT MUSEUM.

Bulletin, Vol. II, No. 2.

ANTHROPOLOGY.

Eurasians of Madras and Malabar;
Note on Tattooing; Malagasy-Nias-Dravidians;
Toda Petition.

With Ten Plates.

BY

EDGAR THURSTON,
SUPERINTENDENT, MADRAS GOVERNMENT MUSEUM.

MADRAS:
PRINTED BY THE SUPERINTENDENT, GOVERNMENT PRESS.

1898.

CONTENTS.

PAGE

EURASIANS OF MADRAS AND MALABAR 69–114

NOTE ON TATTOOING 115–118

MALAGASY-NIAS-DRAVIDIANS 119–127

TODA PETITION 128–130

ANTHROPOLOGY.

EURASIANS OF MADRAS CITY AND MALABAR.

It must be explained, at the outset, that my subjects for measurement and investigation were, with a special object in view, taken from the poorer classes, including the poorest of the poor, who feel more keenly than their more prosperous brethren the struggle for existence and the pinch of poverty, and whose physique I was specially anxious to gauge correctly.

I learn from Sir W. Hunter's 'Brief History of the Indian People' that the first modern Englishman, known to have visited India, was Thomas Stephens, Rector of the Jesuits' College in Salsette, in 1579. The name of the first Eurasian has not, in like manner, been handed down to posterity. The term Eurasian (Eur-asian) may, after the definition in 'Hobson-Jobson,'[1] be summed up as a modern name for persons of mixed European and Native blood, devised as being more euphemistic than half-caste or half-breed, and more precise than East Indian. According to Stocqueler (Handbk. Brit. India, 1854) the name Eurasian was invented by the Marquis of Hastings. By 'Ali Baba'[2] the Eurasian is dismissed, with playful satire, in the following terms: "'The Native papers say 'deport him'; the white papers say 'make him a soldier'; and the Eurasian himself says 'make me a Commissioner, give me a pension.'" In the 'Cyclopædia of India' Dr. Balfour defines East Indian as "a term which has been adopted by all classes in India to distinguish the descendants of Europeans and Native mothers. Other names, such as half-caste, chatikar, and chi-chi are derogatory designations. Chattikar is from chitta (trousers) and kar (a person who uses them). The Muhammadans equally wear trousers, but concealed by their long outer gowns. The East Indians

[1] Yule and Burnell. [2] 'Twenty-one Days in India.'

are also known as Farangi (Franks), a person of Europe. The humbler East Indians, if asked their race, reply that they are Wallandez or Oollanday, which is a modification of Hollandais, the name having been brought down through the seventeenth and eighteenth centuries from the Dutch. East Indians have, in India, all the rights and privileges of Europeans. Races with a mixture of European with Asiatic blood possess a proud and susceptible tone of mind." For the purposes of the Lawrence Asylum, Ootacamund (*q.v.* p. 100), the word "East Indian" is restricted to the children of European fathers by East Indian or Native mothers, or of East Indian fathers and mothers, both of whom are the children of European fathers.

Some Eurasians have, it may be noted, had decorations or knighthood conferred on them, and risen to the highest possible position in, and gained the blue ribbon of Government service. Others have held, or still hold, positions of distinction in the various learned professions, legal, medical, educational, and ecclesiastical.

By a recent ruling of the Government of India it has been decided that Eurasians appointed in England to official posts in India are, if they are not statutory natives, to be treated as Europeans as regards the receipt of "exchange compensation allowance."

The Danes are said (Rush) to have produced, through Hindu women, children of European type and vigour, while such is certainly not the case with other European nations.

It is not generally known that the Anglo-Eurasian owes his origin, in great measure, to the direct influence of pepper. For I learn that "the English East India Company had its origin in the commercial rivalry between London and Amsterdam. In 1599, the Dutch raised the price of pepper against the English from 3*s.* to 6*s.* and 8*s.* per pound. The merchants of London held a meeting on the 22nd September at Founder's Hall, with the Lord Mayor in the chair, and agreed to form an association for the purpose of trading directly with India, and on the 8th October, 1600, the following ships were taken up for the first voyage to the East Indies :—

	Men.	Tons.
"Malice Scourge"	200	600
"Hector"	100	300
"Ascension"	80	240
"Susan"	80	240
A pinnace	40	100

PL. XVI. A.

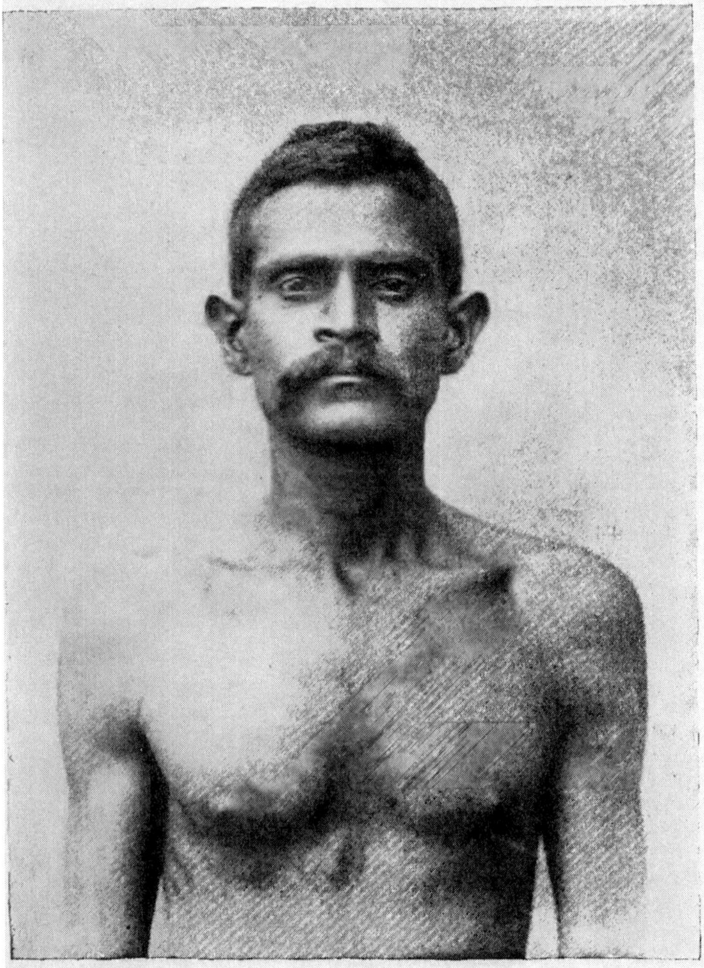

MADRAS EURASIAN.

" Nearly forty years later, in 1639, Mr. Francis Day, the Chief of the British factory at Armagáon, purchased from the Rája of Chandragiri a site called Maderaspatam or Chinipatnam, built Fort St. George, and became the founder of Madras, which was the first territorial possession of the Company in India."

The influence of the various European nations—Portuguese, Dutch, British, Danish, and French—which have at different times acquired territory in peninsular India, is clearly visible in the polyglot medley of Eurasian surnames, *e.g.*, Gomez, Gonsalvez, Pereira, Rozario, Cabral, Da Cruz, Da Costa, Da Silva, Da Souza, Fernandez, Fonseca, Lazaro, Henriquez, Xavier, Mendonza, Rodriguez, Saldana, Almeyda, Luxa, Heldt, Van Spall, Jansen, Augustine, Brisson, Corneille, La Grange, Lavocat, Pascal, Caubo (Corbeau, Mr. Crow ?), De Vine, Aubert, Ryan, McKertish, Macpherson, Harris, Johnson, Smith, &c. Little did the early adventurers, in the dawn of the seventeenth century, think that, as the result of their alliances with the Native women, within three centuries banns of marriage would be declared weekly in Madras churches between, for example, Ben Jonson and Alice Almeyda, Emmanuel Henricus and Mary Smith, Augustus Rozario and Minnie Fonseca, John Harris and Clara Corneille, &c. Yet this has come to pass, and the Eurasian holds a recognised place among the half-breed races of the world resulting from modern 'civilization.'

The pedigree of the early Eurasian community is veiled in some obscurity. But the various modes of creation of a half-breed, which were adopted in those early days, when the sturdy European pioneers first came in contact with the Native females, were probably as follows :—

A. European man (pure)	B. Native woman (pure).
C. Male offspring of A + B (first cross).	D. Native woman.
E. Female offspring of A + B (first cross).	F. European man. G. Native man.
H. Male offspring of C + D.	I. Cross-female offspring of A + B. J. Native woman.
K. Female offspring of C + D.	L. Cross-male offspring of A + B. M. European. N. Native man.

The Eurasian half-breed, thus established, has been perpetuated by a variety of possible combinations:—

European man	..	Eurasian woman. Native woman.
Eurasian man	..	Native woman. Eurasian woman. European woman.
Native man	..	Eurasian woman. European woman.

In the early days of the British occupation of Madras, the traders and soldiers, arriving with an inadequate equipment of females, contracted alliances, regular or irregular, with the women of the country. And in these early days, when our territorial possessions were keenly contested with both European and Native enemies, an attempt was made, under authority from high places, to obtain, through the medium of the British soldier, and in accordance with the creed that crossing is an essential means of improving a race, and rendering it vigorous by the infusion of fresh blood from a different stock, a good cross, which should be available for military purposes. The problem of a Eurasian army is, therefore, no new one, but one which was dealt with long ago in a practical manner, such as is no longer possible in these more advanced times. Later on, as the numbers of the British settlers increased, connexions, either with the Native women, or with the females of the recently founded Eurasian type, were kept up owing to the difficulty of communication with the mother-country, and consequent difficulty in securing English brides by the ordinary rules of sexual selection. Of these barbaric days the detached or semi-detached bungalows in the spacious grounds of the big private houses in Madras remain as a memorial. At the present day the conditions of life in India are, as the result of steamer traffic, very different, and far more wholesome. The Eurasian man seeks a wife as a rule among his own community; and in this manner the race is mainly maintained, though examples of first crosses, and the results of re-crossing between European and Eurasian are frequently met with.

The number of Eurasians within the limits of the Madras Presidency was returned, at the Census, 1891, as 26,643. But on this point I must call Mr. H. A. Stuart, the Census Commissioner, into the witness box. "The number of Eurasians," he writes, "is 26,643, which is 20·76 per cent.

PL. XVII.

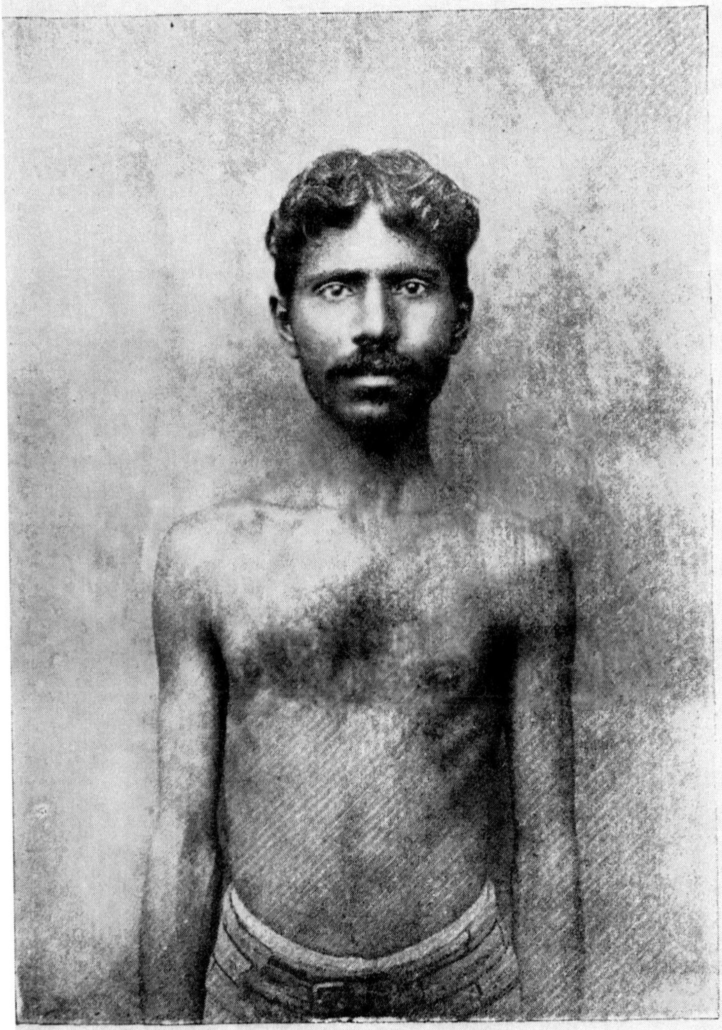

MADRAS EURASIAN.

more than the number returned in 1881." The figures for the last three enumerations are given in the following statement :—

NUMBER OF EURASIANS.

Year.			Total.	Males.	Females.
1871	..	..	26,460	13,091	13,359
1881	..	..	21,892	10,969	10,923
1891	..	...	26,648	13,141	13,502

"It will be seen that, between 1871 and 1881, there was a great decrease, and that the numbers in 1891 are slightly higher than they were twenty years ago. The figures, however, are most untrustworthy. The cause is not far to seek; many persons, who are really Natives, claim to be Eurasians, and some who are Eurasians return themselves as Europeans. It might be thought that the errors due to these circumstances would be fairly constant, but the district figures show that this cannot be the case. Take Malabar, for example, which has the largest number of Eurasians after Madras, and where the division between Native Christians with European names and people of real mixed race is very shadowy. In 1871 there were in this district 5,413 Eurasians; in 1881 the number had apparently fallen to 1,676, while in 1891 it had again risen to 4,193, or, if we include south-east Wynaad, as we should do, to 4,439. It is to be regretted that trustworthy statistics cannot be obtained, for the question whether the true Eurasian community is increasing or decreasing is of considerable scientific and administrative importance.

"The Eurasians form but a very small proportion of the community, for there is only one Eurasian in every 1,337 of the population of the Madras Presidency, and it is more than probable that a considerable proportion of those returned as Eurasians are in reality pure Natives who have embraced the Christian religion, taken an English or Portuguese name, and adopted the European dress and mode of living.

"In the matter of education, or at least elementary education, they are more advanced than any other class of the community, and compare favourably with the population of any country in the world. They live for the most part in towns, nearly one-half of their number being found in the city of Madras."

In connection with the fact that, at times of Census, Native Christians and Pariahs, who masquerade in European clothes, return themselves as Eurasians, and *vice versâ*, it may be accepted that some benefit must be derived by the individual in return for the masking of his or her nationality. And it has been pointed out to me that (as newspaper advertisements testify) many ladies will employ a Native ayah rather than a Eurasian nurse, and that some employers will take Eurasian clerks into their service, but not Native Christians. It occasionally happens that pure-bred Natives, with European name and costume, successfully pass themselves off as Eurasians, and are placed on a footing of equality with Eurasians in the matter of diet, when they are in prison, being allowed the luxury of bread, butter, coffee, &c.

Mr. Stuart had at his command no special statistics of the occupations resorted to by Eurasians, but states that the majority of them are clerks, while very few indeed obtain their livelihood by agriculture. In the course of my enquiry, which included a majority of bread-winners and a sprinkling of loafers, the following varied occupations were recorded. It is noteworthy that, of 130 cases, no less than 33 returned their occupation as " fitter " :—

Accountant.
Attendant, Lunatic Asylum.
Baker.
Bandsman.
Bill-collector.
Blacksmith.
Boarding-house keeper.
Boatswain.
Boilersmith.
Carpenter.
Chemist's assistant.
Clerk, Government.
Clerk, private.
Commission agent.
Compositor.
Compounder.
Contractor.
Copper-smith.
Crane attendant, harbour.
Draftsman.
Electric-tram driver.
Electric-tram inspector.
Engine-driver, Ice factory.
Evangelist.
Filer.
Fitter.
Fireman.
Hammerer.
Harness-maker.
Jewel-smith.
Jointer.
Labourer.
Livery-stable keeper.
Mechanic.
Moulder.
Painter.
Petition-writer.
Police inspector.
Porter.
Printer.
Proof-reader.
Railway—
  Auditor.
  Chargeman.
  Engine-driver.
  Engineer.

PL. XVIII.

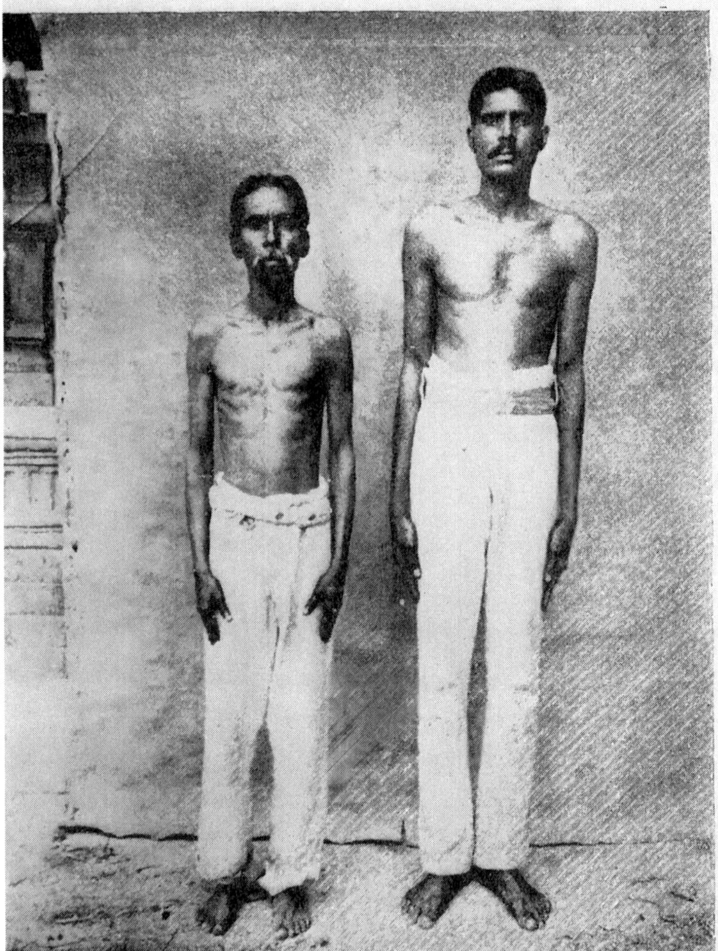

MADRAS EURASIANS.

Railway—
- Goods clerk.
- Guard.
- Locomotive inspector.
- Parcel clerk.
- Prosecuting inspector.
- Shunter.
- Signaller.
- Stationmaster.
- Store-keeper.
- Ticket-collector.
- Tool-keeper.
- Block-signaller.

Railway—
- Carriage examiner.

Reporter.
Rivetter.
Saddler.
Schoolmaster.
Sexton.
Spring-smith.
Stereotyper.
Steward.
Telegraph clerk.
Watch-maker.
Watchman.

The bandsmen, who appeared before me, were tested with the apparatus for estimating appreciation of difference in musical pitch. All responded well to the test, except the performer on the big drum, who broke down hopelessly at a very early stage.

The Eurasians' fancy turns not lightly, but seriously to thoughts of love at a very early age, with the result that they sometimes marry, with all the pomp of bridal dress, cake and wine, when barely out of leading strings, and become burthened with the cares, anxieties, and responsibilities of paternity and maternity when they are mere boys and girls. One of my subjects, indeed, volunteered the information that he married a child-bride before she reached puberty. Whether they marry because, as with the Hindu, an unmarried man is looked down upon as having no social status, and as being an almost useless member of society, or whether for the "causes for which matrimony was ordained," I am unable to state precisely. But I may hazard a guess that it is because they have not acquired the power to "subordinate animal appetite to reason, forethought, and prudence." Whatever the reason, the results are but too frequently disastrous,—a plethora of children, brought up in poverty, hunger, and dirt; but little to earn and many to keep; domestic unrest; insolvency; and destitution. A virtuous state of celibacy has been recently advocated as a substitute for early marriage, and the argument brought forward that, if a man has sufficient intelligence and unselfishness to abstain from dragging a wife and children into poverty and misery, he will be sufficiently intelligent and unselfish to lead a pure life, and not swell the ranks of the illegitimate.

From the analysis of a hundred male cases, in which enquiries were specially made with reference to the married state in individuals ranging in age from 21 to 50, with an average age of 33, I learn that 74 were married at the average age of 22–23; that 141 male and 130 female children had been born to them; and that 26, whose average age was 25, were unmarried. The limits of age of the men at the time of marriage were 32 and 16; of the women 25 and 13. The greatest number of children born to a single pair was 10. In only three cases, out of the seventy-four, was there no issue. In fifty cases, which were investigated, of married men with an average age of 34, 207 children had been born, of whom 91 had died, for the most part in very early life, from "fever" and other causes, among which malnutrition, and consequent marasmus, must take a foremost place. Remembering that house-rent should be paid, and that clothes and food have to be acquired, how, I ask myself, can cases such as the following lead other than a miserable existence, void of the pleasure of life?

Pay per mensem.	Age.	Age of marriage.	Children living.
RS.	YRS.	YRS.	NO.
15	26	21	3
10	27	18	5
15	25	21	2
20	39	19	7
6	38	22	2
18	27	18	6
10	25	19	2
30	40	20	8

To appreciate what misery is indicated here, it is only necessary to convert the rupees into annas, and divide them among the number of mouths to be fed, leaving house-rent and clothes out of the question; and, whether the rent be paid or no, clothes must of necessity be forthcoming—no mere dhoti, langūti, or sari, but clothes of European device, if not of the latest fashion.

The practical result of their want of thrift, and the widespread tendency to allow expenditure to exceed income, is that Eurasians in Government service frequently find themselves caught in the meshes of Rule 39, regulating the conduct of Government servants, which lays down that "it is undesirable that a man, who is in a chronic and hopeless condition of indebtedness, should be retained in the Government service. The anxieties attendant upon such a state must necessarily greatly detract from the value of the

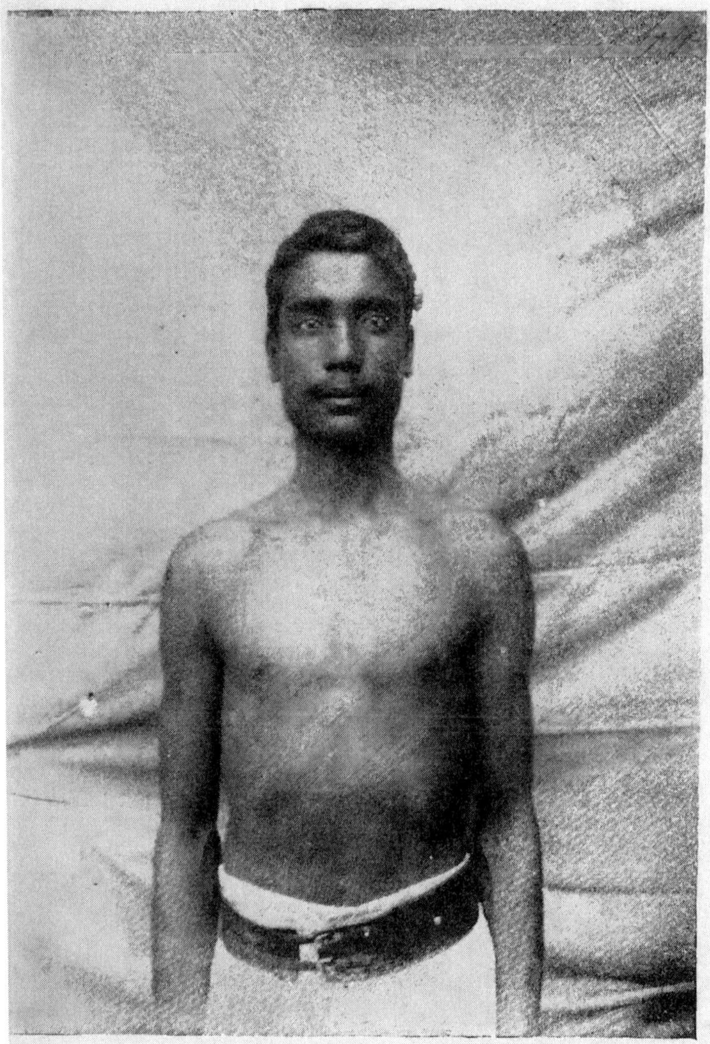

MADRAS EURASIAN.

debtor's work, besides exposing him to temptations to dishonesty, which, in such circumstances, it is very difficult to resist." The following figures, gleaned from the statistics of the Insolvent Court during the five last years, bear directly on the condition referred to :—

Year.	Number of petitions filed by Eurasians.	Number of petitions filed during the year.	Eurasian percentage.
1893	45	233	19
1894	55	255	21
1895	35	237	14
1896	51	268	19
1897	53	297	18
Total ..	239	1,290	18

The percentage is certainly very high, when the Eurasian population is compared with the microscopic minority of Europeans, and the overwhelming majority of the Native community.

As examples of Eurasian improvidence, and a too literal adherence to the old time doctrine of taking no thought for the morrow, for the morrow shall take thought for the things of itself, the following cases may be cited :—

Monthly pay.	Total debt.	Debt in year's pay.
RS.	RS.	
9	3,500	32–33 years.
15	1,400	7–8 ,,
20	1,450	6–7 ,,
30	5,800	16 ,,
40	6,700	13–14 ,,
50	5,550	9–10 ,,
60	8,300	13–14 ,,

The racial position of Eurasians, and the proportion of black blood in their veins, are commonly indicated, not by the terms mulatto, quadroon, octoroon, sambo (or zambo), etc., but, as in the case of cotton, jute, coffee, and other crops, in fractions of a rupee. The European pure breed being represented by Rs. 0–0–0, and the native pure breed by 16 annas (=1 rupee), the resultant cross is, by reference to colour and other tests, gauged as being half an anna in the rupee (faint admixture of black blood; approaching European type); eight annas (half and half);

fifteen annas (predominant admixture of black blood; approaching native type), etc.

The Eurasian body being enveloped in clothes, it was not till they stripped before me, for the purposes of anthropometry, that I became aware how prevalent is the practice of tattooing among the male members of the community. Nearly all the hundred and thirty men, whom I examined in detail, were, in fact, tattooed to a greater or less extent on the breasts, upper arms, fore-arms, wrists, back of the hands, or shoulders. The following varied selection of devices in blue, with occasional red, is recorded in my case-book :—

Anchor.
Ballet girl with flag stars and stripes.
Bracelets round wrists.
Burmese lady carrying umbrella.
Burmese lady playing with parrot.
Bird.
Bugles.
Conventional artistic devices.
Cross and anchor.
Crown and flags.
Crossed swords and pistols.
Dancing girl.
Dancing girl playing with cobras.
Elephant.
Floral devices.
Flowers in pot.
Hands joined in centre of a heart.
Hands joined and clasping a flower.
Heart.
Heart and cross.
Initials of the individual, his friends, relatives, and inamorata, sometimes within a heart or laurel wreath.
Lizard.
Mercy (word on left breast).
Mermaid.
Portraits of youth and his lady-love.
Princess of Wales.
Royal arms and banners.
Sailing boat.
Scorpion.
Solomon's seal.
Steam boat.
Svastika (Buddhist emblem).
Watteau shepherdess.

PL. XX.

MADRAS EURASIANS.

The most elaborate patterns were executed by Burmese artists. The initials, which preponderated over other devices, were, as a rule, in Roman, but occasionally in Tamil characters. In many instances the tattooing was barely visible against the dark skin, and the main objects of the operation—beauty and personal adornment—completely lost. À propos of tattooing in the male sex, the legend goes that the goddesses of the tattooers "swam from Fiji, to introduce the craft to Samoa, and, on leaving Fiji, were commissioned to sing all the way 'Tattoo the women, but not the men'". But they got muddled over it in the long journey, and arrived at Samoa singing "Tattoo the men, but not the women." [3]

In colour the Eurasians afford, as is natural in a mixed race, examples of the entire colour-scale from sooty-black, through sundry shades of brown and yellow, to pale white, and even, as a very rare exception, florid or rosy. The darkening of the skin in Hindu half-breeds with advancing age, and the dark colour of the pudenda, noticed by D'Orbigny and Troyer (Bull. Soc Ethnol. May 22nd, 1846), were very conspicuous in many cases which came under observation. So, too, in individuals with otherwise fair skin, was the tell-tale pigment on the neck, knees and elbows, as also in the axillæ, the glands of which, as in the Native, pour out, under the influence of emotion or exercise, a profuse watery secretion. The pilous or hairy system, which was, in the cases recorded, uniformly black, repeatedly conforms as regards its distribution to the native type ; and the eyebrows are frequently united across the middle line by bushy hairs. The hair of the head may be straight, and, when clipped, recall to mind a Bengali Babu with his close-cropped hair devoid of parting. Or it may be wavy or curly (woolly never), and dressed, like that of a European, in a variety of ways, according to the fancy of the owner. Premature greyness and baldness, arcus senilis, and early senility, were noted in many instances. The colour of the iris, like that of the skin, is liable to great variation, from lustrous-black to light, with a predominance of dark tints. Blue was observed only in a solitary instance.

The Eurasian resists exposure to the sun better than the European, and, while many wear solah topis (sun hats), it is by no means uncommon to see a Eurasian walking about

---

[3] Journ. Anth. Inst., Vol. XVII, 1888, p. 319.

in the middle of a hot day with his head protected only by a straw hat or cap.

In a heated discussion on the "Anglo-Indian in India," which has recently been carried on in the columns of the 'Pioneer,' a retired Indian Staff Corps Colonel suggested the raising of a division of eight regiments, two of cavalry, six of infantry, four of the latter to consist of specially selected Eurasians only, two of Indo-Europeans only. "If," he says, "treated with fair liberality as regards pay, promotion, and prospects, I feel every confidence that a fine, and in every way reliable force may be thus created for general service anywhere (like the Native grandly efficient army) . . . . Such force might be very considerably expanded later on. Three field batteries, one of Indo-Europeans only, and two of Eurasians only, might also be added, rendering the force quite complete in itself." Let us, bearing in mind that the Eurasian community of the Madras Presidency is a limited one on which to draw for military purposes, and that many of those who are physically fitted would be unwilling to enlist, examine the physique of the poorer classes, from the ranks of whom recruits would have to be obtained.

The average height of the Eurasian, according to my measurements of 130 subjects, is 166·6 cm. (5 feet 5½), and compares as follows with that of the English and various Native classes, inhabiting the city of Madras, which have been examined by me :—

	CM.
English	170·8
Eurasians	166·6
Muhammadans	164·5
Brāhmans	162·5
Pallis	162·5
Vellālas	162·4
Pariahs	161·9

The height, as might be expected, comes between that of the two parent stocks, European and Native, and had, in the cases examined, the wide range of 30·8 cm.—the difference between a maximum of 183·8 cm. (6 feet) and a minimum of 153 cm. (5 feet). The high ranges between maxima and minima (*vide* table xvii), which are specially marked in the case of stature and the measurements dependent thereon, and of the nose, are readily explained on the general principle that pure races exhibit a more uniform, and mixed races a variegated type, and this variation increases as the intermixture progresses (Waitz).

The story goes that many years ago, during the fighting days in Southern India, a Highland regiment, as the result of concubinage with the Native women of a certain quarter of the city of Madras, left behind them a half-breed offspring, reared up as Natives, whose descendants, are, owing to their stature, still recognised, at the present day, as the Madras Highlanders.

The average weight of my Eurasians, in clothes with boots, was a mere 7 st. 9½ lbs.; the weight ranging between 12 stone in a flabby individual aged 30 years, and 5 st. 6 lbs. in a man 40 years old. How small this weight is for adults may be emphasised by reference to the fact, based on a series of experiments, that the weight of growing English school boys (in in-door dress with boots on) between the ages of 16 and 17, ranged, in 79·6 per cent. of the cases examined, between 8½ stone and 12 st. 5¼ lbs. Only in 3 out of 103 cases was the weight below 7 stone.[4]

The average chest measurement, taken over the nipples with the arms above the head and hands joined, was 79·1 cm. (31 inches). In the following tabular statement this average is compared with the average chest-girth of the classes noted above, and with the average relative to stature = 100 :—

	Average.	Average relative to stature = 100.
English	93·9	54
Brāhmans	81	49·8
Vellālas	79·8	49·1
Pariahs	79·3	48·9
Pallis	79·2	48·7
Muhammadans	79	48
Eurasians	79·1	47·5

The chest-girth of the Eurasians is, then, relatively to stature, less than that of any of the classes under review. Of far greater importance than actual chest-girth, as everyone who has had to deal with recruiting knows full well, is the play of the chest, viz., the vital capacity, or extreme

[4] Fergus and Rodwell. Journ. Anth. Inst., Vol. IV, 1875, p. 128.

differential capacity of the lungs. This is best estimated by means of a modified gasometer, called the spirometer, which registers the total amount of air which can be given out by the most forcible expiration following upon a most forcible inspiration. Tested with such an instrument, the majority of the Eurasians under examination broke down owing, in great measure, to the feeble development of the pectoral and other inspiratory muscles, whose function is to inflate the lungs.

In the following table the Eurasian shoulder-breadth, measured between the external surfaces of the prominences of the shoulders about 5 cm. below the acromion, is compared with that of the same classes as before :—

	Average.	Average relative to stature = 100.
Vellālas	39·7	24·4
Pariahs	39·4	24·3
Brāhmans	39·3	24·2
Muhammadans	39·8	24 2
Pallis	39·4	24 2
Eurasians	39·2	23·6

The shoulder-breadth is thus seen to be less, both actually and relative to stature, in the Eurasians than in the Native classes. The deficiency in breadth must be attributed both to narrow osteological build, and to the feebly developed condition of the deltoid muscles.

As specimens of the all too common weakly Eurasian humanity, whose living was gained with their hands, the cases in the two following tables, taken from a very large number, may be cited :—

Age. YRS.	Weight. ST. LB.	Height. FT. IN.	Chest. INCHES.	Occupation.
28	9·1	6	31·4	Fitter.
26	7·1	5·7½	29·1	Engine driver.
22	7·9	5·6	29·5	Turner.
21	7·6	5·4½	30·3	Hammerer.
29	7·4	5·4½	29·7	Do.
35	6·6	5·2	26·4	Printer.
37	6·1	5·1½	28 6	Fitter.
23	6·4	5·1½	28 5	Printer.
19	5·9	5·1½	27·1	Blacksmith.

Height.	Girth of upper arm. Relaxed.	Contracted.	Hand-breadth.	Girth round epigastrium (stomach).
FT. IN.	INCHES.	INCHES.	INCHES.	INCHES.
5·7½	..	..	..	23·2
5·1½	7·3	7·9	..	22·8
5·4½	8·4	9·5	..	..
5·8	8·2	9·4	..	..
5·2½	..	..	2·6	..
5 4½	..	..	2·6	..
5 2½	..	..	2·5	..

I have, in the course of the present enquiry, examined many Native women, engaged as coolies in road-repairing, and found arms with good solid muscle, shoulders, and chests, of which some of these feebly developed individuals might well be envious. But the Indian cooly woman is notoriously an excellent beast of burthen, and I recall to mind the legend of the Bhutia woman, who is reputed, in the days before the hill railway was open, to have carried, unaided, a grand piano on her head the whole way from the foot of the hills to Darjiling.

Contrast with the above the following—all the direct result of re-crossing between European man and Eurasian woman. It will be noted that all are, some slightly, others considerably above the average. The physiological significance of this fact, and the possibilities in connection therewith, are obvious, and need not be dilated on at length. Suffice it to state that the product of alliances between British men and Eurasian women show the least signs of physical degeneration, and possess broader shoulders, hips, and hands, greater chest-girth, wider forehead, and more muscle, as the result of re-vivification of the stock by direct British intervention :—

Age.	Weight, average 7 st. 9½ lb.	Height, average 5 ft. 5 in.	Chest, average 31·2 in.	Occupation.
21	9·8	5·7½	31·5	Fitter.
28	9·3	5·7½	33·5	Do.
40	10·9	5·7	34·7	Clerk.
38	9·2	5·7	32·5	Labourer.
22	9 4	5·6	34·3	Boiler-smith.
26	10	5·7½	33	Railway guard.

As a clear indication of the physique, which the poor Eurasian should aspire to with a view to his becoming a soldier, I publish (table xviii) side by side the averages, etc., of a series of physical measurements of 50 sepoys [5] of the 28th Madras Infantry and of my 130 Eurasians; and, further, in table xix, statistics of the same measurements in 50 sepoys and 50 Eurasians between the recruiting ages of 18 and 25.

Leaving hand-grip, as tested by the dynamometer, in which the Eurasians displayed lamentable weakness (an average of only 65 lbs.), out of the question, and considering weight, chest-girth, and shoulder-breadth, the sepoy average was, as shown by the following tabular statement, only reached in four cases out of the 50 examined between the ages of 19 and 25:—

	Weight.	Chest.	Shoulders.
	LB.	CM.	CM.
	127	86·5	41·5
	139	87	42·1
	150	87·5	43·9
	136	84·5	43·3
Sepoy average ...	125	84	41·6

The Eurasian mean above the average, taken as a whole, fell short, as shown below, of the sepoy average:—

	Eurasian mean above the average.	Sepoy average.
Weight	122 lb.	125 lb.
Chest	82 cm.	84 cm.
Shoulders	40·5 „	41·6 „
Dynamometer	72·4 lb.	80 lb.

The figures in tables xviii to xxi suffice, of themselves, to show that the average physique of the Eurasians is far below that required for military purposes. And this deficiency in physique is accentuated by a study of the following tables of comparison drawn up from the detailed figures in tables xx and xxi:—

[5] The periodical fanatical outbreaks in the Moplah (or Máppila) community of Malabar are well known to us in Southern India. It is of interest, therefore, that, since 1895, 150 Moplahs have enlisted in the 25th Madras Infantry, which is stationed at Cannanore, under conditions similar to those applying to the rest of the Native Army. They have, I am told, become most amenable to discipline; and training and good diet have improved their physique, which was good at the commencement.

MADRAS SEPOY.

WEIGHT, LB.

—	80–90	90–100	100–110	110–120	120–130	130–140	140–150	150–160
Sepoys	...	1	4	11	19	9	4	2
Eurasians	6	9	12	13	4	5	1	...

CHEST, CM.

—	60–70	70–80	80–90	90–100
Sepoys	...	5	42	3
Eurasians	3	33	14	...

SHOULDERS, CM.

—	33–37	37–38	38–39	39–40	40–41	41–42	42–43	43–44	44–45	45–46
Sepoys	...	...	4	5	6	15	12	4	2	2
Eurasians	9	10	8	9	10	2	...	2	...	...

Putting the figures in the last three tables in terms of percentages, we obtain the following results, which speak for themselves :—

WEIGHT.

	Below 120 LB.	Above 120 LB.
Sepoys	32	68
Eurasians	80	20

CHEST.

	Below 80 CM.	Above 80 CM.
Sepoys	10	90
Eurasians	72	28

SHOULDERS.

	Below 41 CM.	Above 41 CM.
Sepoys	30	70
Eurasians	92	8

Turning now to head measurements, the average length of the Eurasian head is 18·6 cm. and the breadth 14·1 cm. And it is to be noted that, in 63 per cent. of the cases examined, the breadth exceeded 14 cm. In the length of the head there is nothing distinctive as between the Eurasians and the other classes under review, the difference only amounting to ·1 cm. The breadth of the head, on the contrary, is appreciably greater in Eurasians and Brāhmans (Aryo-Dravidians) than in Muhammadans (some of whom are immigrants with an admixture of Dravidian blood) and the three indigenous classes, Vellālas, Pallis, and Pariahs :—

	Length.	Breadth.	Index.
	CM.	CM.	
Brāhmans ..	18·6	14·2	76·5
Eurasians ..	18·6	14·1	76
Muhammadans ..	18·7	13·9	76·1
Vellālas	18·6	13·8	74·1
Pariahs	18·6	13·7	73·6
Pallis	18·6	13·6	73

The relative breadth of the head is very clearly brought out by the following analysis of forty subjects belonging to each of the six classes, which shows at a glance the preponderance of heads exceeding 14 cm. in breadth in Eurasians, Brāhmans, and (to a less degree) Muhammadans, and of heads below 14 cm. in breadth in the more dolichocephalic Vellālas, Pallis, and Pariahs :—

	12–13	13–14	14–15	15–16
	CM.	CM.	CM.	CM.
Eurasians	..	11	27	2
Brāhmans . ..	1	9	27	3
Muhammadans ..	2	17	21	..
Vellālas	..	24	16	..
Pariahs	..	27	13	..
Pallis	3	30	7	..

The head of a cross-breed, it has been said, generally takes after the father, and the breadth of the Eurasian head is a persisting result of European male influence. The effect of this influence is clearly demonstrated in the following cases, all the result of re-crossing between British men and Eurasian women :—

	Length. CM.	Breadth. CM.
	19	14·5
	18·4	14·2
	19·2	14·2
	20·2	14·6
	19	14·6
	19·4	14·3
Average	19·2	14·4
Eurasian average	18·6	14·1

The character of the nose is, as those who have studied ethnology in India well appreciate, a most important factor in the differentiation of race, tribe, and class, and in the determination of pedigree. "No one," Mr. Risley writes,[6] "can have glanced at the literature of the subject, and in particular at the Védic accounts of the Aryan advance, without being struck by the frequent references to the noses of the people whom the Aryans found in possession of the plains of India. So impressed were the Aryans with the shortcomings of their enemies' noses that they often spoke of them as 'the noseless ones,' and their keen perception of the importance of this feature seems almost to anticipate the opinion of Dr. Collignon that the nasal index ranks higher as a distinctive character than the stature, or even the cephalic index itself." The Eurasian nose, as is natural in a mixed race, exhibits a combination of the long, narrow (leptorhine) type of the higher races, and the broader (mesorhine and platyrhine) type of the lower classes, as shown in the following analysis of the nasal indices of forty Eurasians, Brāhmans, Pallis and Pariahs:—

	Leptorhine. 55–69·9.	Mesorhine. 70–84·9.	Platyrhine. 85–99·9.
Eurasians	19	19	2
Brāhmans	6	24	10
Pallis	3	31	6
Pariahs	2	25	13

It may be noted, *en passant*, that the Brāhman nose belongs to the platyrhine type in 25 per cent. of the cases here analysed (*vide* Bull., Vol. II, No. 1).

Speaking in general terms, it may be said that the noses with high nasal index are possessed by Eurasians of short

[6] Journ. Anth. Inst., Vol. XX, 1891, pp. 249–50; see also Madras Museum Bull., Vol. II, No. 1, pp. 53–58.

stature and dark skin; noses with low index by those of medium stature or tall, and fairer skin. In the following table statistics are given concerning the measurements of the nose and the nasal index in Eurasians and the other classes selected for comparison with them:—

	Length. CM.	Breadth. CM.	Index.
Eurasians	5·1	3·5	69·5
Muhammadans ..	4·9	3·4	70
Vellālas	4·7	3·4	73·1
Brāhmans	4·7	3·6	76·7
Pallis	4·6	3·6	77·9
Pariahs	4·5	3·6	80

Examination of this table shows that there is a gradation from the leptorhine type of the Eurasian to the platyrhine type of the Pariah, and that the change of type from leptorhine to platyrhine is due to shortening of the length of the nose rather than to increase in its breadth. For, as the figures show, while there is a difference of ·6 cm. between the average lengths of the Eurasian and Pariah noses, there is only a difference of ·2 cm. in the average breadths thereof. The difference in the length of the nose is clearly brought out by comparison, in forty members of each of my six classes, of the number of times in which the length reached from 5 to 6 cm. or from 4 to 5 cm.

	Length.	
	5–6 CM.	4–5 CM.
Eurasians	21	19
Muhammadans	16	24
Vellālas	6	34
Brāhmans	5	35
Pallis	5	35
Pariahs	1	39

The results obtained, in like manner, by comparison of the breadth of the nose are not nearly so eloquent, though the greater breadth of the nose in individual Pariahs is en evidence:—

	Breadth.	
	4–5 CM.	3–4 CM.
Eurasians	1	39
Muhammadans	2	38
Brāhmans	0	40
Vellālas	1	39
Pallis	3	37
Pariahs	5	35

In the subjoined table, based on the examination of forty members of each class, who are classified according to their nasal index, the high proportion of Eurasians, Muhammadans and Vellālas with indices ranging between 60 and 70, and of Brāhmans, Pallis, and Pariahs with indices ranging between 80 and 90, is at once manifest, and requires no comment :—

	60–70.	70–80.	80–90.	90–100.
Eurasians	19	17	3	1
Muhammadans ..	17	18	4	1
Vellālas	14	22	3	1
Brāhmans	6	19	14	1
Pallis	3	25	9	3
Pariahs	2	17	19	2

Some final words are necessary on liability to certain diseases, as a differentiating character between Eurasian and European. The Census Commissioner, 1891, states that Eurasians seem to be peculiarly liable to insanity and leprosy. To these should be added elephantiasis (filarial disease), concerning which Surgeon-Major J. Maitland writes as follows [7]: "Almost all the old writers on elephantiasis believed that the dark races were more susceptible to the disease than white people; but it is extremely doubtful if this is the case. It is true that in those countries where the disease is endemic, the proportion of persons affected is much greater amongst the blacks than amongst the whites; but it has to be borne in mind that the habits of the former render them much more liable to the disease than the latter. The majority of the white people, being more civilised, are more careful regarding the purity of their drinking-water than the Natives, who are proverbially careless in this respect. In India, although it is comparatively rare to meet with Europeans affected with the disease, yet such cases are from time to time recorded. Eurasians are proportionately more liable to the disease than pure Europeans, but not so much so as Natives. Doctors Patterson and Hall of Bahia [8] examined the blood of 309 persons in that place, and found the following proportions affected with filaria; of whites, 1 in 26; of blacks, 1 in 10¼; of the mixed race, 1 in 9. Doctor Laville[9] states that in the Society Islands, out of a total of 13 European and American residents,

---

[7] 'Elephantiasis and allied disorders.' Madras, 1891.
[8] 'Veterinarian.' June 1879.
[9] 'Endemic skin and other diseases of India.'—FOX AND FARQUHAR.

11 were affected with elephantiasis. Taking all these facts into consideration, together with our knowledge of the pathology of the disease, I do not think we are justified in saying that the black races are more *susceptible* to the disease than white people. On the other hand, owing to the nature of their habits, they are much more *liable* to the diseases than are the white races."

During the five years, 1893—97, 98 Eurasians suffering from filarial diseases were admitted into the General Hospital, Madras.

To Surgeon-Colonel W. A. Lee, Superintendent of the Government Leper Asylum, Madras, I am indebted for the following note on leprosy in its relation to the Eurasian and European communities:—

"You ask me for information as to the occurrence of leprosy among Europeans and Eurasians, and for statistics of the numbers which were treated in the Government Leper Asylum during the five years, 1893—97. You also add that you wish to bring out the point that leprosy is a distinguishing character as between Eurasians and Europeans.

"Although the latter may possess greater vigour of constitution, and, therefore, a better capacity of resistance, they are by no means immune to the disease, which, in the majority of instance, is contracted by them through coitus with leprous individuals.

"Leprosy is one of the endemic diseases of tropical and sub-tropical countries, to the risk of contracting which Europeans who settle on the plains in India, and their offspring from unions with the inhabitants of the land, as well as the descendants of the latter, become exposed, since, by the force of circumstances, they are thrown into intimate contact with the Native population.

"A portion of the accommodation of the Government Leper Hospital at Madras, which was founded in 1841, is reserved for European and Eurasian lepers; but little can be gleaned from the records as regards the incidence of the disease on the former class, as scanty attention appears to have been bestowed on accuracy of classification. For instance, of 11 'Europeans' who were under treatment in the years 1890—97 (*vide* table xxii), all save two had their birth-place in India or Burma, so that few of them could have been of pure or unmixed European parentage.

"The Eurasian community furnishes a considerable number of lepers, and the disease, once introduced into a family, has a tendency to attack several of its members, and to re-appear in successive generations, occasionally skipping one—a feature akin to the biological phenomenon known as atavism, but of perhaps doubtful analogy, for the possibility of a fresh infection or inoculation has always to be borne in mind. There are numerous instances of such hereditary transmission among the patients, both Native and Eurasian, in the Government Leper Hospital.

"The spread of the disease by contagion is slow, the most intimate contact even, such as that between parent and child, often failing to effect inoculation. Still there is much evidence in support of its being inoculable by cohabitation, prolonged contact, wearing the same clothing, sharing the dwelling, using the same cooking and eating utensils, and even by arm-to-arm vaccination. Influenced by a belief in the last mentioned cause, vaccination was formerly regarded with much suspicion and dislike by Eurasians in Madras. But their apprehensions on this score have abated since animal vaccine was substituted for the humanised material. It has also for long been a popular belief among the same class that the suckling of their infants by infected Native wet-nurses is a common source of the disease.

"Attempts to reproduce leprosy from supposed pure cultures of the leprosy bacillus have invariably failed; and this strengthens the belief that the disease would die out if sufferers from the tubercular or mixed forms were segregated, and intermarriage with members of known leprous families interdicted. Experience shows that, where such marriages are freely entered into, a notable prevalence of the disease results, as in Pondicherry for example, where the so-called creole population is said to contain a large proportion of lepers from this cause."

Writing concerning the prevalence of insanity in different castes, the Census Commissioner, 1891, states that "it appears from the statistics that insanity is far more prevalent among the Eurasians than among any other class. The proportion is 1 insane person in every 410. For England and Wales the proportion is 1 in every 307, and it is significant that the section of the population of Madras, which shows the greatest liability to insanity, is that which has an admixture of European blood. I have no information regarding the prevalence of insanity among Eurasians for any other province or State of India except Mysore, and there the proportion is 1 in 306."

For the statistics relating to insanity given in table xxiv, I am indebted to Surgeon-Captain C. H. Leet Palk, Superintendent of the Government Asylum. It was found impossible to separate Europeans into home-bred and country-bred; and it is very possible that some Eurasians are included among them. The total number of Eurasians, recorded as being admitted into the asylum during the five years 1893—97, was 49, viz., 6·59 per cent. of the total admissions. Leaving out of question the Europeans, in whom, owing to the preponderance of the male sex (including soldiers) in Madras, a greater number of male than female lunatics is to be expected, and considering only Eurasians and Natives, the far higher proportion of female as compared with male lunatics in the Eurasian than in the Native community, is very conspicuous. Taking, for example, the numbers remaining in the asylum in 1894, whereas the proportion of Eurasian males to females was 33 : 31, that of Natives was 30·6 : 6·8, and the high proportion of female Eurasian inmates is visible in the remaining years under review. The subject seems to be one well worthy of further study by those competent to deal with it.

The alleged causes of insanity in the 49 Eurasian cases were as follows :—

Hereditary	10
Domestic trouble	10
Irregular sexual habits	5
Disappointment	4
Epilepsy	4
Nervous shock	4
Love and jealousy	3
Intemperance	2
Sun-stroke	2
Congenital	1
Senile	1
Privation and starvation	1
Religion	1
Fever	1

On the conclusion of my investigation of the Eurasians of the city of Madras, I proceeded to Calicut, the capital of the Malabar district, as being the most convenient centre for comparing the Eurasians of the west, with those of the east coast. My visit was by chance coincident with the commemoration of the four hundredth anniversary of the arrival of Vasco da Gama at Calicut after his discovery of the sea-route from Europe to India, which I celebrated in a unique manner by recording the physique of the community resulting, in the first instance, from alliances between the Portuguese adventurers and the attractive Native women, and left as a legacy to the later British occupants. Concerning the origin of the Indo-Portuguese half-breed I learn[10] that, on his return from the recapture of Goa, Albuquerque brought with him the women he had carried away when the Portuguese were driven out of the place. As soon as affairs became tolerably settled again at that port, he had them converted to Christianity, and married them to Portuguese men. No less than 450 of his men were thus married in Goa, and others who desired to follow their example were so numerous that Albuquerque had great difficulty in granting their requests. The marriage of Portuguese men to Native women had already been sanctioned by Dom Manoel, but this privilege was only to be conceded to men of proved character, and who had rendered good services. Albuquerque, however, extended the permission to marry far beyond what he was authorised to do, and he took care that the women so married were the daughters of the principal men of the land. This he did in the hope of inducing them to become Christians. To those who were married Albuquerque allotted lands, houses and cattle, so as to give them a start in life, and all the landed property which had been in possession of the Moorish mosques and Hindu pagodas he gave to the principal churches of the city, which he dedicated to "Santa Catherina."

The very names of my subjects recalled to mind Pedro Alvares Cabral, who anchored before Calicut in 1500, and established a factory at Cochin; the first Portuguese Governor, Dom Francisco de Almeida; André Furtado de Mendonca, who concluded a treaty with the king of Calicut; and many others, whose exploits are handed down to posterity in the Indo-Portuguese archives. Subjoined is a comparative statement showing the names of the Eurasians, whom I have personally examined in Madras and Malabar. A cursory glance thereat shows a marked preponderance of Portuguese names in Malabar, which is readily explained

---

[10] DANVERS—'The Portuguese in India', 1894.

by reference to the history of the Portuguese in India, aided by a map showing how thickly studded with Portuguese settlements the west coast was as compared with the east coast:—

Eurasians, Madras.	Eurasians, Calicut.
Almeida.	Allamo.
Anthony (2).	Ambrose.
Assey.	Augustine.
Aubert.	
Bantleman.	Barbosa (2).
Bartholomew.	Bastian.
Bastian (2).	Benjamin (2).
Bedford.	Benny.
Bello.	
Binny.	
Bird (2).	
Borgonah.	
Braily.	
Brisson.	
Brown.	
Calderwood.	Cabral (3).
Carless.	Carvalho.
Caubo.	Conceicao (3).
Christian (2).	
Clarke (2).	
Cleary.	
Clegg.	
Collins.	
Corneille.	
Cornelius.	
Da Costa.	Da Cruz (9).
Da Silva (2).	Da Gama.
Daniel.	Da Silva.
David (2).	David.
Davids.	Davis.
Davy.	De Sousa (4).
De Roza.	De Morias (2).
Devine.	Diaz (3).
Dennis.	
Dimney (2).	
Edwards (2).	Escrador (2).
Fernandes (2).	Fernandes (12).
French.	
Gambler.	Gabriel (2).
Goodman.	Gomes (3).
Gragbisse.	Gonsalves.

Günther.
Gwynne.
Hall.
Harris.
Hart.
Heaney.
Heldt.
Henricus (2).
Henriques.
Hogg.
Howell.
Huggins (2).
Hunter (2).
Isaac.
Jansen.
Jennings.
Johnson (5).
Judge.
Langford.
Lavocat.
Lazaro (2).
Lowe.
Luxa.
Mackenzie.
McKertish.
Martin (2).
Morris.
Murray (2).
Newman.
Pascal.
Paul.
Peazold.
Pereira (3).
Peters.
Philbert.
Powell.
Preston.
Renshaw.
Rigley.
Rivett.
Roberts.
Rodgers.
Rose.
Rowland (2).
Rozario (3).
Rozaro.
Ryan (2).

Jacobs.
Joel.
Joseph.
La Grange.
Lopez.
Macarthy.
Macedo.
Mark.
Manoel (2).
Marquise.
Mendonca (3).
Mullen.
Noronha.
Pereira (3).
Phillips.
Pinto (2).
Powell.
Quental.
Rodriques (4).
Rozario (14).

Schooner.
Smith.
Spires.
Stuart (2).
Sturt.
Tanner.
Truss.
Wain.
Wilder (2).
Wood.
Xavier.

Salisbury.
Saldanha.
Van Spall (2).
Van Span.
Varid.
Woolger.
Xavier (2).

Though Portuguese names persist at the present day, it does not follow of necessity that their owners have any Portuguese blood in their veins, for some are merely descendants of Native converts to Christianity, or of household slaves of Portuguese officers. "In Malabar," writes the Census Commissioner, 1881, there is a section of Europeanized Native Christians—Goa Roman Catholics—some of whom have adopted European dress and customs; and these may have been returned in 1871 as Eurasians; and in all districts the popular interpretation of the word "Eurasian" is very liberal. There are many Pariahs and Native Christians, who have adopted a travesty of European clothes, and who would return themselves as Eurasians, if allowed to do so." The division between Native Christians and people of mixed race is, as I have already pointed out, very shadowy in Malabar. Considerable care had, therefore, to be taken in accepting or rejecting some of those who, anxious to secure the modest fee which was offered in return for the loan of their bodies, appeared before me in the rôle of Eurasians. All doubtful cases were rejected, and due attention was paid to the various points—colour, character of nose, type of face, breadth of head, manner of speech, baldness and grey hairs at an early age, etc.—by which one accustomed to close observation of Natives and Eurasians can distinguish racial admixture.

Though the terms are, according to my definition (page 69) synonymous and interchangeable, a social distinction is made at Calicut between Eurasians and East Indians. With a view to clearing up the grounds on which this distinction is based, my interpreter was called on to submit a note on the subject, which eventually arrived, couched in language worthy of "Mark Twain." I, therefore, reproduce it in the original Anglo-Indian.

"Eurasians are classified to those who stand second in the list of Europeans and those born in any part of India, and who are the Pedigree of European descendants, being born of father European and mother East Indian, and notwithstanding those who can prove themselves as really good Indian descendants such as mother and father of the same sex, therefore these are called Eurasians.

"East Indians are those offsprings of Christians of the East, and they atimes gather the offsprings of Eurasians to the entering their marriage to the East Indian females into the East Indian community, thereby they are called East Indians.

"Native Christians are those of Hindu nations converted into Christians by their embracing the poles of Christianity. All Hindus thereby converted and made Christians by a second Baptism are called Native Christians.

"Coaster.—They are alluded to those who belong to the Coast, and who come from a country that has a Sea Coast into that country that has not got a Sea Coast is therefore called a Coaster. A very rude word."

The distinction between Eurasian and East Indian is, as a matter of fact, a very artificial one, and the two types merge imperceptibly one into the other, separated by no sharp line of demarcation. Speaking in general terms, it may be said that the Eurasians are of greater stature, and possess skins of lighter hue than the East Indians, who, as the result of intermarriage with Native Christian women, have reverted in the direction of the Native type.

There are, in North Malabar, many individuals posing as pure-bred Natives, whose fathers were Europeans; but, for caste reasons, their white paternity is lost sight of. Many of them possess very pale skins, and some are in prosperous circumstances. Writing concerning the Tiyan community, Mr. Logan says: [11] "The women are not as a rule excommunicated if they live with Europeans, and the consequence is that there has been among them a large admixture of European blood, and the caste itself has been materially raised in the social scale. In appearance some of the women are almost as fair as Europeans." In recent times the Tiyans of North Malabar have separated into two

---

[11] 'Manual of Malabar'.

factions, which hold different views with reference to the cohabitation of Tiyan women with Europeans, the one being in favour of it, the other against it. On this point the report of the Malabar Marriage Commission, 1894, states "that in the early days of British rule, the Tiyan women incurred no social disgrace by consorting with Europeans, and, up to the last generation, if the Sudra girl could boast of her Brahmin lover, the Tiyan girl could show more substantial benefits from her alliance with a white man of the ruling race. Happily the progress of education, and the growth of a wholesome public opinion, have made shameful the position of a European's concubine; and both races have thus been saved from a mode of life equally demoralizing to each."

The Eurasians examined by me at Calicut, nearly all of whom were Roman Catholics, were earning a modest livelihood, ranging from Rs. 35 to Rs. 12 per mensem, in the following capacities :—

Bandsman.	Municipal inspector.
Boot-maker.	Musician.
Bugler.	Petition-writer.
Carpenter.	Police constable.
Clerk.	Railway guard.
Coffee-estate writer.	Schoolmaster.
Compositor.	Tailor.
Copyist.	Tin-smith.
Mechanic.	Weaver.

No less than 39, out of the 96 cases which came before me for investigation, were tailors. Tailoring is, therefore, to the poor Eurasians of Calicut what "fitting" is to those of Madras.

As in Madras, so in Malabar, tattooing is very prevalent among the male members of the Eurasian community, and the devices are characterised by a predominance of religious emblems and snakes. The following patterns are recorded in my notes :—

Bangle on wrist.	Cross.
Boat.	Cross and crown.
Bird (the Holy Ghost).	Cross and heart.
Chalice.	Cross and I.N.R.I.
Christ crucified.	Crossed swords.
Cobra.	Fish.
Conventional and geometrical designs (done by Koravar women).	Flags.
	Flower.
	Flower with leaves.

Initials.
Ladder.
Sacred heart.
Snake encircling forearm.
Snake coiling round forearm.
Solomon's seal.
Steam boat.

During the course of my visit to Calicut, a resident correspondent of the 'Madras Mail' expressed his fear that, when I came to strike my averages of Calicut "East Indians," I should find the results very poor, as I had measured specimens drawn from the lower section of the community, represented by artisans living on poor food, and amidst surroundings that are not conducive to physical development. This fear was indeed justified, and my remarks on early marriage and physique of the poor Eurasians of Madras apply with equal, if not greater force to those of Malabar. Repetition is unnecessary, and it will suffice to let the figures in table xxv speak for themselves.

Comparing the physique of the younger members of the Calicut "Eurasian and East Indian" community at an age when they would be eligible as recruits, with that of the Eurasians of Madras and sepoys of the same age, the results work out as follows, and demonstrate that a very small proportion of the two former possess the physique necessary to successfully withstand the hardships enforced by active service :—

WEIGHT, LB.

—	70–80	80–90	90–100	100–110	110–120	120–130	130–140	140–150	150–160
Sepoys	...	...	1	4	11	19	9	4	2
Eurasians, Madras ...	...	6	9	12	13	4	5	1	...
„ Calicut ...	3	3	9	15	16	3	1	...	...

CHEST, CM.

—	60–70	70–80	80–90	90–100
Sepoys	...	5	42	3
Eurasians, Madras	3	33	14	...
„ Calicut	1	39	10	...

SHOULDERS, CM.

—	33–37	37–38	38–39	39–40	40–41	41–42	42–43	43–44	44–45	45–46
Sepoys	...	...	4	5	6	15	12	4	2	2
Eurasians, Madras ...	9	10	8	9	10	2	...	2	...	...
,, Calicut ..	12	8	8	17	5	...	...	...	...	...

Putting these figures, as before, in terms of percentages we obtain the following results :—

WEIGHT.

	Below 120 LB.	Above 120 LB.
Sepoys	32	68
Eurasians, Madras	80	20
,, Calicut	92	8

CHEST.

	Below 80 CM.	Above 80 CM.
Sepoys	10	90
Eurasians, Madras	72	28
Calicut	80	20

SHOULDERS.

	Below 41 CM.	Above 41 CM.
Sepoys	30	70
Eurasians, Madras	92	8
,, Calicut	100	0

During a recent visit to Ootacamund, I was, through the courtesy of the Principal, the Rev. A. W. Atkinson, enabled to examine the physique of the elder boys at the Lawrence Asylum, the object of which is "to provide for children of European and East Indian (*i.e.*, Eurasian) officers and soldiers of Her Majesty's Army (British and Native), and of Europeans and East Indians in the Medical Service, Military and Civil, who are serving, or have served within the limits of the Presidency of Madras, a refuge from the debilitating effects of a tropical climate, and from the serious drawbacks to the well-being of children incidental to a barrack life; to afford for them a plain, practical, and religious education; and to train them for employment in different trades, pursuits, and industries." In his last two annual reports the Principal has emphasised the fact that application for the admission of the children of British soldiers, for whom solely this and similar institutions were originally founded, have almost ceased. "There is," he says (6th September, 1897), "not one child of a British soldier eligible for admission on the register to-day-a situation unprecedented in the history of the Asylum. In view then of this lapse of applications for the admission of the kind of children into our Asylum, for whom it primarily exists, ought not the plan to be adopted, as speedily as may be, of drafting such children from Orphanages, and such like Institutions on the enervating plains, and placing them with us here?" In the year 1896–97 four boys enlisted in European regiments, and one boy in a Native régiment. "Compared with the previous year," the Principal reports, "enlistments in European regiments were few, as boys of *pure* European parentage only can be entertained."

As the result of examination of 32 Eurasian boys at the Lawrence Asylum, between the ages of 13 and 17, whose measurements are given in detail in table xxvi, I am able to testify with very great pleasure to the excellence of their physical condition. A good climate, with a mean annual temperature of 58°, good food, and physical training, have produced, in fact, a set of boys well-nourished and muscular, with good chests, shoulders, and body weight, who afford a striking contrast to the lads belonging to the same class in the plains, brought up amid the unwholesome environment of an enervating climate. More eloquent than the columns of figures in table xxvi, which appeal only to those accustomed to anthropometric methods, was examination of the lads themselves as they stood stripped for investigation. But I may, for the purpose of comparison, cite the physical records of a few cases, both pure European and Eurasian, in evidence that, amid wholesome surroundings, the Eurasian (especially of British paternity) is capable of development into a being of good physique, such as is required for the hardships of Military Service:

	Age.	Weight.	Height.	Chest.	Shoulders.
European ..	16–17	135	169·8	84	35·5
" ..	15–16	110	161·8	79·5	34·7
" ..	15–16	100	153·4	81	36·3
" ..	14–15	135	167·6	84	36·6
Eurasian ..	16–17	105	157·4	81	35·3
" ..	16–17	116	162·6	83	39·7
" ..	15–16	102	149·5	80	36·3
" ..	14–15	108	153·6	80	35·2
" ..	13–14	115	167	79·6	37·1

TABLE XVII.

SUMMARY OF MEASUREMENTS.

EURASIANS.

	Max.	Min.	Average.	Range.
Weight	168	79	111·5	89
Height	183·8	153	166·0	30·8
Height, sitting	95·6	78·6	86·6	17
Height, kneeling	136·6	113	123·7	23·6
Height to gladiolus	136·4	110	122·7	26·4
Span of arms	196·8	153·4	172·7	43·4
Chest	93	67	79·1	26
Middle finger to patella	20·4	6·2	12·5	14·2
Shoulders	44·6	34·3	39·2	10·3
Cubit	52·9	40·3	46·1	12·6
Hand, length	20·2	15·5	17·7	4·7
Hand, breadth	8·7	6·5	7·5	2·2
Hips	30·3	21·4	25·4	8·9
Foot, length	29·5	22·4	25·7	7·1
Foot, breadth	10	7·1	8·3	2·9
Cephalic length	20·2	16·8	18·6	3·4
Cephalic breadth	15·6	12·8	14·1	2·8
Cephalic index	87·2	69·5	76	17·7
Bigoniac	12	9	10·1	3
Bizygomatic	14·4	11·8	13	2·6
Maxillo-zygomatic index	85·3	69·9	77·5	15·4
Nasal height	6·1	4·4	5·1	1·7
Nasal breadth	4·2	2·7	3·5	1·5
Nasal index	91·1	53·7	69·5	37·4

Note.—The results are based on the measurement of 130 subjects.

In this and the following tables, the weight is recorded in pounds; the measurements are in centimetres.

TABLE XVIII.

EURASIANS AND SEPOYS.

AVERAGES.

	Eurasians.	Sepoys.
Age	28–29	24–25
Weight	111·5 lbs.	127·5 lbs.
Height	166·6 cm.	168·2 cm.
Chest	79·1 cm.	84·7 cm.
Shoulders	39·2 cm.	41·5 cm.
Dynamometer	65 lbs.	80 lbs.

TABLE XIX.

SEPOYS AND EURASIANS, AGED 18—25.

	Maximum.		Minimum.		Average.		Mean above.		Mean below.	
	Sepoys.	Eur-asians.	Sepoys.	Eur-asians.	Sepoys.	Eur-asians.	Sepoys.	Eur-asians.	Sepoys.	Eur-asians.
Weight	160	150	98	80	125	108	135	122	115	95
Height	178	181	160·6	153·8	167·9	164·8	172·1	170·8	164·3	159
Chest	94	87·5	75·5	68	84	77·6	87·3	82	81	74
Shoulders	45·5	43·9	37·7	33·8	41·6	38·7	42·8	40·5	40	37·1
Dynamometer	113	90	66	50	80	64	87·6	72·4	73·6	56·6

TABLE XX.

DETAILS OF MEASUREMENTS.

EURASIANS, AGED 19—25.

Age.	Weight.	Height.	Chest.	Shoulders.	Dynamometer.	
24	112	167·4	85	40·4	...	Fitter.
22	105	160·4	83	40	...	Fitter.
24	97	153·8	78	37·5	...	Boiler-smith.
21	127	180	86·5	41·5	...	Blacksmith.
21	139	164·8	87	42·1	...	Ticket-collector.
22	135	181	82	40·9	...	Clerk.
23	116	169·6	78·7	38·6	...	Electric tram driver.
21	119	179	79·7	38·7	...	Fitter.
24	110	162	78	39·4	...	Clerk.
23	108	170	76	39·4	...	Carpenter.
23	94	154·6	74·5	36·3	...	Unemployed.
23	90	156·8	72·5	37·2	...	Carpenter.
23	150	180·6	87·5	43·9	...	Electric tram driver.
24	103	167	75·5	38·6	...	Compositor.
21	107	167·2	77	37·2	...	Hammerer.
22	111	170·6	75	37·3	...	Turner.
21	95	160·8	75·5	36·7	...	Mechanic.
23	111	166·8	77	39·5	...	Fitter.
21	115	168·4	83·5	40	...	Fireman.
23	123	162·2	82	40·9	...	Fitter.
24	106	166·8	75·5	40·2	...	Fitter.
24	116	171	75	38·2	...	Fitter.
22	127	169·2	81	40	...	Fireman.
23	109	165·4	77·5	38·5	...	Turner.
24	115	179·4	82·5	41·2	...	Fitter.

TABLE XX—*continued.*

DETAILS OF MEASUREMENTS.

EURASIANS, AGED 19—25.

Age.	Weight.	Height.	Chest.	Shoulders.	Dynamometer.	
24	83	154·7	72	36·5	...	Chemist's assistant.
22	132	171·2	87	40·1	90	Turner.
22	101	165·8	74·5	39·1	70	Clerk.
22	123	160·2	82	40·7	71	Rivetter.
21	103	169·2	76·5	39·1	68	Jointer.
21	137	175·2	80	39·9	60	Fitter.
21	92	154·5	73	33·8	50	Fitter.
24	101	166	79	37·6	69	Railway guard.
19	106	160	78	38·5	67	Turner.
20	96	163·8	72	38·5	56	Cleaner, railway.
20	113	167·2	76·5	39·6	74	Carpenter.
23	136	171·4	84·5	43·3	90	Cobler.
20	87	159·6	76·5	37·7	57	Fitter.
24	80	154·4	68	35·1	56	Clerk.
20	102	163·8	75·5	38·7	55	Fitter.
22	88	158·8	75·5	36·4	62	Printer.
23	94	155·8	75·5	37·6	64	Printer.
19	100	161·4	74	37·5	63	Fitter.
24	118	169	79	39·5	66	Fitter.
19	93	162·6	72	35·6	50	Fitter.
19	95	159·6	72·5	37·1	60	Fitter.
19	80	157·8	69·5	35·9	54	Fitter.
19	111	161·4	74	37	65	Watch-repairer.
20	118	167	79	39·7	66	Fitter.
19	82	157	69	34·8	46	Blacksmith.

TABLE XXI.

DETAILS OF MEASUREMENTS.

SEPOYS, AGED 18—25.

Age.	Weight.	Height.	Chest.	Shoulders.	Dynamometer.
23	131	174	87	45·3	78
24	143	170·4	91·5	42·8	113
20	133	169·2	85	42·3	81
19	126	161·8	80·5	39	71
20	118	160·6	82	41·2	85
19	115	167·1	80	40·7	89
22	131	168·6	82	43·7	81
22	125	167·6	82	41·8	86
19	128	167·4	85	41·7	78
24	122	168·3	84·3	42	69
21	148	171·8	89·5	42·4	81
21	125	165·6	84	42·4	79
18	137	174	88	43·7	83
19	123	173·2	80·5	41·4	73
23	160	175·9	94	41·3	78
23	157	178	90	43·7	88
20	131	175·2	84	42·7	84
23	128	163	85·5	41·3	92
22	139	172·4	89·5	43·4	81
19	124	172	80·5	38·2	80
22	113	161	83	40·2	76
22	129	161·8	84·5	41·8	66
21	141	172·6	88	45·5	97
19	108	162	81	39·5	93
20	123	166	83	40·2	80

TABLE XXI—*continued.*

DETAILS OF MEASUREMENTS.

SEPOYS, AGED 18—25.

Age.	Weight.	Height.	Chest.	Shoulders.	Dynamo-meter.
21	98	166	76	39·6	67
22	127	169	82	39·1	86
20	116	163·2	80	41·1	69
20	129	166·9	89	42·4	77
20	145	177·8	86·5	42·3	75
18	107	166·8	79·5	38·2	66
22	109	160·7	80·5	38·7	84
21	111	161·3	79·5	40·1	75
24	112	165	80·5	39	82
21	118	162	83	40·7	71
19	114	170·8	81·5	41·6	73
18	122	161·2	86	42·2	78
18	120	163·2	83·5	41·8	72
21	127	167	86	41·8	77
22	116	170·4	83	42	82
20	134	173·2	98	42	86
18	113	163·6	79	41·6	76
18	121	167·4	82·5	41·5	77
22	100	165·4	75·5	37·7	75
23	135	169·4	85	41·9	85
23	128	170	88	44	75
24	122	164·6	85·5	42·9	70
19	128	170·2	86	40·8	86
22	114	169·2	83	41·7	73
22	130	172	88	44·8	102

TABLE XXII.

LIST OF SO-CALLED EUROPEANS TREATED IN THE LEPER HOSPITAL FROM 1890-97.

Age.	Race.	Occupation.	Place of birth.	How long ill.	Cause.	Date of Admission.	Date of Discharge.	Date of Death.
						Y. M. D.	Y. M. D.	Y. M. D.
43 ...	European ...	Railway Guard.	Australia ...	15 years ...	Venereal ...	13 9 84	...	28 3 90
25 ...	Irish ...	*Nil*	Madras ...	10 years ...	Unknown ...	13 9 89	...	12 7 91
23 ...	European ...	Interpreter ...	Tanjore ...	9 months ...	Do. ...	12 2 91	13 2 92	...
22 ...	Do. ...	Fitter	Buxar ...	6 years ...	Do. ...	21 2 91	3 2 92	...
34 ...	Do. ...	*Nil*	Negapatam ...	15 years ...	Do. ...	17 3 92	11 3 93	...
27 ...	Do. ...	Accountant ...	Shevaroy Hills.	6 months ...	Do. ...	14 6 92	...	30 7 96
31 ...	French ...	Contractor ...	Pondicherry ...	15 years ...	Do. ...	9 3 93	16 4 93	...
42 ...	European ...	Supervisor, P.W.D.	Bangalore ...	17 years ...	Venereal ...	12 10 94	...	...
20 ...	Do. ...	*Nil*	Tinnevelly ...	12 years ...	Unknown ...	28 3 95	...	14 2 96
27 ...	Do. ...	Sailor	Cardiff ...	$2\frac{1}{2}$ years ...	Do. ...	24 6 97	...	...
32 ...	Do. ...	Soldier	Burma ...	6 years ...	Do. ...	25 10 97	...	11 12 97

TABLE XXIII.

STATISTICS SHOWING THE NUMBER OF CASES OF LEPROSY TREATED DURING THE FIVE YEARS 1893—97.

—	Remained.			Admitted.			Total.			Discharged.			Died.			Remaining.		
	Men.	Women.	Children.	Men.	Women.	Children.	Men.	Women.	Children.	Men.	Women.	Children.	Men.	Women.	Children.	Men.	Women.	Children.
Europeans.																		
1893	1	...	...	1	...	...	2	...	...	1	...	...	...	...	...	1	...	...
1894	1	...	...	1	...	...	2	...	...	...	...	...	...	...	...	2	...	...
1895	2	...	...	1	...	...	3	...	...	...	...	...	...	...	...	3	...	...
1896	3	...	...	...	...	...	3	...	...	...	...	...	2	...	...	1	...	...
1897	1	...	...	2	...	...	3	...	...	...	...	...	1	...	...	2	...	...
Eurasians.																		
1893	22	11	...	7	3	2	29	14	2	5	6	2	4	2	...	20	6	...
1894	20	6	...	7	8	3	27	14	3	6	6	2	4	1	...	17	9	1
1895	17	9	1	8	3	2	25	12	3	9	5	2	...	...	1	16	7	...
1896	16	7	...	16	6	...	32	13	...	12	7	...	...	1	...	20	5	...
1897	20	5	...	6	4	1	26	9	1	2	3	1	3	1	...	21	5	...

TABLE XXIV.

STATEMENT SHOWING THE NUMBER OF LUNATICS TREATED DURING THE FIVE YEARS 1893—97.

—	Remained.		Admitted.		Total.		Discharged.		Died.		Remaining.	
	Men.	Women.	Men.	Women.	Men.	Women.	Men.	Women.	Men.	Women.	Men.	Women.
EURASIANS.												
1893	31	30	6	7	37	37	2	5	2	1	33	31
1894	33	31	8	6	41	37	3	5	1	1	37	31
1895	37	31	10	6	47	37	4	3	3	3	40	31
1896	40	31	2	4	42	35	5	4	...	1	37	30
1897	37	30	3	3	40	33	2	1	1	...	37	32
NATIVES.												
1893	282	78	110	25	392	101	54	19	32	14	306	68
1894	306	68	104	28	410	96	55	13	41	12	314	71
1895	314	71	113	18	427	89	62	12	75	10	290	67
1896	290	67	82	17	372	84	75	13	27	9	270	62
1897	270	62	84	18	354	80	56	6	22	14	276	60
EUROPEANS.												
1893	12	3	15	4	27	9	13	2	1	...	13	7
1894	13	7	19	1	32	8	18	1	...	...	14	7
1895	14	7	11	4	25	11	12	2	1	2	12	7
1896	12	7	5	...	17	7	3	1	1	...	13	6
1897	13	6	14	1	27	7	13	1	...	...	14	6

TABLE XXV.

COMPARISON OF MEASUREMENTS.

EURASIANS, MADRAS AND CALICUT.

	Madras.	Calicut.
Weight	111·5	109
Height	166·6	163·5
Span of arms	172·7	171
Chest	79·1	77·7
Shoulders	39·2	38·7
Hand, breadth	7·5	7·4
Hips	25·4	25·1
Foot, breadth	8·3	8·3
Cephalic length	18·6	18·6
,, breadth	14·1	14
,, index	76	75·4
Bigoniac	10·1	9·9
Bizygomatic	13	12·8
Maxillo-zygomatic index	77·5	77·5
Nasal height	5·1	4·9
,, breadth	3·5	3·4
,, index	69·5	69·3
Dynamometer	65	63

The weights were taken in clothes with boots.

TABLE XXVI.

SUMMARY OF MEASUREMENTS.

EURASIAN BOYS, LAWRENCE ASYLUM.

Age.	Weight.	Height.	Chest.	Shoulders.	Hand, breadth.	Cephalic length.	Cephalic breadth.	Cephalic index.	Dynamometer.
16–17	105	157·4	81	35·3	7·4	18·9	14·2	75·1	50
16–17	116	162·6	83	39·7	7·5	18·2	13·4	73·6	59
16–17	85	145·2	67	33	7·2	18·9	14·2	75·1	43
15–16	118	165·6	79·5	37·4	7·3	17·4	15	86·2	64
15–16	96	155·4	74	33·4	6·8	18	14·8	82·2	49
15–16	97	153·2	73	35	7·3	17·5	14·8	84·6	50
15–16	102	149·5	80	36·3	7·1	17·8	14·6	82	51
15–16	91	149·4	73	35·4	6·8	17·8	14·6	82	42
15–16	104	152·6	76	36	7·4	18·4	13·6	73·9	63
15–16	87	152·4	71·5	35·4	7·1	18·1	14·2	78·5	49
15–16	97	153·6	73·5	35·3	7·2	17·1	14·4	84·2	55
15–16	86	148·7	70·5	32·3	7·4	17·6	13·5	76·4	60
15–16	85	150·2	73·5	32·3	6·9	17·8	13·6	76·4	47
15–16	90	151·2	73·5	32·9	6·4	16·6	14·4	86·7	41
15–16	92	151	70	34·7	7·3	16·9	13·6	80·5	55
15–16	92	144·8	73	33·5	6·9	18	13·4	74·4	44
15–16	97	149·8	72·5	34·1	7	19·5	15·2	76·4	48
15–16	98	150·4	77·5	35·3	7·2	17·2	13·6	79·1	51
15–16	80	140·6	69	30·5	6·7	17·4	13·9	79·9	39
15–16	85	148·9	67·5	33	6·5	17·8	14·2	79·8	38

TABLE XXVI—*continued.*

SUMMARY OF MEASUREMENTS.

EURASIAN BOYS, LAWRENCE ASYLUM.

Age.	Weight.	Height.	Chest.	Shoulders.	Hand, breadth.	Cephalic length.	Cephalic breadth.	Cephalic index.	Dynamometer.
14–15	108	153·6	80	35·2	7·6	16·8	14·2	85·7	67
14–15	93	147·7	76	34·5	7·7	17·6	14	79·5	50
14–15	85	145·6	68·7	32	6·5	18·6	14	75·3	38
14–15	87	150·2	71·5	31·6	6·6	17·8	13·8	77·5	52
14–15	88	148·2	69·5	31·5	6·8	17·6	14	79·5	52
14–15	97	148·7	75	33·2	7·3	18	13·8	76·7	59
14–15	92	148·2	75·3	34·6	6·5	18·2	14·7	80·8	48
14–15	89	146·5	71·5	33·9	7	18·8	13·8	73·4	47
14–15	77	147·6	68	32·8	6·3	18·2	14·2	78	39
14–15	86	143·2	72·5	32·9	6·8	18·5	14·2	76·8	42
14–15	87	146·6	69·5	33·3	7·1	18	14·2	78·9	50
13–14	115	167	79·6	37·1	7·2	18·2	15·8	86·8	57

NOTE ON TATTOOING.

In a paper on tattooing, read at the Anthropological Institute in January, 1888, Miss Buckland refers to the practice of tattooing among the Nāgas of Assam, and to the tattooing of breeches, reaching from the waist to the knee, with which the male Burman is adorned. But, in the map illustrating the paper, peninsular India, south of 20°, is left a perfect and absolute blank. And, in the discussion which followed the reading of the paper, Lieutenant-Colonel Kincaird, recognising this remarkable hiatus, remarked that "his observation led him to believe that this custom is wide-spread on the arms and legs among the women of the lower castes of the Tamil, etc., races in the south and south-east of the peninsula. Among the ethnically allied so-called aboriginal tribes inhabiting the Vindyan and Sathpura hill slopes it is also prevalent, even among the women of the lower orders of Muhammadans, whose fore-fathers were probably low-caste Hindus, before being converted by force. He had observed the same tattoo markings on arms and legs. There is very generally a dot on the chin, and similar dots on the cheek or temple very sparingly placed, forming perhaps, in their ideas, beauty spots similar to the patches of our ladies in former years."

The prevalence of tattooing, frequently with very elaborate devices, among the male sex in the Eurasian community has been dealt with in the preceding chapter. And, in Bulletin No. IV, 1896, I have referred to, and illustrated the primitive patterns of dots and circles on the breasts, arms, hands, legs, and feet of the Toda women of the Nīlgiris, and the more advanced type of lines, dots, and circles, sometimes combined into a simple ornamental pattern, in vogue among the Kota women of the same hill-range.

The following note on the practice of tattooing, as carried out in the city of Madras, is based on information extracted in the course of interviews with professional female tattooers, of whom the first arrived in a state of maudling intoxication. These women belong to the class of Koravas or Yerukalas, "a vagrant tribe found throughout the Madras Presidency. They wander about the country in gangs, selling baskets, carrying salt, telling fortunes, and pilfering and robbing whenever an opportunity occurs. As house-breakers they are especially expert, and burglary is their favourite crime." (Census report, 1881.) The men are also employed in hunting, bird-snaring, and as actors of native plays, which they perform on the road side. Sometimes they masquerade as mendicants, and go about, beating a drum, and begging from house to house in the bazár. The female tattooers leave Madras during the harvest season, and pay professional visits to the neighbouring districts, travelling as far as Pondicherry in the south, and Cuddapah in the north. By these women Brāhmans, 'Sudras' of all classes, Pariahs, and Tamil-speaking Muhammadans (Labbais) are operated on. The patterns range from a dot or straight line to complex geometrical or conventional designs (Plates xxiii–xxiv). Figures of wild animals are not met with, but scorpions, birds, fishes, flowers, and the Vaishnava sect mark, are common. So too, as among the Eurasians, are the initials or name (in Tamil characters) upon the fore-arm. Sometimes Hindu males are tattooed, as an amusement, when boys, or, in some cases among the lower classes, *e.g.*, Pariahs, when grown up. But tattooing with elaborate devices is essentially confined to the female sex. The parts of the body selected for the performance of the operation in its ornamental aspect are the fore-arm, fore-leg, fore-head, cheeks, and chin. But, in some instances, in case of muscular pain or other disorder, the operation is performed as a remedial agent over the shoulder-joint, or on the thigh, upper arm, or other parts of the body. A legend runs to the effect that, many years ago, a Pariah woman wished her upper arms and breast to be tattooed in the form of a bodice. The operation was successfully performed until the region of the heart was reached, and then a vulnerable part was punctured by the needles with the result that the woman died. Whence has arisen a superstitious objection to tattooing of the breasts.

The Tamil equivalent of tattooing is pachai-kuthu-kirathu (= pricking with green). The "marking ink" is prepared in the following manner: Turmeric (kappa manja) powder and agathikeerai (leaves of *Sesbania*

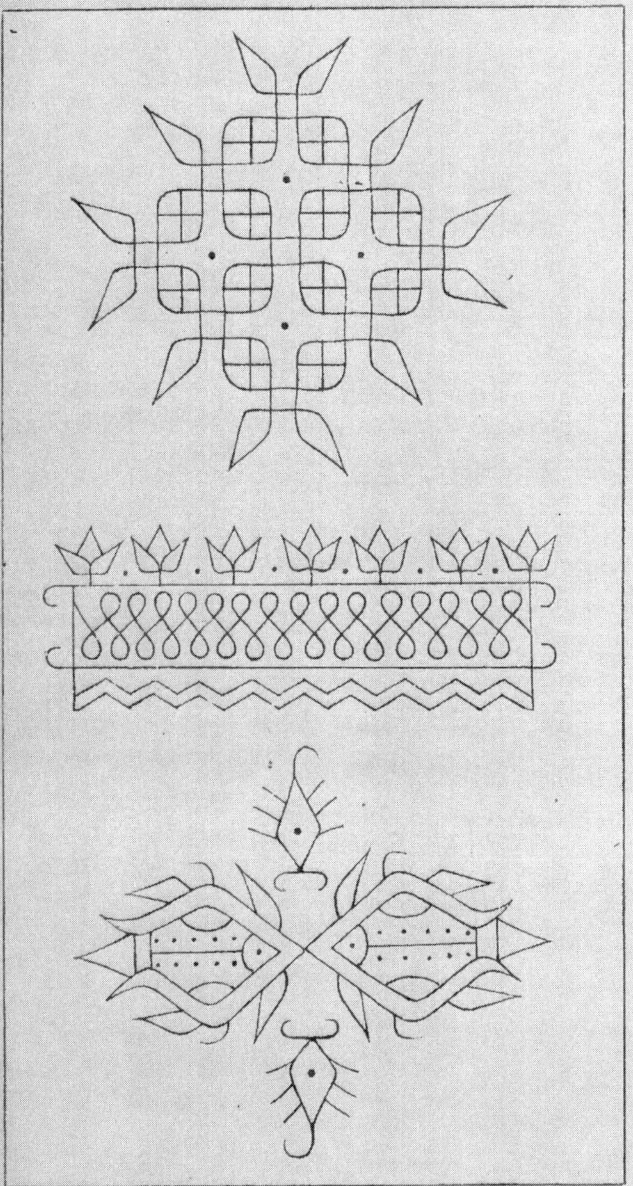

TAMIL TATTOOING.

grandiflora) are rubbed together in a mortar, or on a grinding stone. The mixture is spread on a thin cloth, and rolled up in the form of a wick, which is placed in an open lamp charged with castor-oil. The wick is lighted, and the lamp covered with a new earthen pot, on the inside of which the lamp-black is deposited. This is scraped off and mixed with human milk or water. Instead of agathi-keerai, arumpilloo (green parts of *Cynodon Dactylon*), or karisinagoni (green parts of *Eclipta alba*) may be used in the preparation of the wick. As a pricking instrument, three or four sewing needles are fastened together with thread. In the performance of the operation, the selected pattern is first traced on the skin with a thin stick dipped in the prepared ink, which is pricked in with the needles. The part is then washed with cold water, and a coat of ink rubbed over the surface. To allay the pain, oil is applied, and a small quantity of turmeric powder is rubbed in, to brighten the colour and prevent swelling. The Korava women, being illiterate, are unable to tattoo initials or names unless they are first drawn for them. They are able to execute the complicated patterns, with which they are, from long practice, familiar, with considerable dexterity, and will tattoo any pattern which is new to them, provided that it is first drawn. The woman who described the tattooing process to me traced out very elaborate patterns, with great rapidity, with the blunt stick which she was accustomed to use, but could make no way at all with a pencil. The Burmese patterns are far more artistic, varied, and complicated than those executed by the Koravas. With these patterns sepoys, and Tamil coolies who emigrate to Burma, are freely tattooed by highly skilled Burmese tattooers; and some of these patterns are now being copied by the Madras tattooers. The tattooer's fee is said to range from a quarter-anna for a dot or line to twelve-annas for a complex design. And in up-country villages payment appears to be made in kind, and a present of rice to be the usual remuneration.

The following information was supplied by a Tamil Native, with a European ballet girl tattooed on his upper arm, who was engaged in varnishing cases in one of the Museum galleries: "Some years ago I went to Ceylon with a Native Theatrical Company. While in Colombo I made the acquaintance of a Sinhalese who was a professional tattooer. He had an album of pictures for tattooing. I was attracted by their beauty, and subjected myself to the operation. It was an easy and painless operation as compared with that of the Madras tattooer. The Sinhalese man had the needles tied together in different ways, *e.g.*, for pricking straight lines five or six needles are tied together in a row; for pricking curves the needles are arranged in a curve. The Madras tattooer has the needles tied together in a bundle, and the operation, as performed with them, is painful, and sometimes followed by swelling and ulceration." Asked whether he was glad he had been tattooed, the man said, "I am very sorry I had it done, for, when I got married, I was ashamed of it, and kept it hidden by my cloth."

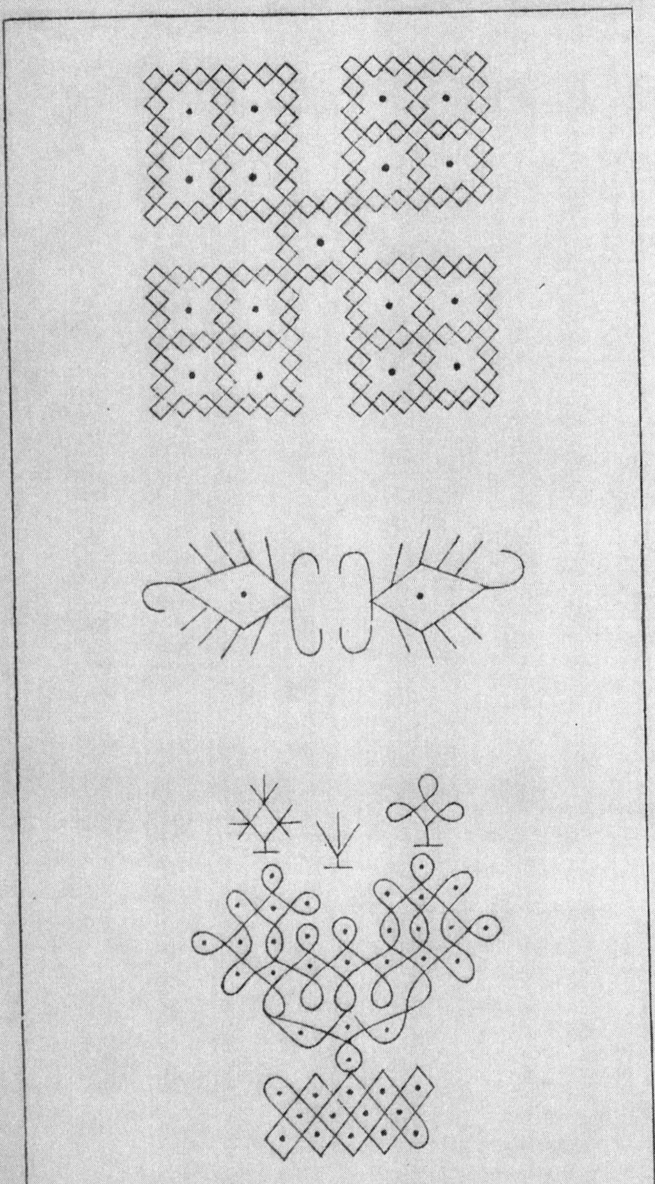

TAMIL TATTOOING.

MALAGASY-NIAS-DRAVIDIANS.

In the course of an article entitled 'Malgaches-Nias-Dravidians,'* M. Zaborowski makes copious reference to the results of my researches among the Irulas, Paniyans, and Kurumbas.† Quoting Modigliani, he says : " I have seen in India, on the Malabar Coast, and especially at Beypur, Calicut, and the surrounding country, various natives of *Malaisoid* type, whose features struck me owing to their close resemblance to those of the Nias. Among the Tiyans, of low caste, this resemblance is great (twisted legs, lobes of the ears widely dilated, the shape of the female breasts, and long arms) ; but those, in whom the resemblance struck me most, were a Kakkai (crow-eating) Kurumba man and woman, mendicants met in the vicinity of Calicut. It was on my return from Nias, and the impression which they produced was a lively one. . . I do not wish to affirm that the Nias are descended from the Tiyans, or from the Kurumbas ; but, from the description of their physical characters, their customs, and their legends, results the possibility of a common origin between Nias and Kurumbas.

Continuing the line of argument, M. Zaborowski writes as follows : " A very important work, which 'M. Edouard' Thurston has just published, allows me to bring this assimilation still closer. The portraits of Irulas, Paniyans, Kurumbas, and a Tamil man, which this author gives with his notes, are sufficient by themselves to clear up many doubts. Mr. Thurston has measured only Dravidians, so that he furnishes us with terms of comparison taken in India itself. A hierarchic classification of all these Indian people is made by the consideration of the nasal index alone. The Irulas, Paniyans, and Kurumbas are shown, by the table of nasal indices, to be specially worthy of attention from the point of view which concerns us. Their extreme platyrhiny is due, as in the Moïs, to shortness of height rather than to excessive breadth."

---

* Bull. Soc. d' Anthropol., Fasc., 2, 1897.

† Madras Museum Bull., Vol. II, No. 1, 1897.

After drawing attention to the profusion of copper rings, and other ornaments which the Irula and Paniyan women wear, and the resemblance between the clothing of Irulas and Malagasy of Madagascar, M. Zaborowski continues: "In studying the customs of our Indo-Chinese wild tribes, I have naturally been struck with the similarity of their taste for interminable rolls of copper, which they wear on the fore-arm, the profusion of bracelets, and especially with the habit of dilating the lobes of the ears, and suspending therein rings of copper, with the tastes and practices of the Dayaks of Borneo. Now I find the same tastes, and almost the same practices among the Dravidian tribes of Southern India. Irulas, Paniyans, and doubtless the Kurumbas, cover themselves with bracelets and rings of copper, and insert in the lobes of the ears light discs, rolls of cajan, doubtless to suspend therein ear-rings, and even rings of copper, which stretch them. This last custom is very widespread at Nias, and it is met with in Madagascar. Its point of departure, its origin, is then not in Borneo, but in Southern India. In addition to their striking physical characters, Irulas, Kurumbas, and Paniyans offer to the careful observer peculiarities of customs which, if not absolutely identical with those of the Moïs, recall no less forcibly their mode of existence, customs, level of culture, moral and social individuality. Close bonds have united them. I do not say that the Nias are Kurumbas, or that the Moïs are Paniyans or Irulas. They are like so much débris of groups disaggregated long ago. They have lived, without communicating one with the other, for perhaps more than a thousand years. And it is undoubtedly more than two thousand years since they were separated, and became subject to the influences of difference in climate and environment. Their separation may even date back to a more remote period. It is, then, marvellous that they present to-day such evident affinities. Traits of custom and character may separate them even under the head of physique. Thus Irulas, Kurumbas, and Paniyans have, as a general rule, the skin of a darker hue than Nias and Moïs, a greater hairy devolpment, and a more Australian type. But the colour of the skin is universally very variable; light skins are met with even among Dravidians. And it must not be forgotten that Malay blood has, for a long time, had a very great influence in Indo-China. So that secondary distinctions cannot make us misinterpret the identity of the primary characters which are preserved in all these groups with remarkable persistence.

It is from India that have proceeded the principal constituent elements of the Nias and Moïs, not to speak of other less well-known groups of Sonda.

As a supplement to my notes on the ornaments worn by Irulas and Paniyans, and as bearing on the subject of dilatation of the ear-lobes referred to by Mr. Zaborowski, I reproduce my notes on the ornaments worn by Cherumans of both sexes at Calicut on the Malabar Coast. The Cherumans are, as I have pointed out elsewhere, a large community of low stature, very dark skinned, with wide nasal index, inhabiting Malabar, where they were formerly agrestic slaves, and now work for the most part as field labourers, and, in the town of Calicut, as grass cutters, &c. With a view to rising in the social scale, many Cherumans are converted to Muhammadanism, and throw in their lot with the Moplahs or Mápillas.

Man, æt. 30. One steel, two brass ear-rings right ear; two brass rings left ear.

Boy, æt. 14–15. Brass ring in each ear.

Man, æt. 30. Three brass rings in each ear; two steel rings and one brass ring left middle finger.

Man, æt. 25. Two brass rings left ear; one brass ring right ear. Three brass rings, and one iron ring right ring finger.

Man, æt. 28. Two brass rings in each ear. One brass, one copper, and five iron rings right little finger. One brass ring with glass ornament left little finger.

Woman, æt. 25. Lobes of both ears widely dilated by rolled leaden ornaments. Brass, and two glass bead necklets. String necklet with flat brass ornaments, the size of a Venetian sequin, with device as in old Travancore gold coins, with two brass cylinders pendent behind, and tassels of red cotton.

Three brass rings on right little finger; two brass rings on left ring finger. One brass, and two steel bangles on left wrist.

Woman, æt. 25. Several bead necklets, and a single necklet of many rows of beads. Brass necklet like preceding, with steel prong and scoop, for removing wax from the ears and picking teeth, tied to one of the necklets. Attached to, and pendent from one necklet, three cajan rolls with symbols and Malayalam inscription to act as a charm to drive away devils.

Three ornamental brass bangles on right fore-arm; two on left fore-arm. Iron bangle on left wrist. Thin brass ring in helix of each ear. Mass (seventy) of thin brass rings (alondôti), with heavy brass ornament (adikyâ) in dilated lobe of each ear.

Woman, æt. 30. Neck and ear-ornaments of same type as preceding, but two brass rings in each helix, and one cajan roll, to drive away cough and fever.

Right hand—

Four brass rings, thumb and middle finger.
Four brass and two copper rings, ring finger.

Left hand—

One copper ring, thumb.
One steel ring, middle finger.
Three copper, and five brass rings, ring finger.

Girl, æt. 12. Ears dilated by small cajan ornaments (gradual dilatation). Necklet with brass ornament with Travancore coin device. Brass ring on right ring finger.

Girl, æt. 13. String round neck to act as a charm in warding off fever. Neck ornament with brass imitation Venetian sequin. Brass bead necklets and ear scoop. Brass and steel bangles on right wrist; brass bangles on left wrist. Three copper, three brass, and two steel rings on right ring finger. Long slit in lobe of each ear for ear ornaments.

Woman, æt. 30. Mass of brass rings and solid brass ornament in lobe of each ear. Thin brass rings in each helix. Neck heavily decorated with glass bead necklets, and necklet with heavy heart-shaped ornaments. Five brass bangles on right fore-arm; steel bangle on left fore-arm. One copper and two brass rings, left ring finger; five copper rings, left little finger.

Woman, æt. 25. Ear ornaments same as preceding. Neck heavily decorated with brass and glass bead necklets, one with ear scoop and tooth-pick pendent from a string. Brass necklet of ornaments with Travancore coin device. String necklet with 5 brass cylinders pendent, 5 brass bangles on right wrist; 6 brass, 2 iron bangles left wrist.

Right hand.

1 copper, 5 brass rings, middle finger.
1 iron, 3 brass rings, little finger.

Left hand.

1 copper, 5 brass rings, middle finger.
3 brass, 2 copper rings, ring finger.
1 brass ring, little finger.

Woman, æt. 25. Cajan roll in lobe of right ear. Rolled leaf in lobe of left ear.

The subject of artificial enlargement of the ear-lobe, and the geographical distribution of this artificial mutilation, by which the lobes are sometimes torn asunder, are treated of in an admirable paper by Mr. J. Park Harrison (Journ. Anth. Inst., Vol. II, 1873). The practice of enlarging the ear-lobe is there recorded from Easter Island, India and Ceylon, Assam, Arakan, Burma and Laos, the Asiatic Islands (Nias, Nicobar, Borneo, etc.), South Pacific, America, and Africa. In his reference to India, Mr. Harrison says: "In the district of Madura, Dr. Shortt mentions that among the Maravars, who form the greater part of the population, the practice of piercing the ear-lobes, and 'so distending them as to touch the shoulders,' is still kept up among the women. The operation is here, as in other countries where the custom prevails, carried out during infancy, and the aperture in the ear-lobe is very gradually enlarged. Salt and water is applied during the first day or two; and at the end of a month weights, each slightly heavier than the last, are attached to the lobe until it is brought to the requisite length. Though ear ornaments of considerable size are common in other parts of India, I have not been able to learn that the lobe of the ear is now distorted in the manner above described in any other districts except Madura and Malabar."

Mr. Harrison further refers to the fact that in one of the earliest fragments of sculpture in India, viz., the frieze of a temple at Bhitari near Benares, the Indian Bacchus, or the sun, has a disc of considerable size in the lobe of the right ear. And he points out that artificial enlargement of the lobe appears originally to have been adopted for the purpose of receiving a solar disc; and that the Ceylon Buddha, when he renounced idolatry, removed the emblem from his ear-lobes, which necessarily hung down in the manner shown in his images.

In the sculptures exhibited in the Madras Museum from the magnificent ruined stûpa at Amarâvati on the Kistna river, which dates back to the first centuries of the Christian

Era, not only is Buddha himself represented with the lobes of his ears dilated (without ornaments), but many of the figures, both male and female, have the lobes dilated, and ornamented with heavy rings with pendents, discs, and spiral rolls, and the upper arms, fore-arms and ankles are adorned either with series of light bangles, or with fewer heavy bangles, after the manner which still prevails at the present day among the females of some of the native tribes of Southern India. Moreover, the T band round the loins (the "bande en T of the Moïs," of M. Zaborowski) is, in the Amarâvati sculptures, everywhere en evidence. It is then possible by a study of these sculptures to trace back the form of jewelry and rude attire which are still in vogue, to the second century A.D. (*vide* Plate xxii).

While the present chapter was being written, I learned that my friend, the Rev. A. Margöschis, of the S.P.G. Mission, Tinnevelly, was an authority on the subject of ear-lobe dilatation. To him I am indebted for the following note on "the long ears of certain classes of women in Southern India." "To produce this artificial deformity," he writes, "is the work of men of the Koravar caste, whose occupations are bird-catching and basket-making. On or about the third day after birth, the troubles of a female infant begin, for the child's ears must be operated on, and for this purpose a knife with a triangular blade is used. Sometimes the ceremony is postponed until the child is sixteen days old. Among the Hindus a "good day" is selected, and Christians choose Sundays. The point of the knife is run through the lobe of the ear until the blade has penetrated for half an inch of its length. Both ears are cut, and a piece of cotton-wool is placed in the wounds, to keep the cut portions dilated. Every other day the Koravan must change the wool, and increase the quantity introduced. If the sores fester, a dressing is used of castor-oil and human milk * in equal parts, and, if there is much suppuration, an astringent, such as tamarind juice lotion, is used. The cut lobes will take not less than one month to heal, and for the whole of that time the process of dilatation is continued by passing through the lobes pledgets of cotton-wool, increasing gradually in size. After the wounds have healed, pieces of cotton cloth are rolled up, and placed in the lobes instead of the cotton-wool, and this is done for a few days only, when

* Human milk, *vide* 'Tattooing,' p. 117.

PL. XXII.

FIGURES FROM AMARAVATI

leaden rings are substituted, which are added to in number until as many as six or eight rings are in each ear. These drag the lobes down more and more, and by the time the infant is one year old, the process of elongating the lobes is complete in so far as the acute stage is concerned, and all that is necessary afterwards is to leave the leaden rings in the lobes, and to let the elongated ears grow as the child grows. Instead of keeping a large number of rings in the ears, they are melted down into two heavy, thick rings, which are kept in the ears until the girl is twelve or thirteen years of age, and by that time the acme of beauty will have been attained so far as the ears are concerned, because the lobes will reach down to the shoulders on each side. This is perfection. The fees for the operation in the first instance are from 3 fanams to $5\frac{1}{4}$ fanams (10 annas to R. 1-1-6). The custom described prevails among the following castes :—Vellālas, Shánars, Maravars, Paravars, shepherds, dyers, tailors, oilmongers, Pallars, and Pariahs. No people of the Telugu castes observe the custom, nor do any Brāhmans. The females of the Paravar caste (Roman Catholic fisher caste) are famous for the longest ears, and for wearing the heaviest and most expensive golden ear jewels made of sovereigns. Ordinary ear jewels cost Rs. 200, but heavy jewels are worth Rs. 1,000, and even more. It is said that the longer the ears the more jewels can be used, and this appears to be the rationale of elongated ears.

"In former days men also had long ears, but it is now reserved for the man who plays the bow and bells at demon dances. With regard to the prevalence of this custom of mangling the human body, and the possibility of its gradual removal, the Missionaries, especially in Tinnevelly, have all along been the sternest foes of the barbarity. In one boarding school alone, consisting of 224 girls, there are 165 with short ears, so that only 59 have them elongated. This is the result of the advice and teaching of the European Missionaries. But, stranger still to relate, of the 165 girls mentioned above, no less than 51 have had their long ears operated on and cut short at the Mission hospital, and this they have consented to as a voluntary act. As it was once the fashion to have long ears, and a mark of respectability, so now the converse is true. Until the last twenty years, if a woman had short ears, she was asked if she was a dancing girl (*devadasi*), because that class kept their ears natural. Now, with the change of customs all round, even dancing girls are found with long ears. Muhammadan women have their ears pierced all round the outer edges, and as many as twenty or twenty-five wire rings, made of iron or gold, are inserted in the holes; but the lobes are not elongated.

"The artificial deforming of the body assumes various phases in different parts of the world, and we have but to refer to the small feet of the Chinese, the flattening of the skull of infants amongst the North American Indians, and the piercing and elongation of the upper lip amongst certain tribes in Central Africa. In all cases these are attempts to improve upon nature, and the results are as revolting as they are often ghastly and wickedly cruel. The torture inflicted upon helpless Tamil babes is so great that it would be humane and righteous for Government to interfere, and to abolish long ears. The number of persons suffering from deafness, and from chronic discharges from the ear, is very considerably increased in consequence of the barbarity described above." Barbaric practices may be regarded from two points of view, humanitarian and ethnographic. And, while sympathising as a human being with the suppression of cruel rites such as the meriah sacrifice, female infanticide, and hook-swinging, as an ethnologist I regard with sorrow the fast approching extinction of less brutal customs, which afford endless 'copy.' If long ears were to be abolished by legislation, so too should be the painful process of squeezing bangles over the hand on to the wrist, and other mild ordeals which native custom requires, or demands.

In connection with the practice of dilating the lobes of the ears among the Kallans of the Madura district, Mr. J. H. Nelson writes * that, "both males and females are accustomed to stretch to the utmost possible limit the lobes of their ears. The unpleasant disfigurement is effected by the mother boring the ears of her baby, and inserting heavy pieces of metal, generally lead, into the apertures. The effect so produced is very wonderful, and it is not at all uncommon to see the ears of a Kallan hanging on his shoulders. When violently angry, a Kallan will sometimes tear in two the attenuated strips of flesh, which constitute his ears, expecting thereby to compel his adversary to do likewise as a sort of *amende honorable*: and altercations between women constantly lead to one or both parties having the ears violently pulled asunder. And formerly, where a

* 'Manual of the Madura District,' 1868.

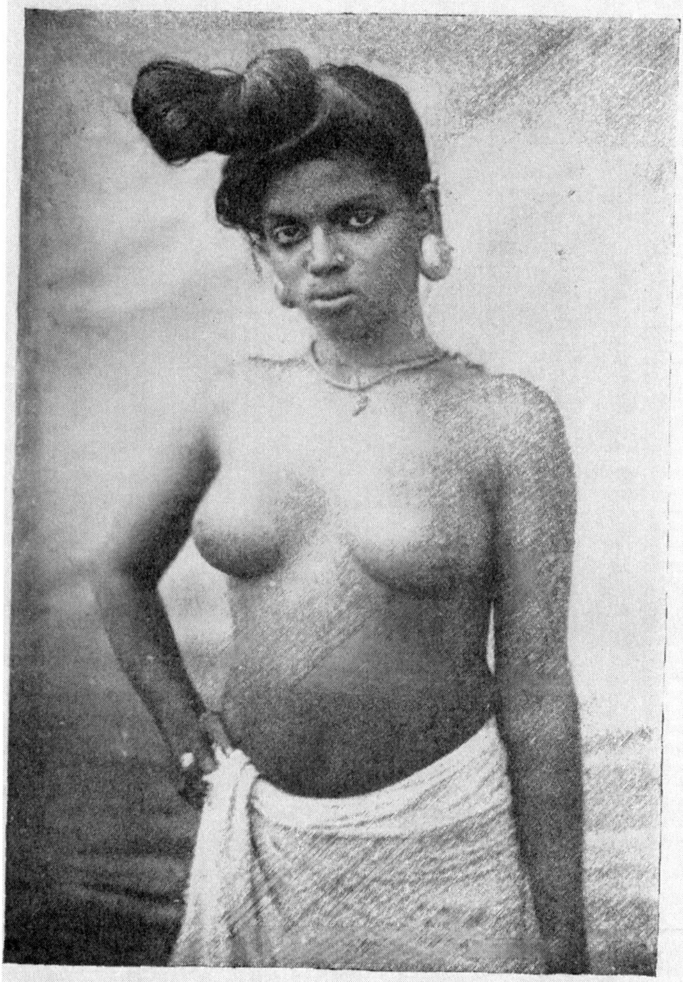

TIYAR WOMAN, MALABAR.

Kalla girl was deputed, as frequently happened, to guide a stranger in safety through a Kalla tract, if any of her caste-people attempted to offer violence to her charge in spite of her protestations, she would immediately tear open one of her ears, and run off at full speed to her home to complain of what had been done. And the result of her complaint was invariably a sentence to the effect, among other things, that the culprits should have both their ears torn in expiation of their breach of the by-laws of the forest."

Mr. H. G. Nicholson, who was some years ago Head Assistant Collector at Ramnád in the Madura district, tells me that the young Maravan princesses used to come and play in his garden, and that, as they ran races, they used to hang on to their ears, lest the heavy ornaments should rend asunder the filamentous ear-lobes.

Among the female Tiyans of Malabar, whom I have recently studied, the practice of dilating the lobes of ears prevails, though the deformity is not carried to such an extreme length as among the Kallans and Maravans. The operation is performed, when the child is a few months or a few years old, either by goldsmiths or by astrologers called Pannikar in South, and Kanisan in North Malabar. The lobe is pierced with a gold pin or thorn, and a thread inserted to prevent the wound from closing up. The ear is dressed daily with butter. After a week or two the thread is replaced by a thin plug of wood, and subsequently gradual dilatation is effected by means of pith soaked in water to make it swell. Further dilatation is effected by means of solid wooden ornaments, or rolls of lead or cajan.

A TODA PETITION.

In my account of the Todas (Bull: No. 4, 1896) reference was made to the fact that the quondam simple-minded and milk-drinking Toda is thoroughly up to date in submitting petitions written in the bazaar by professional petition-writers, appealing to your honour's seat of mercy, &c. In this connection the following petition relating to the slaughter of buffaloes at the Toda funerals (kédus), which was recently submitted to Government through delegates of the Toda community, is not without interest. I therefore reproduce it in its entirety.

To the Honourable Board of Revenue.

The humble petition of one hundred and twenty members of the Toda Community of and near Ootacamund, Nilgiris, through their counsel showeth—

1. That from time immemorial your petitioners' community have, on the death of one of their number, held a kédu, at which they practise certain religious rites peculiar to their tribe.

2. That one of their rites is the sacrifice of buffaloes, so that the dead may not enter the abode of the shades without at least some of the appearance of the respectability he was accustomed to in his lifetime.

3. That the sacrifice of buffaloes at the kédu is the most important of all the rites and ceremonies of the religion which the community of Todas, your petitioners, practise; and that, without its due and proper observance, they believe that they are prejudiced in the next world, while the reputation of the surviving relatives of the dead are lowered in the eyes of the community from the same cause.

4. That, unfortunately for your petitioners' community, it has of late years become the fashion for Europeans to attend their kédus as a kind of theatrical display got up for their benefit; and it is from this fact that an impression has got abroad that unnecessary cruelty is practised on the buffaloes before they receive the "coup de grâce," as in a bull-fight in Spain: an impression that your petitioners maintain is entirely unjustified.

5. That the complaints and allegations of cruelty that have been made from time to time after a kédu have proceeded, not from those who had been present at, and witnessed the ceremony, but by those who have only heard that kédu did take place, buffaloes were killed thereat, and that certain Europeans were present and witnessed the ceremony.

That, if any further proof were needed of this statement, your petitioners would recall to your Honourable Board's recollection that probably the fullest account yet written of what transpires at these kédus came from the pen of the Honourable Mr. J. D. Rees, C.I.E., Collector of the Nilgiri and was published in such a well-known and widely read magazine as the 'Nineteenth Century'; and that this full and descriptive article appeared some ten years ago; that many kédus have taken place since, at which it has been the fashion for Europeans to attend in increasing numbers; and that until quite lately no allegation of cruelties practised at the kédus has been made, or, if made, seriously entertained by the authorities.

6. That the order passed on 30th March 1886 (No. 834, Judicial) restricted the sacrifice of buffaloes to two animals, and that your petitioners have always understood this to mean two buffaloes for each dead person; but that, in the view of the acting Collector of the Nilgiris, Mr. H. Tremenheere, it was by that order intended to restrict the number of the buffaloes sacrificed at any one kédu to two, irrespective of the number of dead Todas for whom such kédu was being held: a view that no previous Collector of Nilgiris adopted; and that, in consequence, the proper holding and observance of a kédu is impossible.

7. That your petitioners desire to draw the Honourable Board's attention to the fact that, according to the custom of their community, unless a certain number of buffaloes are killed (two at least for each Toda), the members of the deceased's family, who, as a rule, subscribe one buffalo apiece for the purposes of the kédu, will no longer make such gifts; and that, if such gifts are not made, the kédu, which involves an outlay of a very considerable number of buffaloes in addition to those sacrificed (as many are always killed for entertaining the Todas present), must altogether cease to exist.

8. That your petitioners crave that your Honourable Board will clear up this point, and lay down, in explicit terms, whether the order was ever intended to impose such a restriction as interpreted by Mr. H. Tremenheere, the acting Collector of Nilgiris.

9. That, in the event of this restriction being found to be the intention of the order, your petitioners beg that your Honourable Board will give the matter their earnest attention, with a view to advising His Excellency the Governor in Council to rescind it, and remove such disabilities as your petitioners suffer from under it.

And your petitioners will ever pray.

On behalf of the 120 Toda petitioners.

*   *   *   *

Petitioners' Counsel.

OOTACAMUND,
20th February, 1897.

In passing orders on the petition, the Government ruled that the interpretation put upon the existing orders in the matter by the District Magistrate (Collector) was correct; and that the number of animals killed at any one kédu should be restricted to two, whatever may be the number of Todas, in connection with whose decease the kédu is held.

MADRAS GOVERNMENT MUSEUM.

Bulletin, Vol. II, No. 3.

ANTHROPOLOGY.

Kādirs of the Ānaimalais; Malaiālis of the Shevaroys; Syllabus of Demonstrations on Anthropology; The Dravidian Head; The Dravidian Problem.

With Seven Plates.

BY

EDGAR THURSTON,

SUPERINTENDENT, MADRAS GOVERNMENT MUSEUM; CORRESPONDANT ÉTRANGER, SOCIÉTÉ D'ANTHROPOLOGIE DE PARIS.

MADRAS:

PRINTED BY THE SUPERINTENDENT, GOVERNMENT PRESS.

1899.

Madras Government Museum Bulletins.

BY EDGAR THURSTON.

Vol. I.

No. 1.—Pearl and Chank Fisheries of the Gulf of Manaar.

No. 2.—Note on Tours along the Malabar Coast.

No. 3.—Rámésvaram Island and Fauna of the Gulf of Manaar.

No. 4.—Anthropology of the Todas and Kotas of the Nilgiri Hills; and of the Bráhmans, Kammálans, Pallis and Pariahs of Madras City.

Vol. II.

No. 1.—Anthropology of the Badagas and Irulas of the Nilgiris; Paniyans of Malabar; Chinese-Tamil Cross; Cheruman Skull; Kuruba or Kurumba; Summary of Results.

No. 2.—Eurasians (Poorer Classes) of Madras and Malabar; Note on Tattooing; Malagasy-Nias-Dravidians; Toda Petition.

MADRAS GOVERNMENT MUSEUM.

Bulletin, Vol. II, No. 3.

ANTHROPOLOGY.

Kādirs of the Anaimalais; Malaiālis of the Shevaroys; Syllabus of Demonstrations on Anthropology; The Dravidian Head; The Dravidian Problem.

With Seven Plates.

BY

EDGAR THURSTON,

SUPERINTENDENT, MADRAS GOVERNMENT MUSEUM; CORRESPONDANT ÉTRANGER, SOCIÉTÉ D'ANTHROPOLOGIE DE PARIS.

MADRAS:
PRINTED BY THE SUPERINTENDENT, GOVERNMENT PRESS.

1899.

CONTENTS.

	PAGE
KÁDIRS OF THE ÁNAIMALAIS	131-151
MALAIÁLIS OF THE SHEVAROYS	152-169
SYLLABUS OF DEMONSTRATIONS	170-180
NOTE ON THE DRAVIDIAN HEAD	181
THE DRAVIDIAN PROBLEM	182-197

ANTHROPOLOGY.

KĀDIRS OF THE ĀNAIMALAIS.

In striking and pleasant contrast to the suspicious Malaiālis, who are dealt with in the next chapter, were the friendly Kādirs, who inhabit the Ānaimalai hills (= elephant hills) and the mountain range which extends thence southward into Travancore. This study was undertaken with a view to acquiring an addition to our existing fragmentary knowledge of the short, broad-nosed tribes of Southern India, round whom, as the living remnant of an ancient, and once more numerous race, much interest will be found to centre when, if ever, these stray notulæ are amalgamated in book form.

A night journey by rail to Coimbatore, and forty miles thence by road at the mercy of a typically obstinate jutka pony, which landed me in a dense patch of prickly-pear (*Opuntia Dillenii*), brought me to the foot of the hills at Séthumadai, where I came under the kindly hospitality of the Conservator of Forests, Mr. H. A. Gass, and the District Forest Officer, Mr. F. A. Lodge. To the former, who has had long experience of the Kādirs, I am indebted for much information on forest and tribal matters, gathered during a fortnight of camp life at Mount Stuart, situated 2,350 feet above sea-level in the midst of a dense bamboo jungle, and playfully named after Sir Mountstuart Grant-Duff, who visited the spot during his Madras quinquennium.

At Sēthumadai I made the acquaintance of my first Kādir, not dressed, as I hoped, in a primitive garb of leaves, but wearing a coloured turban and the cast-off red coat of a British soldier, who had come down the hill to carry up my camp bath, which acted as an excellent umbrella, to protect him from the driving showers. Very glad was I of his services in helping to convey my clothed, and consequently helpless self, across the mountain torrents swollen by a recent burst of monsoon rain. Mount Stuart is easily accessible by a ghât road fit for bullock-cart traffic, and I lodge a protest against the short cut, up the steep and slippery boulders of which a pilot forest-guard conducted me, as being a severe trial to both lungs and legs of one fresh from city life in the plains, and a course of a daily maximum of 98° to 104° in the shade.

The Kādir forest-guards, of whom there are several serving under the Government, looked, except for their noses, very unjungle-like by contrast with their fellow-tribesmen, being smartly dressed in regulation Norfolk jacket, knickerbocker-trousers, pattis (leggings), buttons, and accoutrements.

On arrival at the forest depôt, with its comfortable bungalows and Kādir settlement, I was told by a native servant that his master was away, as an "elephant done tumble in a fit." My memory went back to the occasion, many years ago, when I took part in the autopsy of an elephant, which died in convulsions at the London Zoological Gardens. Its brain, I remember, weighed twelve pounds, and was very difficult of extraction owing to splintering of the cancellous tissue lining the air-sinuses. It transpired later in the day that a young and grown-up cow elephant had tumbled, not in a fit, but into a pit made with hands. The story has a philological significance, and illustrates the difficulty which the Tamulian experiences in dealing with the letter P.

An incident is still cherished at Mount Stuart in connection with a sporting 'globe-trotter,' who was accredited to the Conservator of Forests for the purpose of putting him on to 'bison' (the gaur—Bos gaurus) and other big game. On arrival at the depot he was informed that his host had gone to see the "ellipence." Incapable of translating the pigeon-English of the Pariah butler, and concluding that a financial reckoning was being suggested, he ordered the servant to pay the baggage coolies their elli-pence, and send them away. To a crusted Anglo-Indian it is clear that ellipence could only mean elephants.

The salient characteristics of the Kādirs, which will be dealt with in detail hereafter, may be briefly summed up as follows: short stature; dark skin; platyrhine. Men and women have the incisor teeth chipped. Women wear bamboo combs in the back-hair. Those whom I met with spoke a Tamil patois, running up the scale in talking, and

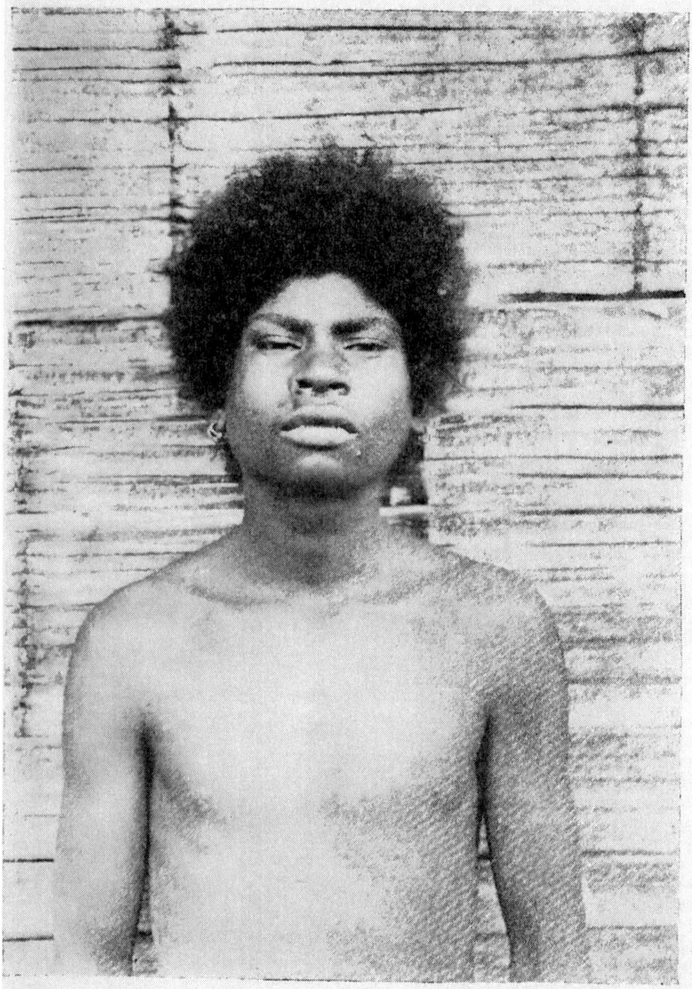

KADIR MAN.

finishing, like a Suffolker, on a higher note than they commenced on. But I am told that some of them speak a mixture of Tamil and Malayālam.

The Kādirs afford a typical example of happiness without culture. Unspoiled by education, the advancing wave of which has not yet engulfed them, they still retain many of their simple "manners and customs." Quite refreshing was it to hear the hearty shrieks of laughter of the nude curly-haired children, wholly illiterate, and happy in their ignorance, as they played at funerals, or indulged in the amusement of making mud pies, and scampered off to their huts on my appearance. The uncultured Kādir, living a hardy out-door life, and capable of appreciating to the full the enjoyment of an "apathetic rest" as perfect bliss, has, I am convinced, in many ways, the advantage over the poor under-fed student with a small-paid appointment under Government as the narrow goal to which the laborious passing of examination tests leads.

Living an isolated existence, confined within the thinly-populated jungle, where Nature furnishes the means of obtaining all the necessaries of life, the Kādir possesses little, if any, knowledge of cultivation, and objects to doing work with a māmuti, the instrument which serves the gardener in the triple capacity of spade, rake, and hoe. But armed with a keen-edged bill-hook he is immense. As Mr. O. H. Bensley says [1]: "The axiom that the less civilised men are, the more they are able to do every thing for themselves, is well illustrated by the hill-man, who is full of resource. Give him a simple bill-hook, and what wonders he will perform. He will build houses out of etâh, so neat and comfortable as to be positively luxurious. He will bridge a stream with canes and branches. He will make a raft out of bamboo, a carving knife out of etâh, a comb out of bamboo, a fishing-line out of fibre, and a match from dry wood. He will find food for you where you think you must starve, and show you the branch which, if cut, will give you drink. He will set traps for beasts and birds, which are more effective than some of the most elaborate products of machinery." A European, overtaken by night in the jungle, unable to light fire by friction or to climb trees to gather fruits, ignorant of the edible roots and berries, and afraid of wild beasts, would

[1] Lecture delivered at Trivandrum. M.S.

in the absence of comforts, be quite as unhappy and ill-at-ease as a Kādir surrounded by plenty at an official dinner-party.

At the forest depôt the Kādir settlement consists of neatly constructed huts, made of bamboo deftly split with a bill-hook in their long axis, thatched with leaves of the teak tree (*Tectona grandis*) and bamboo (*Beesha travancorica*), and divided off into verandah and compartments by means of bamboo partitions. But the Kādirs are essentially nomad in habit, living in small communities, and shifting from place to place in the jungle, whence they suddenly re-appear as casually as if they had only returned from a morning stroll instead of a long camping expedition. In this way the wondrous type figured in Plate XXVI, of whom I knew by repute, turned up to my joy during my stay at Mount Stuart, and was instantly photographed, lest he should disappear again as mysteriously as he arrived. When wandering in the jungle, the Kādirs make a rough lean-to shed covered over with leaves, and keep a small fire burning through the night, to keep off bears, elephants, tigers, and leopards. They are, I am told, fond of dogs, which they keep chiefly as a protection against wild beasts at night. The camp fire is lighted by means of a flint and the floss of the silk-cotton tree (*Bombax malabaricum*), over which powdered charcoal has been rubbed. Like the Kurumbas, the Kādirs are not, in a general way, afraid of elephants, but are careful to get out of the way of a cow with young, or a solitary rover, which may mean mischief. On the day following my descent from Mount Stuart, a Wudder cooly woman was killed on the ghât road by a solitary tusker. Familiarity with wild beasts, and comparative immunity from accident, have bred contempt for them, and the Kādirs will go where the European, fresh to elephant land, fears to tread, or conjures every creak of a bamboo into the approach of a charging tusker. As an example of pluck worthy of a place in Kipling's 'Jungle-book,' I may cite the case of a hill-man and his wife, who, overtaken by night in the jungle, decided to pass it on a rock. As they slept, a tiger carried off the woman. Hearing her shrieks, the sleeping man awoke, and followed in pursuit in the vain hope of saving his wife. Coming on the beast in possession of the mangled corpse, he killed it at close-quarters with a spear. Yet he was wholly unconscious that he had performed an act of heroism worthy of the bronze cross 'for valour.'

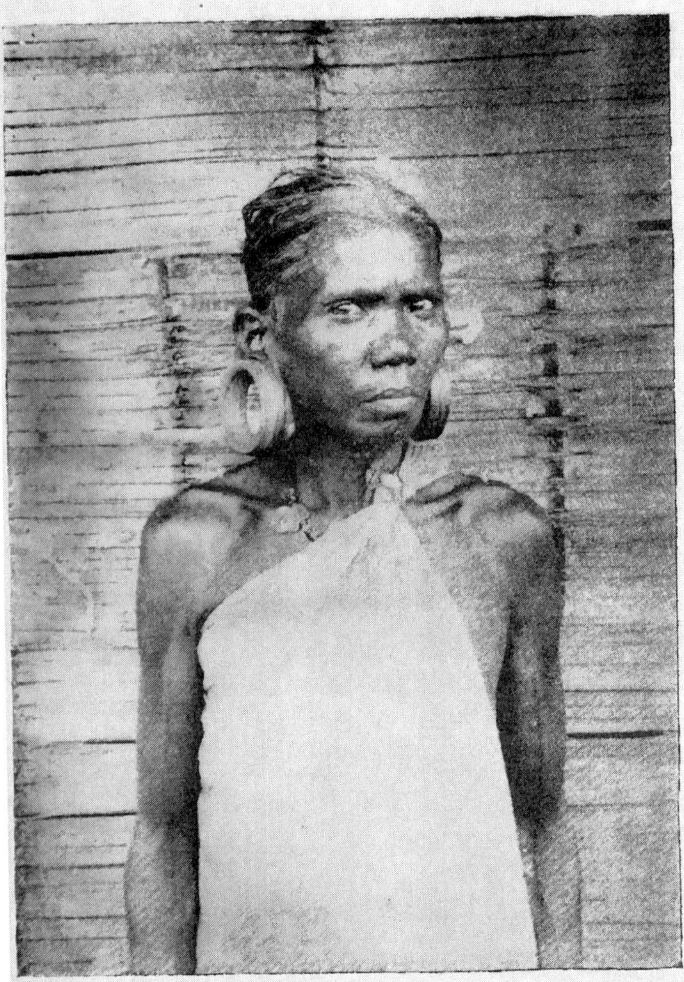

KADIR WOMAN.

The Kādirs carry loads strapped on the back over the shoulders by means of fibre, instead of on the head in the manner customary among coolies in the plains; and women on the march may be seen carrying the cooking utensils on their backs, and often have a child strapped on the top of their household goods. The dorsal position of the babies, huddled up in a dirty cloth, with the ends slung over the shoulders and held in the hands over the chest, at once caught my eye, as it is contrary to the usual native habit of straddling the infants across the loins as a saddle.

The Kādirs have never claimed, like the Todas, and do not possess any land on the hills. But the Government has declared the absolute right of the hill tribes to collect all the minor forest produce, and to sell it to the Government through the medium of a contractor, whose tender has been previously accepted. The contractor pays for the produce in coin at a fair market rate, and the Kādirs barter the money so obtained for articles of food with contractors appointed by Government to supply them with their requirements at a fixed rate, which will leave a fair, but not exorbitant margin of profit to the vendor. The principal articles of minor forest produce of the Ānaimalai hills are wax, honey, cardamoms, myrabolams, ginger, dammar, turmeric, deer horns, elephant tusks, and rattans. And of these, cardamoms, wax, honey, and rattans are the most important. Honey and wax are collected at all seasons, and cardamoms from September to November. The total value of the minor produce collected, in 1897–98, in the South Coimbatore division (which includes the Ānaimalais) was Rs. 7,886. This sum was exceptionally high owing to a good cardamom crop. An average year would yield a revenue of Rs. 4,000—5,000, of which the Kādirs receive approximately 50 per cent. They work for the Forest department on a system of short advances for a daily wage of four annas. And, at the present day, the interests of the Forest department and planters, who have acquired land on the Ānaimalais, both anxious to secure hill men for labour, have come into mild collision.

Some Kādirs are good trackers, and a few are good shikāris. A zoological friend, who had nicknamed his small child his "little shikarēē" (= little sportsman) was quite upset because I, hailing from India, did not recognise the word with its misplaced accent. One Kādir, named Viapoori Muppan, is still held in the memory of Europeans, who made a good living, in days gone by, by shooting tuskers, and had one arm blown off by the bursting of a gun. He is reputed to have been a much married man, greatly addicted to strong drinks, and to have flourished on the proceeds of his tusks. At the present day, if a Kādir finds tusks, he must declare the find as treasure-trove, and hand it over to Government, who rewards him at the rate of Rs. 15 to Rs. 25 per maund of 25 lbs. according to the quality. Government makes a good profit on the transaction, as exceptionally good tusks have been known to sell for Rs. 5 per lb. If the find is not declared, and discovered, the possessor thereof is punished for theft according to the Act. By an elastic use of the word cattle, it is, for the purposes of the Madras Forest Act, made to include such a heterogeneous zoological collection of mammalia as elephants, sheep, pigs, goats, camels, buffaloes, horses—and asses. A classification which recalls to mind the occasion on which the Flying-fox or Fox-bat was included in an official list of the insectivorous birds of the Presidency; and, further, a report on the wild animals of a certain district, which was triumphantly headed with the "wild tattu," the long-suffering, but pig-headed country pony, at whose hands most touring officers have "suffered much misery" (as the Natives expressed their feelings when a certain fast-bowling Colonel went on in a cricket match).

Often, when out on the tramp with the late Government Botanist, Mr. M. A. Lawson, I have heard him lament that it is impossible to train arboreal monkeys to collect specimens of the fruit and flowers of lofty forest trees, which are inaccessible to the ordinary man. Far superior to any trained Simian is the Kādir, who, by means of pegs or notches, climbs even the tallest masts of trees with an agility which recalls to memory the celebrated picture in 'Punch,' representing Darwin's 'Habit of climbing plants.' For the ascent of comparatively low trees, notches are made with a bill-hook, alternately right and left, at intervals of about thirty inches. To this method the Kādir will not have recourse in wet weather, as the notches are damp and slippery, and there is the danger of an insecure foot-hold. In the system of scaling a tree by means of pegs (*vide* Plate XXVIII), a number of pegs, made of sharp-pointed bamboo, are carried round the loins, and driven securely into the tree by sharp blows with a bill-hook. The pegs are left in the tree, and a fresh set used for the next tree.

KADIR TREE-CLIMBING.

I gather, from an anonymous account of the process by one who had considerable knowledge of the Kādirs, that "they will only remove the hives during dark nights, and never in the day-time or on moonlight nights. In removing them from cliffs, they use a chain made of cane or rattan, fixed to a stake or a tree on the top. The man, going down this fragile ladder, will only do so while his wife or son watches above to prevent any foul play. They have a superstition that they should always return the way they go down, and decline to get to the bottom of the cliff, although the distance may be less, and the work of re-climbing avoided. For hives on trees, they tie one or more long bamboos to reach up to the branch required, and then climb up. They then crawl along the branch until the hive is reached. They devour the bee-bread and the bee-maggots or larvæ, swallowing the wax as well." In a note on a shooting expedition in Travancore,[2] Mr. J. D. Rees, describing the collection of honey by the Kādirs, of the southern hills, says that they "descend giddy precipices at night, torch in hand, to smoke out the bees, and take away their honey. A stout creeper is suspended over the abyss, and it is established law of the jungle that no brother shall assist in holding it. But it is more interesting to see them run a ladder a hundred feet up the perpendicular stem of a tree, than to watch them disappearing over a precipice. Axe in hand, the honey-picker makes a hole in the bark for a little peg, standing on which he inserts a second peg higher up, ties a long cane from one to the other, and by night—for the darkness gives confidence—he will ascend the tallest trees, and bring down honey without any accident." I have been told, with how much of truth I know not, that, when a Kādir goes down the face of a rock or precipice in search of honey, he sometimes takes with him, as a precautionary measure, and guarantee of his safety, the wife of the man who is holding the ladder above.

An important ethnographic fact, and one which is significant, is that the detailed description of tree-climbing by the Dyaks of Borneo, as given by Wallace,[3] might have been written on the Ānaimalai hills, and would apply equally well in every detail to the Kādir. "They drove in," Wallace writes, "a peg very firmly at about three feet from the ground, and, bringing one of the long bamboos, stood it upright close to the tree, and bound it firmly to the two first

---

[2] *Nineteenth Century*, 1898.

[3] 'Malay Archipelago'.

pegs by means of a bark cord and small notches near the head of each peg. One of the Dyaks now stood on the first peg and drove in a third about level with his face, to which he tied the bamboo in the same way, and then mounted another step, standing on one foot, and holding by the bamboo at the peg immediately above him, while he drove in the next one. In this manner he ascended about twenty feet, when the upright bamboo became thin; another was handed up by his companion, and this was joined on by tying both bamboos to three or four of the pegs. When this was also nearly ended, a third was added, and shortly after the lowest branch of the tree were reached, along which the young Dyak scrambled.

"The ladder was perfectly safe, since, if any one peg were loose or faulty, the strain would be thrown on several others above and below it. I now understood the use of the line of bamboo pegs sticking in trees, which I had often seen." Such is the description given by Wallace, and it may be compared with Plate XXVIII, which represents a tree with a line of pegs left in it, and an agile young Kādir climbing a tree by means of pegs with bamboos bound to them.

In their search for produce in the evergreen forests of the higher ranges, with their heavy rainfall, the Kādirs become unpleasantly familiar with leeches and blue bottle flies, which flourish in the moist climate. And it is recorded that a Kādir, who had been gored and wounded by a bull 'bison,' was placed in a position of safety while a friend ran to the village to summon help. He was not away for more than an hour, but, in that short time, flies had deposited thousands of maggots in the wounds, and, when the man was brought into camp, they had already begun burrowing into the flesh, and were with difficulty extracted. On another occasion, the eye-witness of the previous unappetising incident was out alone in the forest, and shot a tiger two miles or so from his camp. Thither he went to collect coolies to carry in the carcase, and was away for about two hours, during which the flies had, like the child in the story, 'not been idle,' the skin being a mass of maggots and totally ruined. I have it on authority that, like the Kotas of the Nīlgiris, the Kādirs will eat the putrid and fly-blown flesh of carcases of wild beasts, which they come across in their wanderings. To a dietary which includes succulent roots, which they upturn with a digging stick, sheep, fowls, rock-snakes (Python), deer, porcupines, rats (field, not

KADIR BOY.

house), wild pigs, monkeys, &c., they do credit by displaying a hard, well-nourished body. The mealy portion of the seeds of the *Cycas* tree, which flourishes on the lower slopes of the Ānaimalais, forms a considerable addition to the ménu. In its raw state the fruit is said to be poisonous, but it is evidently wholesome when cut into slices, thoroughly soaked in running water, dried, and ground into flour for making cakes, or baked in hot ashes. The Kādir is said to prefer roasting and eating the flesh of animals with the skin on. For catching rats, jungle-fowl, &c., he resorts to cunningly devised snares and traps made of bamboo and fibre, as a substitute for a gun. Porcupines are caught by setting fire to the scrub jungle round them as they lie asleep, and thus smoking and burning them to death.

When a Kādir youth's thoughts turn towards matrimony, his parents, who select his bride, go to the parents of the girl, and ask their consent to the proposed alliance. If this is accorded, a dinner-party is given at the home of the bridegroom-elect. During the period of engagement the young man's parents give meals of rice and other things to their future daughter-in-law. They make presents too, in view of purchase money, of a new turban and cloth to the girl's father, and a new cloth to her mother. On the wedding day a feast of rice, sheep, fowls, and other luxuries, is given by the parents of the bridegroom, to which the Kādir community is invited. The bride and bridegroom stand beneath a pandāl (arch) decorated with flowers, which is erected outside the home of the bridegroom, while men and women dance separately to the music of drum and pipe. The bridegroom's mother or sister ties the tāli (marriage badge) of gold or silver round the bride's neck, and her father puts a turban on the head of the bridegroom. The contracting parties link together the little fingers of their right hands as a token of their union, and walk in procession round the pandāl. Then, sitting on a reed mat of Kādir manufacture, they exchange betel. The marriage tie can be dissolved for incompatibility of temper, disobedience on the part of the wife, adultery, &c., without appeal to any higher authority than a council of elders, who hear the arguments on both sides, and pronounce judgment on the evidence. As an illustration of the manner in which such a council of hill-men disposes of cases, Mr. Bensley cites the case of a man who was made to carry forty basket-loads of sand to the house of the person against whom he had offended. He points out how absolute is the control exercised by the council. Disobedience would be followed by expulsion, and expulsion would mean being turned out into the jungle, to obtain a living in the best way one could.

By one Kādir informant I was assured, as he squatted on the floor of my bungalow at "question time," that it is essential that a wife should be a good cook, in accordance with the maxim that the way to the heart is through the mouth. How many men in civilised western society, who suffer from marrying a wife wholly incompetent, like the first Mrs. David Copperfield, to conduct the housekeeping, might well be envious of the system of marriage as a civil contract to be sealed or unloosed according to the cookery results! Polygyny is indulged in by the Kādirs, who agree with Benedick that "the world must be peopled," and hold more especially that the numerical strength of their own tribe must be maintained. The plurality of wives seems to be mainly with the desire for offspring, and the father-in-law of one of the forest-guards informed me that he had four wives living. The first two wives producing no offspring, he married a third, who bore him a solitary male child. Considering the result to be an insufficient contribution to the tribe, he married a fourth, who, more prolific than her colleagues, gave birth to three girls and a boy, with which he remained content. In the code of polygynous etiquette, the first wife takes precedence over the others, and each wife has her own cooking utensils.

Special huts are maintained for women during menstruation and parturition. For three months after the birth of a child, the woman is considered unclean. When the infant is a month old, it is named without any elaborate ceremonial, though the female friends of the family collect together. Sexual intercourse ceases on the establishment of pregnancy, and the husband indulges in promiscuity. Widows are not allowed to re-marry, but may live in a state of concubinage. No ceremony is performed when boys or girls reach puberty. Women are said to suckle their children till they are two or three years old, and a mother has been seen putting a lighted cigarette to the lips of a year old baby immediately after suckling it. If this is done with the intention of administering a sedative, it is less baneful than the pellet of opium administered to Anglo-Indian babies rendered fractious by troubles climatic, dental,

PL. XXX.

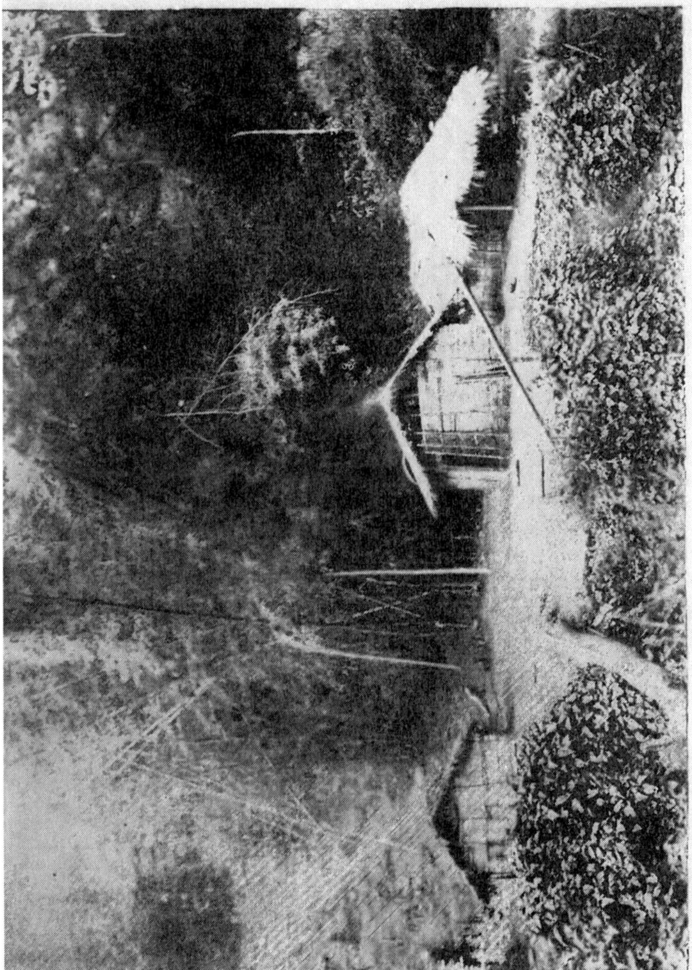

KADIR HUTS.

and other. The Kādir women chew tobacco. The men smoke the coarse tobacco as sold in the bazārs, and showed a marked appreciation of Spencer's Torpedoes No. 1, which I had to distribute among them in lieu of the cheaper cheroots, which generally travel with me for the purposes of bribery and conciliation.

The religion of the Kādirs is a crude polytheism, and vague worship of stone images or invisible gods. It is, as Mr. Bensley expresses it, "an ejaculatory religion, finding vent in uttering the names of the gods and demons." The gods, as enumerated and described to me, were as follows :—

(1) Paikutlātha—a projecting rock overhanging a slab of rock, on which are two stones set up on end. Two miles east of Mount Stuart.

(2) Athuvisariammā—a stone enclosure, 10 to 15 feet square, almost level with the ground. It is believed that the walls were originally ten feet high, and that the mountain has grown up round it. Within the enclosure there is no representation of the god. Eight miles north of Mount Stuart.

(3) Vanathavāthi has no shrine, but is worshipped anywhere as an invisible god.

(4) Iyappaswāmi—a stone set up beneath a teak tree, and worshipped as a protector against various forms of sickness and disease. In the act of worshipping, a mark is made on the stone with ashes. Two miles and a half from Mount Stuart, on the ghât road to Sēthumadai.

(5) Māsanyātha—a female recumbent figure in stone on a masonry wall in an open plain near the village of Anaimalai, before which trial by ordeal is carried out. The goddess has a high repute for her power of detecting thieves or rogues. Chillies are thrown into a fire in her name, and the guilty person suffers from vomiting and diarrhœa.

When Kādirs fall sick, they worship the gods by saluting them with their hands to the face, burning camphor, and offering up fruits, cocoanuts and betel.

The Kādir dead are buried in a grave, or, if death occurs in the depths of the jungle, with a paucity of hands available for digging, the corpse is placed in a crevice between the rocks, and covered over with stones. The grave is dug from four to five feet deep. There is no special burial ground, but some spot in the jungle, not far from the scene of death, is selected. A band of music—drum and pipe—plays weird dirges outside the hut of the deceased, but does not accompany the funeral party to the grave. The body is carried on a bamboo stretcher, lying on a mat, and covered over with a cloth and mat. As it leaves the hut, rice is thrown over it. The funeral ceremony is simple in the extreme. The corpse is laid in the grave on a mat in the recumbent posture with head towards the east, and covered over with a mat and leaves. The grave is then filled in with earth. No stone, or sepulchral monument of any kind, is erected, to indicate the spot. Two years after death a memorial festival, called karrumanthram, is held, at which the Kādirs are invited to a feast with drinks and a dance. The Kādir believes that the dead go to heaven, which is up in the sky, but has no views as to what sort of place it is, as there is no one who can tell him. He is, in a mild way, a philosopher.

On a certain Monday in the months of Ādi and Āvani (July-September) the Kādirs observe a festival called nōmbu, during which a feast is held, after they have bathed and anointed themselves with oil. It was, they say, observed by their ancestors, but they have no definite tradition as to its origin or significance.

Turning now to the characteristics of the Kādirs. They belong to the curly-haired gentes dolichocephalæ orthognathæ of Retzius, which, being translated, signifies that they are long-headed people with the upper jaw straight when viewed in profile, and have no resemblance to the prognathous (prominent-jawed) and woolly-haired Negro. According to Mr. Bensley "the Kādir has an air of calm dignity, which leads one to suppose that he had some reason for having a more exalted opinion of himself than that entertained for him by the outside world. A forest officer of a philanthropic turn had a very high opinion of the sturdy independence and blunt honesty of the Kādir, but he once came unexpectedly round a corner, to find two of them exploring the contents of his portmanteau, and subsequent search revealed that they had abstracted a pair of scissors, a comb, and a looking-glass." "The Kādirs," Mr. Nicholson writes[4] "are, as a rule, rather short in stature and deep-chested, like most mountaineers; and, like many true mountaineers, they rarely walk with a straight leg. Hence their thigh muscles are often abnormally developed at the

[4] 'Manual of the Coimbatore District.'

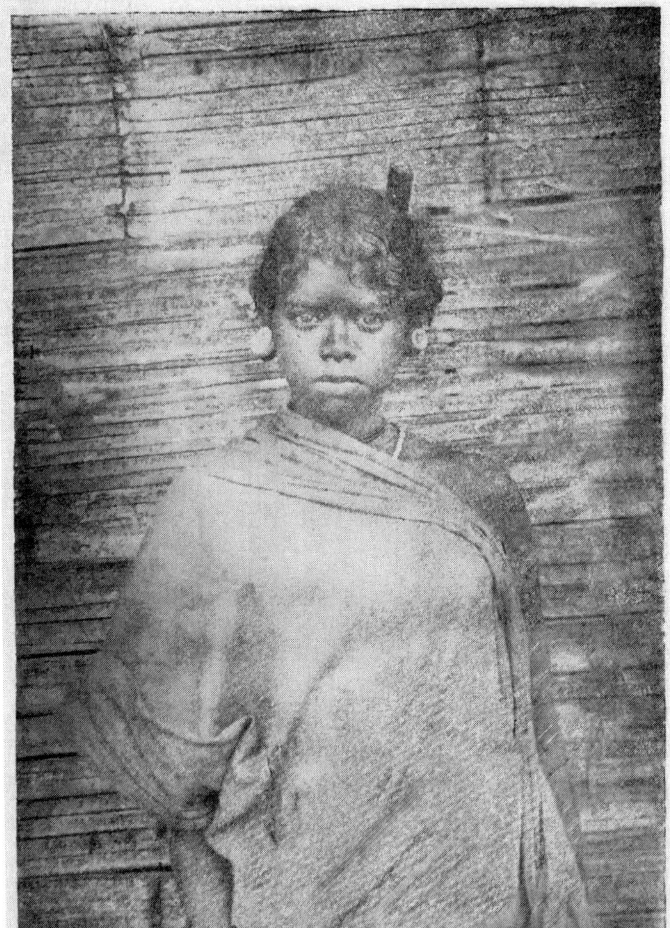

KADIR GIRL.

expense of those of the calf. Hence, too, in part, their dislike to walking long distances on level ground, though their objection, mentioned by Colonel Douglas Hamilton, to carrying loads in the plains is deeper rooted than that arising from mere physical disability. This objection is mainly because they are rather a timid race, and never feel safe out of the forests. They have also often affirmed that the low-country air is very trying to them." As a matter of fact, they very rarely go down to the plains, even as far as the village of Ânaimalai, only fifteen miles distant from Mount Stuart. One woman, whom I saw, had, however, been as far as Palghât by railway from Coimbatore, and had returned thence very much up-to-date in the matter of jewelry and the latest barbarity in imported piece-good sāris.

With the chest-girth of the Kādirs, as well as their general muscular development, I was very much impressed; and the following comparative series of figures shows that, so far as wind is concerned, they would, like other jungle tribes of short stature, be valuable camp-followers in a mountaineering expedition.

	Average height. CM.	Average chest. CM.	Average chest relative to stature 100.
Paniyans	157·4	81·5	51·8
Kādirs	157·7	80·5	51·4
Kurumbas	157·5	79·2	50·3
Tamil Pariahs	162·1	79·3	48·9
Eurasians (poorer classes) ..	166·6	79·1	47·7

The most interesting custom, which prevails among the Kādirs, and among them alone, so far as I know, of the entire population of the Indian peninsula, is that of chipping all or some of the incisor teeth, both upper and lower, into the form of a sharp-pointed, but not serrated cone. The operation, which is performed with a chisel or bill-hook and file by members of the tribe skilled thereat, on boys at the age of eighteen, and girls at the age of ten or thereabouts, has been thus described: "The girl to be operated on lies down, and places her head against a female friend, who holds her head firmly. A third woman takes a sharpened bill-hook, and chips away the teeth till they are shaded to a point, the girl operated on writhing and groaning with the pain. After the operation she looks dazed, and in a very few hours the face begins to swell. Swelling and pain last for a day or two, accompanied by severe headache." Whether this practice is one which the Kādir has hit on spontaneously in comparatively modern times, or whether it is a relic of a custom resorted to by their ancestors of long ago, which remains as a stray survival of a custom once more widely practised among the remote inhabitants of Southern India, cannot be definitely asserted, though I incline to the latter view. Let us, however, see from the available literature on the subject what is the present-day geographical distribution of the practice of tooth chipping or filing, as a possible clue to the source from which it was derived. In 'Anthropological Notes and Queries' it is stated that "it is chiefly in Africa that the custom of deforming the teeth is practised ; and, as different modes of doing it prevail among different tribes, the characters afforded in this way will probably be found of considerable ethnographical importance. The practice appears in general to be limited to the front or incisor teeth, and consists either in extracting, or, more usually perhaps, in breaking off one or more of them, or of filing them either to a sharp single point, or in serrate fashion." Westermarck[5] informs us that, when the age of puberty draws near, "in several parts of Africa and Australia they knock out some teeth, knowing that they would otherwise run the risk of being refused on account of ugliness. Mr. Crawfurd tells us that, in the Malay Archipelago, the practice of filing and blackening the teeth is a necessary prelude to marriage, the common way of expressing the fact that a girl has arrived at puberty being that 'she has had her teeth filed,' and, with reference to some of the Natives of the Congo countries, Tuckey says that the two upper front teeth are filed by the men, so as to make a large opening, and scars are raised on the skin, both being intended by the men as ornamental, and principally done with the idea of rendering themselves agreeable to the women." Further, Darwin writes[6] "The Natives of the Upper Nile knock out the four front teeth, saying that they do not wish to resemble brutes. Further south, the Batokas knock out only the two upper incisors, which, as Livingstone remarks, gives the face a hideous appearance; but these people think the presence of the incisors most unsightly, and, on beholding some Europeans, cried out 'Look at the great teeth'! In parts of Africa

[5] 'History of Human Marriage.' [6] 'Descent of Man.'

and the Malay Archipelago the Natives file the incisors into points like a saw, or pierce them with holes, into which they insert studs." I have somewhere read that the practice of tooth-filing is resorted to, not for ornament or as a means of sexual attraction, but that the Natives may not degrade themselves by using all their teeth in eating like a cow. Be its origin what it may among the Kādirs, I cannot but think that the geographical distribution of the practice of tooth chipping, of the use of the boomerang, and the custom of dilating the lobes of the ears, are important links of evidence in connection with the Dravidian problem, which is discussed later on.

A friendly old woman, with huge discs in the widely dilated lobes of the ears, and a bamboo five-pronged comb in her back-hair, who acted as spokesman on the occasion of a visit to a charmingly situated settlement in a jungle of magnificent bamboos by the side of a mountain stream, pointed out to me, with conscious pride, that the huts were largely constructed by the females, while the men worked for the sircar (Government). The females also carry water from the streams, collect fire-wood, dig up edible roots, and carry out the sundry household duties of a housewife. Both men and women are clever at plaiting bamboo baskets, necklets, &c. I was told one morning by a Kādir man, whom I met on the road, as an important item of news, that the women in his settlement were very busy dressing to come and see me—an event as important to them as the dressing of a débutante for presentation at the Court of St. James'. They eventually turned up without their husbands, and evidently regarded my methods as a huge joke organised for the amusement of themselves and their children. The hair was neatly parted, anointed with a liberal application of cocoanut oil, and decked with wild flowers. Beauty spots and lines had been painted with coal-tar dyes on the forehead, and turmeric powder freely sprinkled over the top of the heads of the married women. Some had even discarded the ragged and dirty cotton cloth of every-day life in favour of a colour-printed imported sári. One bright, good-looking young woman, who had already been through the measuring ordeal, acted as an efficient lady-help in coaching the novices in the assumption of the correct positions. She very readily grasped the situation, and was manifestly proud of her temporary elevation to the rank of standard-bearer to Government. The Kādir women, when they meet a European on the road, with their body-cloths wrapped round them in such a way as to expose the upper halves of their breasts, manifest symptoms of shyness and modesty, and stand aside with face averted so that they cannot see the stranger, on the same principle which prompts some Eastern women, if surprised when taking a bath, to turn the face, no further concealment being necessary. Ideas of modesty, it has been said, are altogether relative and conventional, and it is not the feeling of shame that has given rise to the covering of the body, but the covering that has provoked the feeling of shame. This is well illustrated by the difference in the behaviour of the Native females of Malabar and the Tamil women of the East Coast. In Malabar the body-clothing of the Nāyar, Tiyan, Cheruman females, etc., above the loins is exceedingly scanty. As Mr. Logan says: [7] "The women clothe themselves in a single white cloth of fine texture reaching from the waist to the knees, and occasionally, while abroad, they throw over the shoulder and bosom another similar cloth. But by custom the Nāyar women go uncovered from the waist. Upper garments indicate lower caste, or sometimes, by a strange reversal of Western notions, immodesty." The observant Abbé Dubois noticed that, "of all the women in India, it is especially the courtesans (dancing-girls or deva-dasis) who are the most decently clothed, as experience has no doubt taught them that for a woman to display her charms damps sensual ardour instead of exciting it, and that the imagination is more easily captivated than the eye."

A Tamil woman, young or old and wizen, going along the high road, with breasts partially uncovered by her ample body-cloth, will, when she sees a European coming, pull the cloth over them from a feeling of shame in the presence of the foreigner, which is absent in the presence of her fellow country-men. So, too, a Tamil woman, when undergoing the process of measurement at my hands, is most particular in arranging her upper garment so as to conceal her breasts, whereas a Malabar woman has no hesitation in appearing with breasts completely exposed, or in throwing off the slender wrapper which may cover her shoulders, and considers the exposure in no way immodest. I have heard that the women of a tribe (I think in South Canara), whose leafy clothing is, in their home surroundings, reduced to slender proportions, when they come into a town,

[7] 'Manual of Malabar.'

walk in Indian file, concealing their nakedness by means of a series of cloths stitched together, spread out between them and extending down the line. A friend, bartering for the two bead necklets, which constituted the full-dress of a jungle girl, had no difficulty in securing one, but no bribe would tempt her to part with the second, as, in its absence, she would be naked.

The chief characteristics of the Kādirs, their system of personal adornment, etc., will be gathered from the following illustrative cases. It may be noted that the Kādirs do not practise tattooing.

Man, æt. 25. Height 157·4 cm. Nasal index 102·3. Chest girth 86·4 cm. Abundant curly hair, parted in the middle line, tied with string in a bunch (kudumi) behind, and saturated with cocoanut oil. Skin dark-brown. Slight moustache. Hair feebly developed on trunk and extremities. Upper and lower incisor teeth chipped. Only stump remaining of one tooth, which was broken during the operation. Dirty plain cotton loin-cloth. Two brass ornaments in lobe of each ear. Carries bill-hook and pegs for tree-climbing, hanging by fibre rope from left loin.

Man, æt. 30. Hair long and wavy, tied in a loose bunch behind. Three brass ornaments in lobe of each ear. Brass rings on right ring and little fingers.

Man, æt. 27. White turban. Glass bead necklet. Hair clipped short in front in observance of a death ceremony.

Man, æt. 23. Skin as dark as that of a typical Irula of the Nīlgiris. Unparted and untrimmed mass of long curly hair. Very sturdy build. Hard, well developed muscles. Height 156·2 cm. Chest girth 87·5 cm. Shoulders 42 cm. Nasal index 100.

Man, æt. 30. Slight billy-goat beard as well as moustache (unusual). Steel bangle on left upper arm.

Man, æt. 28. Steel ring on left second toe.

Boy, æt. 18. Hair worn in a curly fringe in front, plastered down on top with cocoanut oil, and tied in a compact bunch behind. Brass, bead, and plaited grass necklets. Brass ornament in lobe of each ear. Brass ring with ornament pendent from link-chain in helix of each ear.

It is sometimes difficult to distinguish adolescent youths, with curly fringe, breasts concealed by a cotton cloth, and necklets, from girls. And I was myself several times caught in an erroneous diagnosis of sex.

Boy, æt. 15—16. Plaited grass necklet, and necklet of big brass and glass beads. Brass ring with pendent ornament in helix of left ear. Brass ornament in left lobe. Plug of wood in right nostril.

Boy, æt. 15—16. Mass of long curly hair. Flat bridge to nose. Upper and lower lips conspicuously everted (*cf.* Plate XXVI). Brass and glass bead ornament in right helix. Three brass ornaments, and brase wire with pendent ornaments in left helix. Two brass ornaments in left lobe. Plaited grass necklet. Brass bangle on left wrist.

Boy, æt. 5—6. Clean-shaved on top and front of head. Wooden plug in lobe of each ear. Four upper incisor teeth chipped.

Boy, æt. 5. Hair shaved on top and front of head, tied in a bunch behind. Chunám (lime) smeared over forehead for ornament. Brass ring in lobe of each ear. Steel ring on right wrist.

Boy, æt. 5. Hair a mass of short curls without parting.

Infant in arms. Head shaved all over, except frontal lock. Bead necklace with dried tortoise foot pendent to ward off fever.

Infant in arms. String round neck with wooden imitation of tiger's claw to act as a charm.

Infant in arms. Steel necklet with jungle-worn crocodile tooth pendant, mimicking a phallic emblem, and also supposed to ward off attacks from a mythical water elephant, which is believed to live in the mountain streams.

Infant in arms. Glass bead necklets. Steel bangle on right upper arm. Steel wire round left ankle.

Infant in arms. Necklet made of the seeds of *Coix lachryma* (Job's tears) strung together.

Woman, æt. 23. Height 142·8 cm. Nasal index 94·6. Dirty cotton body and loin cloths. Upper and lower incisor teeth chipped. Hair parted in middle, smoothed with cocoanut oil, and tied in a knot behind. Turmeric powder sprinkled on top of head (forbidden to unmarried girls and widows). Dark blue coal-tar dye streak in mid-frontal line and white spot on glabella. Brass and steel rings in right helix; steel rings in left helix. Cajan roll in dilated lobe of each ear. String and bead necklets. Five steel bangles on right wrist; three steel bangles on left wrist.

Woman, æt. 22. Lantana flowers in hair. White spot on glabella. Wooden plug in each helix. Brass ring in lobe of right ear. Plaited grass and bead necklets.

Woman, æt. 40. Thread round neck, with bases of porcupine quills pendant.

Woman, æt. 45. Bamboo comb, with ornamental geometric patterns scratched on it, worn in back hair and used for doing hair. Lobes of ears widely dilated, pendulous and as elastic as India-rubber. Length of slit in lobes 5·5 cm. Wears no ornaments, as she is a widow.

Woman, æt. 25. Turmeric powder on top of head. Blue and white beauty spots on glabella. Brass and bead ornament in septum of nose. Brass ornament in left nostril. Solid wooden disc in lobe of right ear; cajan roll in left lobe. Wooden plug and brass pendant ornament in each helix. Brass and glass bead necklet with imitation Venetian sequins. Steel bangles on right upper arm and forearm. Steel and six armlets on left upper arm. Three steel armlets on left fore-arm. Spiral steel ring on right thumb and little finger, and left thumb.

Girl, æt. 4. Plug of wood in lobe of each ear. Glass bead necklets. Steel ring on right first finger. Brass bangle on left wrist.

Since writing the above account, I have come across the following note, relating to the Kādirs, by Captain Cotton, in the 'Madras Journal of Literature and Science,' 1858. "These little dwarfish people," he says, "file their front teeth into points, to facilitate their eating the hardest roots. There is some nerve shown in this, and we may look with wonder and respect upon the exiled lords of the ancient land, when we see that, rather than serve those who usurped the country, they chose to live where the food was beyond their natural powers, and could be eaten only by such a preparation of their teeth. It is possible that, in the absence of better arms, they reckoned upon these pointed teeth as weapons, in case their conquerors should follow them to their mountain home."

TABLE XXVII.

SUMMARY OF MEASUREMENTS.

KĀDIR MEN.

	Max.	Min.	Average.
Height	169·4	148·6	157·7
Height, sitting	85·4	70·4	80·3
Height, kneeling	124	109	116·3
Height to gladiolus	126·6	109·2	117·4
Span of arms	184	158·8	168·8
Chest	87·5	74·5	80·5
Middle finger to patella	14·4	6·8	10·7
Shoulders	41·9	36·5	38·8
Cubit	49·1	41·8	45·1
Hand, length	19·5	16·7	17·8
Hand, breadth	8·2	7	7·5
Hips	25·5	22·5	24·1
Foot, length	26·3	21·9	23·8
Foot, breadth	9·1	7·4	8·3
Cephalic length	19·4	17·2	18·4
Cephalic breadth	13·8	12·5	13·4
Cephalic index	80	69·1	72·9
Bigoniac	11	9·1	10
Bizygomatic	13·6	12	12·9
Maxillo-zygomatic index	84·6	70·7	77·4
Nasal height	4·8	3·8	4·3
Nasal breadth	4·5	3·2	3·9
Nasal index	115·4	72·9	89·8

NOTE.—In this and the following tables the measurements are in centimetres.

TABLE XXVIII.

SUMMARY OF MEASUREMENTS.

KĀDIR WOMEN.

	Max.	Min.	Average.
Height	149	133	143
Height, sitting	78·4	69	73·3
Height, kneeling	110·1	98·8	106·2
Span of arms	159	138·8	149·8
Shoulders	36·3	30·6	33·8
Hand, length	16·8	14·7	16·1
Hand, breadth	6·9	5·9	6·6
Foot, length	22·1	19·2	20·8
Foot, breadth	7·6	6·1	7
Cephalic length	18	15·8	17·3
Cephalic breadth	13·4	12·4	12·8
Cephalic index	79·1	71·6	74·2
Bigoniac	10	8·8	9·3
Bizygomatic	12·8	11·4	12
Maxillo-zygomatic index	83·3	72·6	77
Nasal height	4·4	3·2	3·9
Nasal breadth	3·9	3·2	3·4
Nasal index	100	77·3	88

MALAIĀLIS OF THE SALEM DISTRICT.

EXCEPT from a climatic point of view, I have no pleasurable recollections of my sojourn on two occasions among the Malaiālis, who dwell on the summit and slopes of the Shevaroy hills, and earn their living by cultivating grain and working on coffee estates. Suspicious and superstitious to a degree, they openly expressed their fear that I was the dreaded settlement officer, and had come to take possession of their lands in the name of the Government, and transport them, with their wives and families, to the penal settlement in the Andaman Islands. When I was engaged in the innocent occupation of photographing a village, my camera was mistaken for a surveying instrument, and a mild protest raised. Mistaking my motive, they objected strongly to being examined as to their "manners and customs." Many of them, while willing to part with their ornaments of the baser metals, were loth to sell or let me examine their gold and silver jewelry, from fear lest I should use it officially as evidence of their too prosperous condition. Only with great difficulty, and through the kindly assistance of my planter friends, was I enabled to scrape together fifty men for measurement. One man, indeed, told me to my face that he would rather have his throat cut than submit to the measuring operations, and fled precipitately from my bed-room (doing duty as an impromptu research laboratory), which was pervaded with a distinct Malaiāli aroma. The women stolidly refused to entrust themselves in my hands. Nor would they bring their children (unwashed specimens of humanity) to me, lest they should fall sick under the influence of my mild, but to them evil eye. And it was only through the intervention of the Native revenue officer (tāhsildar) that I was enabled to snap the group represented in plate XXXII, just as a thunder-storm burst over the throng collected at the weekly shandy (market).

In the account which follows I am, except as regards physical records, largely indebted to Mr. H. LeFanu's admirable and at times amusing 'Manual of the Salem District,' and to the answers to a series of ethnographic questions, which had been recently circulated through the Collector of the district.

The word Malaiāli denotes inhabitant of the hills (malai = hill or mountain). The Malaiālis have not, however, like the Todas of the Nīlgiris, any claim to be considered as an ancient hill tribe, but are a Tamil-speaking people, who migrated from the plains to the hills in comparatively recent times. As a shrewd, but unscientific observer put it concisely to me, they are Tamils of the plains with the addition of a kambli or blanket; which kambli is a luxury denied to the females, but does duty for males, young and old, in the triple capacity of great coat, waterproof, and blanket. According to tradition, the Malaiālis originally belonged to the Vellāla caste of cultivators, and emigrated from the sacred city of Kānchipūram (Conjeeveram) to the hills about ten generations ago, when Muhammadan rule was dominant in Southern India. When they left Kānchi, they took with them, according to their story, three brothers, of whom the eldest came to the Shevaroy hills, the second to the Kollimallais, and the youngest to the Pachaimallais (green hills), all in the Salem district. The Malaiālis of the Shevaroys are called the Peria (big) Malaiālis, those of the Kollimallais the Chinna (little) Malaiālis. According to another version "the Malaiāli deity Karirāman, finding himself uncomfortable at Kānchi, took up a new abode. Three of his followers, named Perianan, Naduvanan, and Chinnan (the eldest the middle-man, and the youngest) started with their families to follow him from Kānchi, and came to the Salem district, where they took different routes, Perianan going to the Shevaroys, Naduvanan to the Pachaimalais and Anjūr hills, and Chinnan to Manjavādi."

The Malaiālis of the Shevaroy hills all have Goundan as their second name, which is universally used in hailing them. The first name is sometimes derived from a Hindu deity, and my notes record Mr. Black, Mr. Green, Mr. Little, Mr. Short, Mr. Large, and Mr. Big-nose.

As regards the conditions under which the Malaiālis hold land, I learn from the Manual that, in 1866, the Collector of the Salem district fixed an area around each village for the cultivation of the Malaiālis exclusively, and, in view to prevent aggression on the part of the planters, had the boundaries of these areas surveyed and demarcated. This area is known as the "village green." With this survey the old system of charging the Malaiālis on ploughs and hoes appears to have been discontinued, and they are now charged at one rupee per acre on the extent of their holdings. The lands within the green are given under the ordinary darakhāst [1] rules to the Malaiālis, but outside it they are sold under the special waste land rules of 1863. In 1870 the Board of Revenue decided that, where the lands within the green are all occupied, and the Malaiālis require more land for cultivation, land outside the limits of the green may be given them under the ordinary darakhāst rules. In 1871 it was discovered that the planters tried to get lands outside the green by making the Malaiālis first apply for it, thereby evading the waste land rules. The Board then ordered that, if there was reason to suspect that a Malaiāli was applying for lands outside the green on account of the planters, the patta (deed of lease) might be refused.

Subscribing vaguely to the Hindu religion, the Malaiālis, who believe that their progenitors wore the sacred thread, give a nominal allegiance to both Siva and Vishnu, as well as to a number of minor deities, and believe in the efficacy of a thread to ward off sickness and attacks by devils or evil spirits. "In the year 1852," Mr. LeFanu writes, "a searching enquiry into the traditions, customs, and origin of these Malaiālis was made, and probably nothing more is to be ascertained. They then stated that 'smearing the face with ashes indicates the religion of Shiva, and putting nāmam that of Vishnu, but that there is no difference between the two religions; that, though Sivarātri sacred to Shiva, and Strirāmanavami and Gokalashtami sacred to Vishnu, appear outwardly to denote a difference, there is really none.' Though they observe the Saturdays of the month Peratāsi sacred to Vishnu, still worship is performed without reference to Vishnu or Shiva. They have, indeed, certain observances, which would seem to point to a division into Vaishnavas and Saivas, the existence of which they deny; as for instance, some, out of respect to Shiva, abstain from sexual intercourse on Sundays and Mondays; and others, for the sake of Vishnu, do the same on Fridays and Saturdays. So, too, offerings are made to Vishnu on Fridays and Saturdays, and to Shiva on

---

[1] Darakhāst: application for land for purposes of cultivation; or bid at an auction.

PL. XXXII.

GROUP OF MALAIALIS.

Sundays and Mondays; but they denied the existence of sects among them."

In April, 1896, I paid a visit to the picturesquely-situated village of Kiliūr, not far distant from the town of Yercaud, on the occasion of a religious festival. The villagers were discovered, early in the morning, painting pseudo-sect-marks on their foreheads with blue and pink coal-tar dyes, with the assistance of hand looking-glasses of European manufacture purchased at the weekly market, and decorating their turbans and ears with the leafy stems of *Artemisia austriaca*, var. *orientalis*, and hedge-roses. The scene of the ceremonial was in a neighbouring sacred grove of lofty forest trees, wherein were two hut temples, of which one contained images of the goddess Draupādi and eight minor deities, the other images of Perumāl and his wife. All the gods and goddesses were represented by human figures of brass and clay. Two processional cars were gaily decorated with plantain leaves and flags, some made in Germany. As the villagers arrived, they prostrated themselves before the temples, and whiled away the time, till the serious business of the day began, in gossiping with their friends, and partaking of light refreshment purchased from the fruit and sweet-meat sellers, who were doing a brisk trade. At 10 A.M. the proceedings were enlivened by a band of music, which played at intervals throughout the performance, and the gods were decorated with flowers and jewelry. An hour later, pūja (worship) was done to the stone image of the god Vignaswaram, in the form of a human figure, within a small shrine built of slabs of rock. Before this idol cooked rice was offered, and camphor burnt. Then plantain stems, with leaves, were tied to a tree in the vicinity of the temples, and cooked rice and cocoanuts placed beneath the tree. A man holding a sword, issued forth, and, in unison with the collected assemblage, screamed out "Govinda, Govinda" (the name of their god). The plantain stems were next removed from the tree, carried in procession with musical honours, and placed before the threshold of one of the temples. Then some men appeared on the scene to the cry of "Govinda," bearing in one hand a light, and ringing a bell held in the other. Holy water was sprinkled over the plantain stems, and pūja done to the god Perumāl by offering sāmai (grain) and burning camphor. Outside one of the temples a cloth was spread on the ground, and the images of Draupādi and the eight minor deities placed thereon. From the other temple Perumāl and his wife were brought forth in state, and placed on the two cars. A yellow powder was distributed among the crowd, and smeared over the face. A cocoanut was broken, and camphor burnt before Perumāl. Then all the gods, followed by the spectators, were carried in procession round the grove, and a man, becoming inspired and seized with a fine religious frenzy, waved a sword wildly around him, but with due respect for his own bodily safety, and pointed it in a threatening manner at the crowd. Asked, as an oracle, whether the omens were propitious to the village, he gave vent to the oracular (and true) response that for three years there would be a scarcity of rain, and that there would be famine in the land, and consequent suffering. This performance concluded, a bamboo pole was erected, bearing a pulley at the top, with which cocoanuts and plantains were connected by a string. By means of this string the fruits were alternately raised and lowered, and men, armed with sticks, tried to hit them, while turmeric water was dashed in their faces just as they were on the point of striking. The fruits, being at last successfully hit, were received as a prize by the winner. The gods were then taken back to their temples, and three men, overcome by a mock convulsive seizure, were brought to their senses by stripes on the back administered with a rope by the pujāri (officiating priest). A sheep being produced, mantrams (prayers) were recited over it. The pujāri, going to a pool close by, bathed, and smeared turmeric powder over his face. A pretence was made to cut the sheep's throat, and blood drawn with a knife. The pujāri, after sucking the blood, returned to the pool and indulged in a ceremonial ablution, while the unhappy sheep was escorted to the village, and eventually eaten at a banquet by the villagers and their guests.

To Mr. W. Mahon Daly I am indebted for the following account of a Malaiāli bull dance, at which he was present as an eye witness. "It is the custom on the Shevaroy hills, as well as in the plains, to have a bull dance after the pongul festival, and I had the pleasure of witnessing one in a Malaiāli village. It was held in an open enclosure called the munthay. This piece of land adjoins the village, and faces the Mariamma (goddess of small-pox) shrine, and is the place of resort on festive occasions. The village panchāyats (councils), marriages, and other ceremonies are held here. On our arrival, we were courteously invited to sit under a wide spreading fig-tree. The bull dance would literally mean a bull dancing, but I give the translation of the Tamil 'yerothoo-attum', the word attum meaning dance. This is a sport which is much in vogue among the Malaiālis, and is celebrated with much ēclat immediately after pongul, this being the principal festival observed by them. No doubt they have received the custom from those in the plains. A shooting excursion follows as the next sport, and, if they be so fortunate as to hunt down a wild boar or deer, or any big game, a second bull dance is got up.

"We were just in time to see the tamāsha (spectacle). The munthay was becoming crowded, a regular influx of spectators, mostly women arrayed in their best cloths, coming in from the neighbouring villages. These were marshalled in a circle round the munthay, all standing. I was told that they were not invited, but that it was customary for them to pour in of their own accord when any sports or ceremonial took place in a village; and the inhabitants of the particular village were prepared to expect a large company, whom they fed on such occasions. After the company had collected, drums were beaten, and the long brass bugles were blown; and, just at this juncture, we saw an elderly Malaiāli bring from his hut a coil of rope made of leather, and hand it over to the pujāri or priest in charge of the temple. The latter placed it in front of the shrine, worshipped it thrice, some of the villagers following suit, and, after offering incense, delivered it to a few respectable village men, who in turn made it over to a lot of Malaiāli men, whose business it was to attach it to the bulls. This rope the oldest inhabitant of the village had the right to keep. The bulls had been previously selected, and penned alongside of the munthay, from which they were brought one by one, and tied with the rope, leaving an equal length on either side. The rope being fixed on, the bull was brought to the munthay, held on both sides by any number who were willing, or as many as the rope would permit. More than fifteen on either side held on to a bull, which was far too many, for the animal had not the slightest chance of making a dart or plunge at the man in front, who was trying to provoke it by using a long bamboo with a skin attached to the end. When the bull was timid, and avoided his persecutors, he was hissed and hooted by those behind, and, if these modes of provocation failed to rouse his anger, he was simply dragged to and fro by main force, and let loose when his strength was almost exhausted. A dozen or more bulls are taken up and down the munthay, and the tamāsha is over. When the munthay happens to have a slope, the Malaiālis have very little control over the bull, and, in some instances, I have seen them actually dragged headlong to the ground at the expense of a few damaged heads. The spectators, and all the estate coolies who were present, were fed that night, and slept in the village.

"If a death occurs in the village a few days before the festival, I am told that the dance is postponed for a week. This certainly, as far as I know, is not the custom in the plains."

A very tame affair is this bull dance, when compared with the buffalo 'drive' at a Toda funeral [2], or the bull baiting (jellikattu) practised chiefly by the Maravan and kindred castes, which is thus graphically described by Mr. J. H. Nelson: [3] "This is a game worthy of a bold and free people, and it is to be regretted that certain Collectors should have discouraged it under the idea that it was somewhat dangerous. The jellikattu is conducted in the following manner:—On a certain day large crowds of people, chiefly males, assemble together in the morning in some extensive open place, the dry bed of a river perhaps, or of a tank (pond), and many of them may be seen leading ploughing bullocks, of which the sleek bodies, and rather wicked eyes, afford clear evidence of the extra diet they have received for some days in anticipation of the great event. The owners of these animals soon begin to brag of their strength and speed, and to challenge all and any to catch and hold them: and in a short time one of the beasts is selected to open the day's proceedings. A new cloth is made fast round his horns, to be the prize of his captor, and he is then led out into the middle of the arena by his owner, and there left to himself, surrounded by a throng of shouting and excited strangers. Unaccustomed to this sort of treatment, and excited by the gestures of those who have undertaken to catch him, the bullock usually lowers his head at once, and charges wildly into the midst of the crowd, who nimbly run off on either side to make way for him. His

---

[2] *Vide* Bull. No. IV, 1896.
[3] 'Manual of the Madura District,' 1868.

speed being much greater than that of the men, he soon overtakes one of his enemies and savagely makes at him, to toss him. Upon this the man drops on the sand like a stone, and the bullock, instead of goring him, leaps over his body, and rushes after another. The second man drops in his turn, and is passed like the first; and, after repeating this operation several times, the beast either succeeds in breaking the ring and galloping off to his village, charging every person he meets on the way, or is at last caught, and held by the most vigorous of his pursuers. Strange as it may seem, the bullocks never by any chance toss or gore any one who throws himself down on their approach; and the only danger arises from their accidentally reaching, unseen and unheard, some one who remains standing.

"After the first two or three animals have been let loose one after the other, two or three, or even half a dozen, are let loose at a time, and the scene becomes wildly exciting. The crowd sways violently to and fro in various directions in frantic efforts to escape being knocked over; the air is filled with shouts, screams and laughter, and the bullocks thunder over the plain as fiercely as if blood and slaughter were their sole occupation. In this way perhaps two or three hundred animals are run in the course of the day; and, when all go home towards evening, a few cuts and bruises, borne with the utmost cheerfulness, are the only evil results of an amusement which requires great courage and agility on the part of the competitors for the prizes—that is for the cloths and other things tied to the bullocks' horns—and not a little on the part of the mere by-standers. The only time I saw this sport (from a place of safety) I was highly delighted with the entertainment, and no accident occurred to mar my pleasure. One man, indeed, was slightly wounded in the buttock: but he was quite able to walk, and seemed to be as happy as his friend."

To return to the Malaiālis. The man of highest rank is the guru, who is invited to settle disputes in villages, to which he comes, on pony-back or on foot, with an umbrella over him, and accompanied by music. The office of guru is hereditary, and, when he dies, his son succeeds him, unless he is a minor, in which case the brother of the deceased man steps into his shoes. If, in sweeping the hut, the broom touches any one, or when a Malaiāli has been kicked by a European or released from prison, he must be received back into his caste. For this purpose he goes to the guru, who takes him to the temple, where a screen is put up between the guru and the applicant for restoration of caste privileges. Holy water is dedicated to the swâmi (God) by the guru, and a portion thereof drunk by the man, who prostrates himself before the guru, and subsequently gives a feast of pork, mutton, and other delicacies. The Malaiālis, it may be noted, will eat sheep, pigs, fowls, various birds, and black monkeys.

Each village has its own headman, an honorary appointment, carrying with it the privilege of an extra share of the good things, when a feast is being held. A kangāni is appointed to do duty under the headman, and receives annually from every hut two ballams of grain. When disputes occur, *e.g.*, between two brothers regarding a woman or partition of property, the headman summons a panchâyat (village council), which has the power to inflict fines in money, sheep, etc., according to the gravity of the offence. For every group of ten villages there is a pattakāram (head of a division), who is expected to attend on the occasion of marriages and car festivals. A bridegroom has to give him eight days before his marriage a rupee, a packet of betel-nut, and half a measure of nuts. Serving under the pattakāram is the mānia keeran, whose duty it is to give notice of a marriage to the ten villagers, and to summon the villagers thereto. Among the Peria Malaiālis weddings take place on Wednesday and Thursday in the month Chittaray (April-May). For eight days before the ceremony, bride and bridegroom must anoint themselves with turmeric paste.

In the auspicious month of April, 1898, on the receipt of news of a wedding in a distant village, I proceeded thither through coffee estates rich with white flowers bursting into blossom under the grateful influence of copious thunder-showers. *En route*, a good view was obtained of the " Golden Horn," an overhanging rock with a drop of 1,000 feet, down which the Malaiālis swing themselves in search for honey. On the track through the jungle a rock, known from the fancied resemblance of the holes produced by weathering to hoof-marks, as the kudre panji (horse's foot-prints), was passed. Concerning this rock the legend runs that a horse jumped on to it at one leap from the top of the Shivarâyan hill, and at the next leap into the plains at the foot of the hills. The village, which was to be the scene of the festivities, was, like other Malaiāli villages, made up of detached bee-hive huts of bamboo, thatched with palm-leaves and grass, and containing a central room surrounded by a verandah,—the home of pigs, goats, and fowls. Other huts, of similar bee-hive shape, but smaller, were used as store-houses for the grain collected at the harvest season. These grain-stores have no entrance, and the thatched roof has to be removed to take out the grain for use. Tiled roofs, such as are common in the Badaga villages on the Nilgiris, are forbidden, as their use would be an innovation, which would excite the anger of the Malaiāli gods. Huts built on piles contain the flocks, which, during the day, are herded in pens that are removable, and, by moving these pens from one place to another, the villagers manage to get the different parts of their fields manured. Round the whole village a low wall usually runs, and, close by, are the coffee, tobacco, and other cultivated crops. Outside the village, beneath a lofty tree, was a small stone shrine, capped with a stone slab, wherein were stacked a number of neolithic celts, which the Malaiālis reverence as thunder-bolts fallen from heaven. On my arrival at the village, I learned that the bride was not expected to arrive from her own village till long after dark. "She has," said the headman, "a stomach, which must be fed before she comes here." I was, however, presented to the youthful and anxious bridegroom, who was already dressed up in his marriage finery, and stripped before the assembled villagers, in order that I might record his wedding garments. His entire body was enshrouded in a new Salem cotton cloth with silk-woven border, and a clean white turban and coloured cotton langūti completed the clothing. For jewelry he wore gold ornaments in each helix, and a marriage hoop ornament of gold encircling each ear, a heavy silver necklet, five rows of silver armlets on the right upper arm, and a silver chain round his hips. Fingers and toes were decorated with silver rings. The neck was smeared with chunam (lime), and the chest and abdomen daubed with symbolical marks in turmeric. Unfortunately, the arrival of a case of cholera in the village gave rise to a hitch in the proceedings, and I had to rely on native evidence for details of the marriage ceremonial. On the first day, the bridegroom, accompanied by his relations, takes the modest dowry of grain and money (usually five rupees) to the bride's village, and arranges for the performance of the nalungoo ceremony on the following day. If the bride and bridegroom belong to the same village, this ceremony is performed by the pair seated on a cot. Otherwise it is performed by each separately. The elders of the village take a few drops of castor-oil, and rub it into the heads of the bride and bridegroom; afterwards washing the oil off with poonac and alum water. One of the elders then dips betel-leaves and arugum-pillu (*Cynodon Dactylon*) in milk, and with them describe a circle round the heads of the young couple, who do obeisance by bowing their heads. The proceedings wind up with a feast of pork and other luxuries. On the following day the ceremony of tying the tāli (marriage emblem) round the bride's neck is performed. The bride, escorted by her party, comes to the bridegroom's village, and remains outside it, while the bridegroom brings a light, a new mat, and three bundles of betel-nut and half a measure of nuts, which are distributed among the crowd. The happy pair then enter the village, accompanied by music. Beneath a pandal there is a stone, representing the god, marked with the nāmam, and decorated with burning lamps and painted earthen pots. Before this stone the bride and bridegroom seat themselves in the presence of the guru, who is seated on a raised dais. Flowers are distributed among the wedding guests, and the tāli, made of gold, is tied round the bride's neck. This done, the feet of both bride and bridegroom are washed with alum water, and presents of small coin received. The contracting parties then walk three times round the stone, before which they prostrate themselves, and receive the blessing of the assembled elders. The ceremony concluded, they go round the village, riding on the same pony. The proceedings again terminate with a feast. I gather that the bride lives apart from her husband for eleven or fifteen days, during which time he is permitted to visit her at meal times, with the object, as my interpreter expressed it, of " finding out if the bride loves her husband or not. If she does not love him, she is advised by the guru and head man to do so, because there are many cases in which the girls, after marriage, if they are matured, go away with other Malaiālis. If this matter comes to the notice of the guru, she says that she does not like to live with him. After enquiry, the husband is permitted to marry another girl."

A curious custom prevailing among the Malaiālis of the Kollimallais, and illustrating the Hindu love of offspring, is thus referred to by Mr. LeFanu: " The sons, when mere children, are married to mature females, and the father-in-law of the bride assumes the performance of the procreative function, thus assuring for himself and his son a descendant to take them out of 'Put.' When the putative father comes of age, and in their turn his wife's male offspring are married, he performs for them the same office which his father did for him. Thus, not only is the religious idea involved in the words Putra and Kumāran[4] carried out, but also the premature strain on the generative faculties, which this tradition entails, is avoided. The accommodation is reciprocal, and there is something on physiological grounds to recommend it." Concerning this custom the Rev. H. N. Hutchinson writes as follows:[5] "A man who has young sons, mere children, takes new wives for himself, who are, however, called his sons' wives, and the children they bear to him are called his sons' children, and so it goes on from one generation to another. This appears to be a relic of what is called the matriarchal system, which still prevails in various countries, as once in India." Widow re-marriage among the Peria Malaiālis is, I am informed, forbidden, though widows are permitted to contract irregular alliances. But, writing concerning the Malaiālis of the Dharmapuri taluk (division) of the Salem district, Mr. LeFanu states that: "It is almost imperative on a widow to marry again. Even at eighty years of age, a widow is not exempted from this rule, which nothing but the most persistent obstinacy on her part can evade. It is said that, in case a widow be not re-married at once, the Pattakār sends for her to his own house, to avoid which the women consent to re-enter the state of bondage." Of the marriage customs of the Malaiālis of the Javādi hills the same author writes that "these hills are inhabited by Malaiālis, who style themselves Vellālars and Pachai Vellālars, the latter being distinguished by the fact that their females are not allowed to tattoo themselves, or tie their hair in the knot called 'kondai'. The two classes do not intermarry. In their marriage ceremonies they dispense with the service of a

---

[4] Putra means literally "one who saves from put," a hell into which those who have not produced a son fall. Hindus believe that a son can, by the performance of certain rites and ceremonies, save the souls of his ancestors from this place of torture. Hence the anxiety of every Hindu to get married, and beget male offspring. Kumāran is the second stage in the life of an individual, which is divided into infancy, childhood, manhood, and old age.

[5] 'Marriage Customs in many Lands,' 1897.

Brāhman. Monday is the day chosen for the commencement of the ceremony, and the tāli is tied on the following Friday, the only essential being that the Monday and Friday concerned must not follow new moon days. They are indifferent about choosing a 'lakkinam' (muhūrtham or auspicious day) for the commencement of the marriage, or for tying the tāli. Widows are allowed to re-marry. When a virgin or a widow has to be married, the selection of a husband is not left to the woman concerned, or to her parents. It is the duty of the Úrgoundan to inquire what marriageable women there may be in the village, and then to summon the pāttan, or headman of the caste, to the spot. The latter, on his arrival, convenes a panchāyat of the residents, and, with their assistance, selects a bridegroom. The parents of the happy couple then fix the wedding day, and the ceremony is performed accordingly. The marriage of a virgin is called 'kaliānam' or 'marriage proper'; that of a widow being styled 'kattigiradu' or 'tying' (*cf.* Anglice noose, nuptial knot). Adultery is regarded with different degrees of disfavour according to the social position of the co-respondents. If a married woman, virgin or widow, commits adultery with a man of another caste, or if a male Vellālan commits adultery with a woman of another caste, the penalty is expulsion from caste. Where, however, the paramour belongs to the Vellāla caste, a caste panchāyat is held, and the woman is fined Rs. 3-8-9, and the man Rs. 7. After the imposition of the fine, Brāhman supremacy is recognised, the guru having the privilege of administering the 'tirtam', or holy water, to the culprits for their purification. For the performance of this rite his fee varies from 4 annas to 12 rupees. The tirtam may either be administered by the guru in person, or may be sent by him to the nattan for the purpose. The fine imposed on the offenders is payable by their relatives, however distant; and, if there be no relatives, then the offenders are transported from their village to a foreign country. Where the adulteress is a married woman, she is permitted to return to her husband, taking any issue she may have had by her paramour. In special cases a widow is permitted to marry her deceased husband's brother. Should a widow re-marry, her issue by her former husband belongs to his relatives, and are not transferable to the second husband. The same rule holds good in successive re-marriages. Where there may be no relatives of the deceased husband forthcoming to take charge of the children, the duty of caring for them devolves on the Ūrgoundan, who is bound to receive and protect them. The Vellālars generally bury their dead, except in cases where a woman quick with child, or a man afflicted with leprosy has died, the bodies in these cases being burnt. No ceremony is performed at child-birth; but the little stranger receives a name on the fifteenth day. When a girl attains puberty, she is relegated for a month to a hut outside the village, where her food is brought to her during that period, and she is forbidden to leave the hut either day or night. The same menstrual and death customs are observed by the Peria Malaiālis, who bury their dead in the equivalent of a cemetery, and mark the site by a mound of earth and stones. At the time of the funeral, guns are discharged by a "firing party," and, at the grave, handfulls of earth are, as at a Christian burial service, thrown over the corpse.

The Malaiālis of the Shevaroy hills snare with nets, and shoot big game—deer, leopards, tigers, bears, and pigs—with guns of European manufacture; and Mr. LeFanu narrates that, during the pongal feast, all the Malaiālis of the Kalrāyans go ahunting, or, as they term it, for 'par vēttai.' "Should the Pālaiagar fail to bring something down, usage requires that the pujāri should deprive him of his kudimi or top-knot. He generally begs himself off the personal degradation, and a servant undergoes the operation in his stead."

In games the Malaiālis seem to be deficient, and, despite the manual labour which work on coffee estates and their own lands imposes on them, they are wanting in muscular development. "How", said the possessor of a miserable hand-grip of 48 lbs. in reply to a question, "can any of us be strong, when we have to work all day for the European"? A rough-and-tumble game, resembling prisoner's base, called sathurappāri vilayāttu, is played in a square court, of which the lines are marked by means of the feet in the dust, with water on moonlight nights, or with chunām (lime wash) in mimicry of the lines of a lawn-tennis court. The players, eight in number, divide into an in and out side. The square is defended at the corners by the former, while the latter try to force their way within the lines.

The finest specimen of a Peria Malalāli, which I have seen, was a man, aged 25, named Dāsan Goundan, working on a coffee estate, whose record was as follows :—

		Malaiāli. average.
Weight ..	.. 157 lbs.	99 lbs.
Height ..	.. 173·2 cm.	163·4 cm.
Span of arms	.. 179·8 ,,	172·1 ,,
Chest ..	.. 93·5 ,,	79·7 ,,
Shoulders	.. 42·6 ,,	38·5 ,,
Hips	.. 27 ,,	35·5 ,,
Foot, length	.. 26·7 ,,	25·3 ,,

The leading characteristics of the Malaiālis, and their personal adornment are summed up in the following cases :—

1. Man, æt. 25. A lean and long-legged individual with very thin calves. Height 164 cm. Hair of head clipped short on top, long and tied in a knot behind. Diffuse hairs over middle of chest. Median strip of hairs on abdomen. Clothing consists of white turban decorated with roses, brown kambli (blanket) with white border pattern, dhūti and langūti. Bag containing betel-leaf and tobacco slung over left shoulder. Carries bill-hook and gourd water-vessel. Coffee walking stick. Silver belt round loins. Brass ring in lobe of each ear and gold ornament in left helix. Silver bangle on each wrist. Two silver rings on right ring and little fingers. Silver ring on such second toe.

2. Man, æt. 30. Will not sit on a chair to have his head measured, as it would be disrespectful, and make his god angry. No objection to standing upon it. Hair extensively developed over chest, abdomen, shoulders, back and extensor surface of fore-arms. Silver belt round loins. Silver armlet on right upper arm, and bangle on each wrist. Three silver rings on right ring finger. Two silver rings on right little finger. Silver ring on each second toe. Stores his money away in the hollow bamboos of his hut.

3. Man, æt. 25. Brass ring in left nostril. Four brass rings in right ear lobe ; two in left. Two silver rings on right third finger.

4. Man, æt. 28. Caste spots on forehead and root of nose, painted with coal-tar magenta dyes. Smeared with

chunām (lime) over both deltoids, chest and neck. Mutton-chop whiskers and billy-goat beard.

5. Man, æt. 30. Woollen anklet round left ankle, worn as a charm to drive away pain.

6. Man, æt. 26. Wooden plug in lobe and helix of each ear.

7. Man, æt. 26. Blue sect spot on forehead and blue line in mid-frontal region. Wooden plug in lobe of each ear. Gold ornament in left helix. Silver bangle on right wrist. Two silver rings on right ring and little fingers. Two brass rings on left little finger. Silver ring on left second toe.

Little girl. Gold ornament in right nostril. Silver and bead necklets. Tattooed (blue) with mark like masonic compasses on forehead, circle surrounded by ring of dots on right cheek, sun and half moon on left cheek, spot on chin, and unknown symbols outside orbits. Tattooing is done by Korava women, who come on circuit from the plains about once a month. The devices on the face constitute distinctive tribal marks. Gold ornament in right nostril. Silver and bead necklets. Two leaden bangles on right wrist, and a single leaden bangle on left wrist. Two silver rings on left fore-finger. Two brass rings on left second finger.

Woman, æt. 35. Tattooed with the same symbols as the preceding on forehead and outside orbits. Sun and half moon on right cheek. Rayed circle on left cheek. Scorpion on metacarpus of right thumb. Elaborate geometrical and conventional devices, as among women of the plains, over right deltoid, both fore-arms, and back of left hand. Gold ornament in each ear lobe, and in helix, the latter connected with a silver link chain fixed into back hair, which is tied in a bunch. Gold ring in right nostril, and gold ornament in left nostril. Gold tāli tied with string round neck. Silver and bead necklets with tooth-pick and ear-scoop pendent. Two silver armlets on right upper arm. Leaden bangle on right wrist. One leaden, and two composition bangles on left wrist. Silver ring on each second toe. Sári (dress) made of florid imported printed cotton. Smokes tobacco of local cultivation, wrapped in a leaf of *Gmelina arborea*.

The averages of my Malaiāli measurements are, in Table XXX, compared with those of two of the Tamil classes of Madras City (Vellālas and Pallis) and support the theory that the Malaiālis emigrated from the Tamil-speaking area of the plains at no very remote period.

TABLE XXIX.

SUMMARY OF MEASUREMENTS.

MALAIĀLIS. 50.

	Max.	Min.	Average.
Weight	120	87	99
Height	173·2	153·2	163·4
Height, sitting	87·2	77·1	82
Height, kneeling	125·7	111·4	120
Height to gladiolus	131	112·8	122·7
Span of arms	188·6	161	172·1
Chest	90	74	79·7
Middle finger to patella ...	14·8	6·4	10·8
Shoulders	43·2	35·1	38·5
Cubit	50·2	43·1	46·6
Hand, length	19·6	16	17·8
Hand, breadth	9·1	7·4	8·1
Hips	27·2	23·6	25·5
Foot, length	26·9	23·1	25·3
Foot, breadth	10·1	8·1	8·8
Cephalic length	19·3	16·9	18·3
Cephalic breadth	14·6	12·8	13·6
Cephalic index	82·8	61	74·3
Bigoniac	10·8	8·2	9·6
Bizygomatic	13·9	11·7	12·7
Maxillo-zygomatic index ...	85·2	65·6	75·8
Nasal height	5·2	3·9	4·6
Nasal breadth	4·1	3	3·5
Nasal index	100	63·8	77·8

TABLE XXX.

SUMMARY OF MEASUREMENTS OF MALAIÂLIS, VELLÀLAS, AND PALLIS.

	Vellālas.	Malaialis.	Pallis.
Weight	103·3	99	104·6
Height	162·4	163·4	162·5
Height, sitting	83·4	82·1	83·6
Height, kneeling	119·3	120	118·8
Height to gladiolus	121·9	122·8	121·5
Span of arms	174·1	172·1	172·6
Chest	79·8	79·7	79·2
Middle finger to patella ...	10·4	10·8	9·5
Shoulders	39·7	38·5	39·4
Cubit	46·9	46·6	46·2
Hand, length	18·3	17·8	17·9
Hand, breadth	8·2	8·1	8·1
Hips	25·6	25·5	25·5
Foot, length	25·7	25·3	25·5
Foot, breadth	8·7	8·8	8·9
Cephalic length	18·6	18·3	18·6
Cephalic breadth	13·8	13·6	13·6
Cephalic index	74·1	74·3	73
Bigoniac	10	9·6	9·9
Bizygomatic	12·9	12·7	12·7
Maxillo-zygomatic index ...	76·7	75·8	78
Nasal height	4·7	4·6	4·6
Nasal breadth	3·4	3·5	3·6
Nasal index	73·1	77·8	77·9

SYLLABUS OF A COURSE OF DEMONSTRATIONS ON PRACTICAL ANTHROPOLOGY GIVEN AT THE MUSEUM, OCTOBER 1898.

Demonstrations primarily for the benefit of students in the University classes of History, which, as laid down by the local University, includes some knowledge of ethnology and comparative philology. No facilities for practical instruction at the colleges. Questions in examination papers, bearing on the cephalic index and body measurements, which cannot be answered in a style worthy of Degree examination by candidates who have not seen practical application of methods on skull and living subject. Demonstrations, practical and semi-popular, to supplement theoretical knowledge acquired from books and lectures.

Anthropology, a branch of natural history, which treats of Man and the races of Man, conveniently separated into two main divisions :—

(*a*) Ethnography, which deals with man as a social and intellectual being, his " manners and customs, " knowledge of arts and industries, tradition, language, religion, etc.

Illustrations. Show-cases of tribal jewelry, models of dwelling-huts, implements, and photographs. Meriah sacrifice (buffaloes sacrificed at present day instead of human beings). Toda polyandry and female infanticide. Hook-swinging. Dravidian languages. Animistic religion of hill and forest tribes. Burial and cremation. Decline of indigenous weaving industry, and degeneration in Native female dress as result of imported colour-printed piece-goods.

(*b*) Anthropography, which deals with Man and the varieties or " species " of the human family from an animal point of view, his structure and the functions of his body.

Necessary for the purposes of study of anthropology, so far as Indian peninsula is concerned, to keep in mind three primary links of evidence :—

(*a*) Evidence of " prehistoric " people, bearing in mind that, like the geologist, the anthropologist does not reckon by days or years; and that " the 6,000 years (Creation said to have occurred 4004 B.C.) which were till lately looked on as the sum of the world's age are to him but as a unit of measurement in the long succession of past ages." Prehistoric man in Southern India very largely represented by tumuli, cairns, cromlechs and kistvaens of Shevaroy, Palni, and Nīlgiri mountain ranges; by the large earthenware burial urns or sarcophagi found at Pallávaram near Madras, in the Tinnevelly district, etc.; and by the palæolithic and neolithic implements (celts, hammer-stones, scrapers, saws, etc.), concerning which Mr. R. Bruce Foote is preparing a catalogue raisonné based on his own and the museum collections.

Illustrations. Quartzite implements found in lateritic formation at Pallávaram; stone implements from the Bellary district and Shevaroy hills, stored by Natives in small shrines, and worshipped as thunderbolts fallen from heaven; earthenware sarcophagus, 105 cm. high, from Tinnevelly; earthenware vessels impressed with rude ornamentation. Models of large-horned buffaloes, birds, fabulous animals, and bearded men on horseback, bronze vessels, and iron arrow or javelin heads, excavated on the Nīlgiri hills. Evidence that Nīlgiris were inhabited by a people earlier than the Todas, who possess not even the most elementary knowledge of arts and industries. Todas live on products of semi-feral buffalo, and by soliciting alms (inám) from European visitors to their mands. Pottery and human bones (heads and necks of femora) from Coimbatore district; pottery and chank shells (*Turbinella rapa*) from Guntakal.

(*b*) Evidence of oldest existing people, now confined to jungle tribes dispersed in small communities, for the most part in the jungles on the slopes of the mountains.

Examples: Irulas, Kurumbas, Kādirs, Paniyans, and Sholigas, all possessing two marked characters in common, viz. (*a*) shortness of stature; (*b*) short, broad nose with consequent high nasal index. "Aryans so impressed with the flat, snub noses of their enemies, that they often spoke of them as the noseless ones" (Risley).

	Average height. CM.	Average nasal index. CM.
Paniyans	157·4	95·1
Kādirs	157·7	89·8
Kurumbas	157·4	89·6
Irulas	159·8	84·9

(*c*) Evidence of influence of immigration of foreign races, *e.g.*, 'Aryans,' whose influence may, *mutatis mutandis*, be argued by analogy with influence of European immigration (Portuguese, Dutch, British, French, and Danish) on indigenous population of Southern India during last five centuries, with, as starting point, alliances between Portuguese adventurers under Alboquerque with Native women of Malabar.

Important division of anthropography is anthropometry, *i.e.*, measurement and estimation of physical data relating to people belonging to different races, castes and tribes, by means of which their characteristics can be compared together. Anthropometry for purposes of criminal identification. Bertillonage. Measurements, to be relied on, must be taken by experts. Fingerprint records more reliable for criminal purposes.

As a means of gauging physique, three pieces of apparatus used in museum laboratory, viz., weighing machine, dynamometer, spirometer.

(*a*) Weighing machine. Record actual weight, and weight relatively to uniform stature of 100 cm. for purpose of comparison of different castes and tribes.

Examples:

	Average height.	Average weight.	Average weight relative to stature = 100.
	CM.	LBS.	LBS.
Brāhmans (poorer classes).	162·5	115	70·8
Pariahs	162·1	106	65·4
Pallis	162·5	104·6	64·4
Kammālans ..	159·7	100·4	62·9

European inhabitants of a hill station objected to my weighing local tribesmen in meat scales of butcher's shop.

(*b*) Spirometer, or gasometer, which records play of chest or vital capacity, *i.e.*, total quantity of air, which can be given out by the most forcible expiration following on a most forcible inspiration. Play of chest of far greater importance than actual girth, as every one knows who has had to examine recruits or applicants for life-insurance. No use possessing a 40-inch chest if lungs emphysematous, and chest walls have not corresponding power of expansion and contraction.

(*c*) Hand-dynamometer for testing hand grip.

Examples:

	Average. LBS.
Europeans, Madras City	88
Sepoys, 28th Madras Infantry	80
Todas	79
Kotas	70
Eurasians (poorer classes), Madras City ..	65

Note that Todas, who do no manual labour, have a greater average grip than the Kotas of the Nīlgiris, many of whom are blacksmiths or carpenters. Maximum recorded in Madras 113 lbs., Native musketry instructor 28th M.I.

Results of anthropometry depend essentially on calculation of averages. In small communities, *e.g.*, jungle-tribes, measurement of 20 to 25 subjects sufficient for all practical purposes. In larger communities, measurement of 40 subjects yields sufficiently accurate results. Necessary, when investigating Eurasians, to measure over a hundred individuals owing to great variation in stature and other characters. Women, as well as men, should be measured if possible. Not always easy to establish confidence among them. Two-anna pieces most effective means of conciliation, supplemented by cheroots for men, cigarettes for children, and, as a last resource, alcohol. Measuring appliances sometimes frighten the subjects, especially goniometer for determining facial angle, which is mistaken for an instrument of torture.

Before measuring individual, record notes on personal characteristics, ornaments, dress, etc.

(*a*) Name. May be derived from a god or goddess, personal characteristic, a colour, etc. Natives have equivalent of Mr. Black, Green, Short, Large, and further Mr. Big-nose, Mr. Brownish-black, and Mr. Greenish-blue.

(*b*) Age. Difficult to estimate accurately in uneducated classes, as, after childhood, they lose all count of age. In taking measurements of Europeans, limits of age 25 to 40. Useless to record measurements of individuals not fully developed, or of those who have begun to shrink from age. In dealing with Natives, I accept 40 as maximum and 20 as minimum. Development earlier in the east than in Europe.

(*c*) Skin-colour. Fair, as in high-caste Brāhmans, dark-brown, or even blackish-brown in some jungle-tribes, notably Irulas of Nīlgiris, who are so dark that it has been jestingly said, charcoal leaves a white mark on them. Skin-colour can be roughly described according to number on Broca's colour scale. Typical Dravidian brown colour not represented therein.

(*d*) Tattooing. Originally resorted to as ornament, and as a means of sexual attraction. In Samoa, for example, until a young man is tattooed, he cannot think of marriage. Tattooing in blue performed even on dark skins, on which blue is invisible, and original object of the practice lost. In South India tattooing conspicuously absent on west coast. In other parts pattern ranges from simple devices of dots, lines, and circles among women of hill-tribes to elaborate geometrical and conventional devices among women of the plains. Prevalence of religious symbols (chalice, dove, crucifix, sacred heart, etc.) among Eurasians of west coast. Most elaborate patterns executed by Burmese professional tattooers on Tamil emigrants to Burma.

(*e*) Malformations. Refer to pinched in feet of Chinese women, compression of infant skull among Peruvians, and effects of tight-lacing. Contrast Native female and European waists, undistorted foot of Native, and foot of European distorted by badly-fitting boots. In latter long axis of great toe not parallel to central axis of foot as in Natives.

Most characteristic malformations in Southern India :—

1. Circumcision, a Muhammadan practice, but, curiously enough, resorted to by Kallans of Madura district, and said to be survival of forcible conversion to Muhammadanism.

2. Dilatation of lobes of ears, which become, from stretching, as elastic as india-rubber, and sometimes snap across. Native Christian girls in Tinnevelly have long ears operated on, and cut short at Mission hospital. Objection that short ears make them look like deva-dasis (dancing girls) dying out. In statues of Buddha, as far back as 2nd century A.D., ears dilated, but void of ornaments.

3. Chipping and filing of incisor teeth, practised by Kādirs of Ānaimalai hills. Practice common to some tribes in Africa and Malay Archipelago. Whence did Kādirs inherit the custom?

4. Amputation of terminal phalanges of ring and little fingers, practised on women of Vakkaliga sect in Mysore. Operation performed when their children have the ear and nose-boring ceremony carried out.

Odour of skin. Missionary Huc could distinguish between smell of Tibetan, Hindu, Negro and Chinaman, by sense of smell. Characteristic odour of Todas. Mosquitoes mercilessly attack Europeans newly arrived in India. Old stagers comparatively free from attack, and said to be protected by smell of skin, which develops as result of climatic conditions, and is distasteful to mosquito.

Skin of body. Extent of development of hair and areas of distribution. Median strip of hair on abdomen common Dravidian type. Todas characterised by excessive development of hairy system, which may form thick fur on chest. Todas have this character in common with Australians and Ainus of Japan.

Hair of head, straight, wavy, curly, frizzly, or woolly. Woolly hair, in which little curls interlock, and form tufts resembling wool, characteristic of Negroes; curly or wavy of inhabitants of Southern India. Repeatedly asserted that Paniyans of Malabar woolly-haired, and of African descent. No evidence. Their hair curly, not woolly. Native hair universally black in adult; frequently light-brown in infancy. Mode of doing hair; dyeing with henna (leaves of *Lawsonia alba*). Photograph of Cheruman with hair in long matted plaits in observance of death ceremonial.

Colour of iris, or diaphragm of eye. Natives, as a rule, have dark eyes, but sometimes blue as inherited character. Badaga family, in which grandfather, father, and grandchildren all had light blue eyes. In Madras City two Native albinoes with pink skin, white hair, and pink eyes, from absence of pigment.

Shape of face--long, narrow; short, broad; pyramidal, etc.

Nose. Shape when viewed in profile. Concave nose common among Dravidians, due to hollowing out of nasal bones.

Cheek-bones, flat or prominent. Prominence of cheek-bones, and obliquely-set eyes characteristic of Mongolians. Irulas of Nilgiris have prominent cheek-bones, but straight eyes.

Prominence of superciliary (brow) ridges. Characteristic of Neanderthal skull, Pithecanthropus, Australians, etc. Compare skull of higher ape with that of European. Tamil skulls with ridges well developed, and other Australian characters.

Lips, thin, thick, or everted. Photograph of Kādir with upper and lower lips conspicuously everted.

Lower jaw, prognathous or orthognathous, when viewed in profile.

Measurements recorded in centimetres and millimetres (2·54 cm. = 1 inch), divided into (*a*) essential; (*b*) accessory. Necessary, for purpose of comparison of various tribes and castes of Indian peninsula, to have notes on body-colour, and accurate statistics relating to body height, length and breadth of head, and height and width of nose. With these data to work on, easy to fit any tribe or caste in its correct place in the anthropological puzzle. Training necessary before measurements, *e.g.*, of nose and head, can be accepted. Accuracy most essential in smaller measurements. Anthropometric results based on average of sum of measurements of a number of individuals.

1. Standing height. Classification. Tall, 170 cm. and upwards; middle height 170—160 cm.; short 160 cm. and below. In South India no tall race, tribe, or caste, though Todas nearly reach this dignity (average 169·6 cm.). Compare heights on standard. Patagonians tallest, Stanley's dwarfs (African) shortest. Jungle tribes of South India are about same height as a number of Australians measured in Sydney. Standing height one of the measurements used for purposes of criminal identification.

Examples:	Average. CM.
English	170·8
Todas	169·6
Eurasians	166·6
Brāhmans	162·5
Pariahs	161·9
Paniyans	157·4

2. Relative length of upper extremities, best determined by comparison of span of arms outspread at right angles to body with stature, and of distance from tip of middle finger to patella (knee-cap) in altitude of attention with extensor muscles of thigh relaxed.

Examples: Span of arms.	Average relative to stature = 100.
Eurasians	103·6
Pariahs	106·2
Kādirs	107
Negroes	108·1

Examples : Middle finger to knee-cap.

	Average relative to stature = 100.
English	7·5
Brāhmans	6·2
Pariahs	5·8
Paniyans	4·6
Negroes	4·4

Hands of long-armed Ráma said, in Hindu epic, to have reached to his knees. Compare skeleton of Negro with that of Orang-utan, in which hands reach far below knees.

3. Chest. Physical rather than racial test. Measurement taken with tape over nipples with arms above head, and hands joined.

Examples :	Average relative to stature = 100.
Paniyans	51·8
Kādirs	51
Sepoys, 28th M.I.	50·4
Brāhmans	49·8
Pariahs	48·9

Paniyans and Kādirs (jungle-tribes), short of stature and deep-chested ; well adapted for mountaineering.

4. Hip-breadth. Measured across anterior spines of ilia (hip-bones). Ratio between breadth of hips and length of foot important as distinguishing character between races, castes, and tribes of Southern India. Frequently come across Natives with foot-length considerably greater than hip-breadth. In Europeans hip-breadth considerably in excess of foot-length.

Head measurements estimated with callipers and compasses.

5. Maximum length and breadth of head. Length from glabella or ophryon to occipital point. Breadth : greatest breadth across parietal bones. Easiest to measure, on living subject, heads clean-shaved in observance of religious ceremony, on which shape of head easily studied. Difficulty in measuring heads of Todas, whose dense locks offer obstacle to shifting of callipers in search for right spot.

Examples :

	Average.	
	Length. CM.	Breadth. CM.
Pariahs	18·6	13·7
Brāhmans (poorer clases).	18·6	14·2
Civil Servants, Madras ..	19·6	15·3
Other Europeans, Madras.	19·4	15

Ratio of length to breadth represented by cephalic index determined by formula.

$$\frac{\text{Breadth} \times 100.}{\text{Length.}}$$

More nearly breadth and length correspond, higher the index. Longer the head in proportion to breadth, lower the index. Heads range in type from long, narrow (dolichocephalic) to short, broad (brachycephalic). Intermediate type, mesaticephalic, common among half-breeds. Dolichocephalic type characteristic of Dravidians. Todas have longest, Brahmans broadest heads among Natives of Southern India. Character of Dravidian skull is absence of convexity of posterior portion of skull, with result that back of head forms a flattened are of a considerable length almost at right angles to base of skull. Corresponding shortness of head and diminished brain-space. Compare series of Tamil skulls with those of European, Jew, etc. Cephalic indices, European 74·7 ; Tamil 74·4 ; Negro 72·5 ; Andamanese 83·2 ; Sinhalese 85·1 ; Burmese 86·6. Shape of skull does not necessarily indicate size of brain. Section of Negro skull with large bump on top caused by bony thickening and large frontal sinus. Relative sizes of brains, or cranial capacity, estimated on skull by plugging foramina (holes) with cotton wool, and filling up skull through foramen magnum (large hole at base) with small shot or mustard seed, Calculate by pouring shot or seed into glass vessel graduated in cubic centimetres. Estimate cubic capacity of skulls of various Dravidian classes.

6. Relation of greatest breadth of facial portion of head across zygomatic arches to greatest breadth of lower jaw (bigoniac).

$$\frac{\text{Bigoniac} \times 100}{\text{Zygomatic}} = \text{maxillo-zygomatic index.}$$

7. Facial angle. Estimated with goniometer. Some Natives object to holding it between their teeth, as being source of pollution. Diagrams of classic Greek head with forehead thrown forward, heads of Dravidian, Negro, and Chimpanzee. Facial angle of Dravidian averages from 67° to 70°. Dravidians as a whole orthognathous, *i.e.*, line of upper jaw more or less vertical when viewed in profile. Negro conspicuously prognathous, *i.e.*, upper jaw projects forwards, with corresponding lowering of facial angle. Measure true sub-nasal prognathism. Demonstrate facial angle of Brāhman and Negro skulls. Prognathism indicated on skull by basi-alveolar length, *i.e.*, distance between front of foramen magnum and alveolar point in centre of upper jaw. Show Tamil skull, possessing not only prominent superciliary ridges, but also well-marked prognathism. Australian affinities. Use of boomerang by Kullans and Maravans of Southern India. Refer to skulls of Man and ape, in which line drawn from glabella to basion indicates predominance of cranial or brain-bearing portion in former, and of facial portion of latter. Show sections of skull of horse and elephant, demonstrating small size of brain relatively to that of head.

8. Nose—facial feature, which is most likely to be transmitted from one generation to another. Nasal character, in India, most important factor in differentiation of race, tribe, and class, and in determination of pedigree from broad-nosed ancestors. Shape not so important as relation of height to breadth.

$$\frac{\text{Breadth} \times 100}{\text{Height}} = \text{Nasal index.}$$

Examples:

Brāhman.

Height 5·5 cm. } Breadth 3·4 ,, } $\frac{3{\cdot}4 \times 100}{5{\cdot}5} = 61{\cdot}8$ = nasal index.

Paniyan.

Height 4 cm. } Breadth 4 ,, } $\frac{4 \times 100}{4} = 100$ = do.

Kurumba.

Height 3·8 cm. } Breadth 4 ,, } $\frac{4 \times 100}{3{\cdot}8} = 105{\cdot}3$ = do.

Nasal index lowest in Aryans, highest in jungle-tribes. Index increases as body height diminishes. High nasal index, and short stature of individuals belonging to various castes and tribes, must be attributed to lasting influence of short, broad-nosed ancestor.

	Average Height.	Average Nasal index.
	CM.	CM.
Lambādis (Aryan language)	164·5	69·1
Eurasians	166·6	69·5
Tiyans	163·7	75
Pariahs	162·1	80
Kurumbas	157·6	87
Paniyans	157·4	95·1

Contrast nasal indices on skulls of European, Tamil, and Negro. European 37·5; Tamil 57·8; Negro 60·9. In absence of nostrils, nasal index never nearly so high in skeleton as in living subject.

NOTE ON THE DRAVIDIAN HEAD.

I recently came across a passage in Taylor's 'Origin of the Aryans' (Contemporary Science Series), wherein it is stated that "the Todas are fully dolichocephalic, differing in this respect from the Dravidians, who are brachycephalic." As this statement is not in accord with my own observations, it is right that I should place on record the results obtained from the measurement of a large number of Native tribes and castes of Southern India other than Brāhmans and Muhammadans, which have been investigated by me in the course of the last few years. The figures, published below, show that the average cephalic index of 639 members of 19 different tribes and castes was 74·1; and that in only 19 out of the 639 individuals did the index exceed 80. So far, then, from the Dravidian being separated from the Todas by reason of their higher cephalic index, this index is, in the Todas, actually higher than in some of the remaining Dravidian peoples, *e.g.*, the Badagas, Pallis, Muppas, and Ambattans.

	Number of men examined.	Average cephalic index.	Number of times in which cephalic index exceeded 80.
Badagas	40	71·7	
Muppas	24	72·3	
Tiyans	60	72·8	1 (80·3)
Pallis	40	72·9	
Kādirs	23	73	
Todas	25	73·3	
Ambattans ..	29	73·4	
Cherumans ..	60	73·4	2 (80·1; 81·9)
Pariahs	40	73·6	
Paniyans ..	25	74	1 (81·1)
Kotas	25	74·1	
Vellālas	40	74·1	1 (81·1)
Malaiālis ..	50	74·3	1 (82·8)
Malasars ..	23	74·5	
Kammālans ..	40	75	5 (80·1; 80·1; 80·2; 80·6; 81·5)
Kurubas ..	25	75·8	2 (80·1; 82·1)
Irulas	25	75·8	1 (80·9)
Kongas	20	77	2 (80·3; 81·7)
Koravas	25	77·5	3 (82·4; 83·7; 83·7)
	639	74·1	19 (max. 83·7).

THE DRAVIDIAN PROBLEM.

THE manifold views, which have been brought forward as to the origin and place in nature, of the indigenous population of Southern India, are scattered so widely in books, manuals, and reports, that it will be convenient, not only for my own purpose hereafter, but for the purpose of those interested in, or urged by the University syllabus into a pseudo-interest in the subject of South Indian ethnology, if I bring together the evidence derived from sundry authoritative sources.

The original name for the Dravidian family, it may be pointed out, was Tamulic, but the term Dravidian was substituted by Bishop Caldwell, in order that the designation Tamil might be reserved for the language of that name. Drávida is the adjectival form of Dravida, the Sanskrit name for the people occupying the south of the Indian Peninsula (the Deccan of European writers), and Tamil is merely another form of Dravida.

Accepting, with one small addition (Máhl, the mother-tongue of the Natives of Minicoy Island), the classification of Bishop Caldwell, Mr. H. A. Stuart, Census Commissioner, 1891, gives the following list of the Dravidian languages and their dialects, with the numbers of those who returned each :—

Language.	Dialect.	Total.
Tamil ..	Tamil ..	14,076,989
	Yerukala or Korava ..	37,536
	Irula	1,614
	Kasuva ..	316
Telugu ..	.. .. ..	13,653,674
Malayálam	.. .. ..	2,688,332
Máhl ..	.. .. ..	3,167
Canarese ..	Canarese ..	1,445,650
	Badaga ..	30,656
	Kurumba ..	3,742
Tulu ..	Tulu	461,176
	Koraga ..	1,868
	Bellara ..	668
Khond ..	.. .. ..	190,893

Language.	Dialect.	Total.
Gond ..	Gond	6,694
	Gotte	353
	Kóya	36,503
Tóda ..	.. .. ..	736
Kôta ..	.. .. ..	1,201
Kodagu ..	.. .. ..	947

According to Haeckel[1] three of the twelve species of Man—the Dravidas (Deccans; Sinhalese) Nubians, and Mediterranese (Caucasians, Basque, Semites, Indo-Germanic tribes)—"agree in several characteristics, which seem to establish a close relationship between them, and to distinguish them from the remaining species. The chief of these characteristics is the strong development of the beard, which, in all other species, is either entirely wanting, or but very scanty. The hair of their heads is in most cases more or less curly. Other characteristics also seem to favour our classing them in one main group of curly-haired men (Euplocomi). At present the primæval species, Homo Dravida, is only represented by the Deccan tribes in the southern part of Hindustan, and by the neighbouring inhabitants of the mountains on the north-east of Ceylon. But, in earlier times, this race seems to have occupied the whole of Hindustan, and to have spread even further. It shows, on the one hand, traits of relationship to the Australians and Malays; on the other to the Mongols and Mediterranese. Their skin is either of a light or dark brown colour; in some tribes of a yellowish brown, in others almost black brown. The hair of their heads is, as in Mediterranese, more or less curled; never quite smooth, like that of the Euthycomi, nor actually woolly, like that of the Ulotrichi. The strong development of the beard is also like that of the Mediterranese. The oval form of face seems partly to be akin to that of the Malays, partly to that of the Mediterranese. Their forehead is generally high, their nose prominent and narrow, their lips slightly protruding. Their language is now very much mixed with Indo-Germanic elements, but seems to have been originally derived from a very peculiar primæval language."

In the chapter devoted to 'Migration and Distribution of Organisms,' Haeckel, in referring to the continual changing of the distribution of land and water on the surface of

---

[1] 'History of Creation.'

the earth, says: "The Indian Ocean formed a continent, which extended from the Sunda Islands along the southern coast of Asia to the east coast of Africa. This large continent of former times Sclater has called Lemuria, from the monkey-like animals which inhabited it, and it is at the same time of great importance from being the probable cradle of the human race. The important proof, which Wallace has furnished by the help of chronological facts, that the present Malayan Archipelago consists in reality of two completely different divisions, is particularly interesting. The western division, the Indo-Malayan Archipelago, comprising the large islands of Borneo, Java, and Sumatra, was formerly connected by Malacca with the Asiatic continent, and probably also with the Lemurian continent just mentioned. The eastern division, on the other hand, the Austro-Malayan Archipelago, comprising Celebes, the Moluccas, New Guinea, Solomon's Islands, etc., was formerly directly connected with Australia."

On the evidence of the very close affinities between the plants and animals in Africa and India at a very remote period, Mr. R. D. Oldham concludes that there was once a continuous stretch of dry land connecting South Africa and India. "In some deposits," he says [Man. Geol. Ind.] "found resting upon the Karoo beds on the coast of Natal, 22 out of 35 species of Mollusca and Echinodermata collected and specifically identified, are identical with forms found in the cretaceous beds of Southern India, the majority being Trichinopoli species. From the cretaceous rocks of Madagascar six species of cretaceous fossils were examined by Mr. R. B. Newton in 1889, of which three are also found in the Ariyalur group [Southern India]. The South African beds are clearly coast or shallow water deposits, like those of India. The great similarity of forms certainly suggests continuity of coast line between the two regions, and thus supports the view that the land connection between South Africa and India, already shown to have existed in both the lower and upper Gondwána periods, was continued into cretaceous times."

It is worthy of note that Haeckel defines the nose of the Dravidian as a prominent and narrow organ. For Mr. Risley [2] lays down that, in the Dravidian type, the nose is thick and broad, and the formula expressing the proportionate dimension (nasal index) is higher than in any known

---

[2] 'Tribes and Castes of Bengal.'

PL. XXXIII

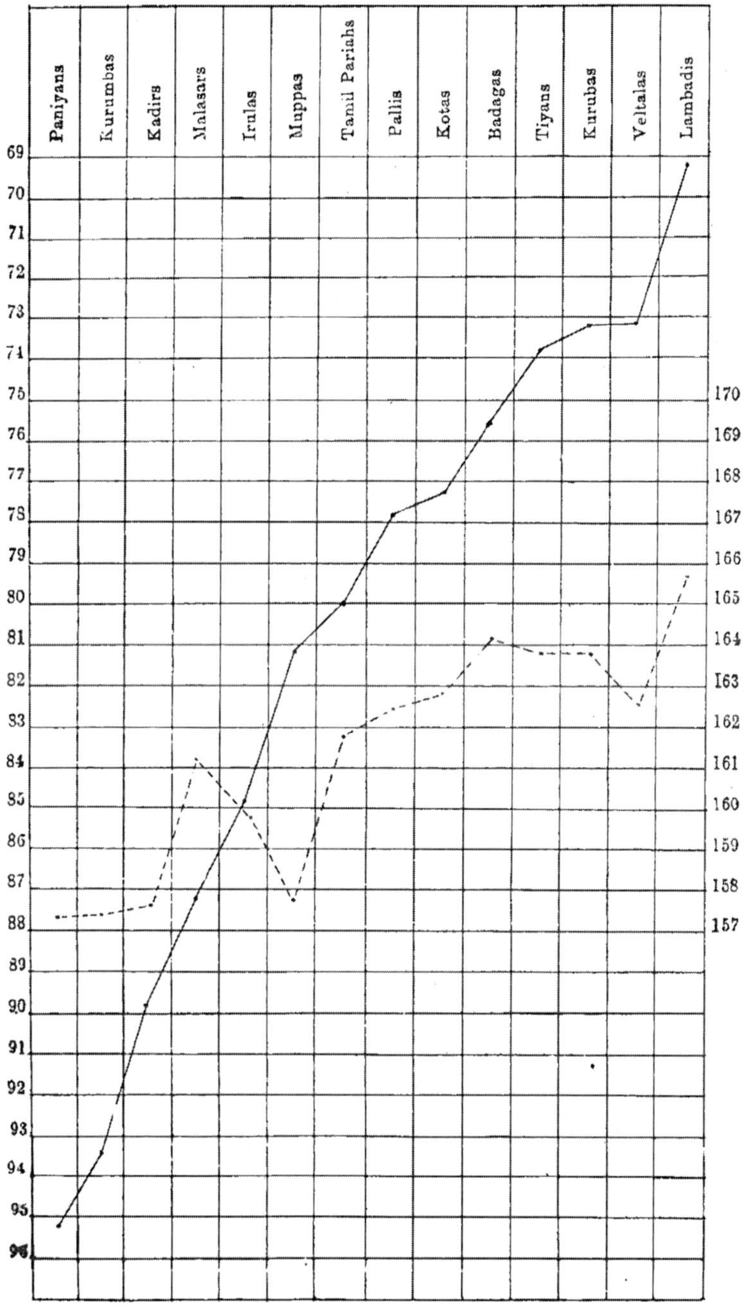

Photo-Print., Survey Office, Madras

race, except the Negro; and that the typical Dravidian, as represented by the Mále Pahária (nasal index 94·5), has a nose as broad in proportion to its length as the Negro, while this feature in the Aryan group can fairly bear comparison with the noses of sixty-eight Parisians, measured by Topinard, which gave an average of 69·4. In this connection a study of table XXXIII, based on the results of my measurements, is not without interest. In this table I have brought together, for the purpose of comparison, the nasal indices (lined) and stature (dotted) of jungle tribes, Dravidians of the plains, and the nomad Lambādis, who speak an Aryan language. The table demonstrates very clearly a progressive and unbroken series ranging from the typical jungle-man, whom I may term archi-Dravidian, dark-skinned, short of stature, and platyrhine, through various mixed Dravidian classes of the plains, to the comparatively fair-skinned, leptorhine Lambádi. The influence of crossing through many ages on the Dravidian type is referred to hereafter. But I may draw attention to the indisputable fact that it is to the lasting influence of a broad nosed ancestor, such as is represented at the present day by the jungle tribes, that the very high nasal index and short stature of many of the modern inhabitants of Southern India (Dravidian, Muhammadan, Eurasian, and 'Aryan') must be attributed. Viewed in the light of this remark, the connection between the following mixed collection of individuals, all of very dark colour, short of stature, and with nasal index exceeding 90, calls for no further explanation :—

	Stature.	Nasal Index.
	CM.	CM.
Saiyad Muhammadan	160	91·3
Vellāla	154·8	91·6
Muppa	151·2	91·9
Malaiāli	158·8	92·5
Konga	157	92·7
Kādir	156·5	92·7
Pattar Brāhman	157·6	92·9
Kurumba	159·6	93·2
Malasar	149·2	95
Smārta Brāhman	159	95·1
Palli	157·8	95·1
Irula	155·4	95·1
Paniyan	157·8	95·1
Irula	158·6	100
Tamil Pariah	160	105
Paniyan	158·8	105·3
Kādir	148·6	110·5

By Huxley[3] the races of mankind are divided into two primary divisions : the Ulotrichi with crisp or woolly hair (Negros ; Negritos), and the Leiotrichi with smooth hair. And the Dravidians are included in the Australioid group of the Leiotrichi "with dark skin, hair, and eyes, wavy black hair, and eminently long, prognathous skulls, with well-developed brow ridges, who are found in Australia and in the Dekhan." There is, in the collection of the Royal College of Surgeons' Museum, an exceedingly interesting 'Hindu' skull from Southern India, conspicuously dolichocephalic, and with highly developed superciliary ridges. Some of the recorded measurements of this skull are as follows :—

Length	19·6 CM.
Breadth	13·2 ,,
Cephalic index	67·3
Nasal height	4·8 CM.
,, breadth	2·5 ,,
,, index	52·1

Another 'Hindu' skull, in the collection of the Madras Museum, with similar marked development of the superciliary ridges, has the following measurements :—

Cephalic length	18·4 CM.
,, breadth	13·8 ,,
,, index	75
Nasal height	4·9 CM.
,, breadth	2·1 ,,
,, index	42·8

I was quite recently much impressed by a Tamil Pariah, who by a happy chance came before me for examination, and of whom the following measurements were recorded :—

Height	161·8 CM.
Cephalic length	19·7 ,,
,, breadth	14·2 ,,
,, index	72·1
Nasal height	4·4 CM.
,, breadth	4·2 ,,
,, index	95·5 ,,

With his prominent superciliary ridges and brushy eyebrows, hairy chest, abdomen, back, arms, and legs, and long, dolichocephalic head, this man might, save for his broad nose, have passed for a Toda of short stature, such as is frequently met with among the Toda community.

---

[3] 'Anatomy of Vertebrated Animals.'

I am unable to subscribe to the general prognathism of the Dravidian tribes of Southern India, though there are some notable exceptions. Wavy and curly black hair are common types, but I have seen no head of hair to which the term woolly could be correctly applied.

By Flower and Lydekker [4] a white division of Man, called the Caucasian or Eurafrican, is made to include Huxley's Xanthochroi (blonde type) and Melanochroi (black hair and eyes, and skin of almost all shades from white to black); and the Melanochroi are said to "comprise the greater majority of the inhabitants of Southern Europe, Northern Africa, and South West Asia, and consist mainly of the Aryan, Semitic, and Hamitic families. The Dravidians of India, the Veddahs of Ceylon, and probably the Ainos of Japan, and the Maoutze of China, also belong to this race, which may have contributed something to the mixed character of some tribes of Indo-China [5] and the Polynesian islands, and have given at least the characters of the hair to the otherwise Negroid inhabitants of Australia. In Southern India they are largely mixed with a Negrito element, and in Africa, where their habitat becomes coterminous with that of the Negroes, numerous cross-races have sprung up between them all along the frontier line. The ancient Egyptians were nearly pure Melanochroi."

In describing the 'Hindu type,' Topinard [6] divides the population of the Indian peninsula into three strata, viz., the Black, the Mongolian, and the Aryan. "The remnants of the first," he says, "are at the present time shut up in the mountains of Central India under the name of Bhils, Mahairs, Ghonds, and Khonds; and in the south under that of Yenādis, Maravers, Kurumbas, Veddahs, etc. Its primitive characters, apart from its black colour and low stature, are difficult to discover, but it is to be noticed that travellers do not speak of woolly hair in India. The second has spread over the plateaux of Central India by two lines of way, one to the north-east, the other to the north-west. The remnants of the first invasion are seen in the Dravidian or Tamil tribes, and those of the second in the Jhats. The third more recent, and more important as to quality than as to

---

[4] Mammals, living and extinct.

[5] *Vide* Madras Museum Bull. No. 2, Vol. II, p. 119, sq: also Tooth-chipping, Kādirs, antea, p. 143.

[6] 'Anthropology.' Translation.

number, was the Aryan." In speaking further of the Australian type, characterised by a combination of smooth hair with Negroid features, Topinard states that "it is clear that the Australians might very well be the result of the cross between one race with smooth hair from some other place, and a really Negro and autochthonous race. The opinions expressed by Huxley are in harmony with this hypothesis. He says the Australians are identical with the ancient inhabitants of the Deccan. The features of the present blacks in India, and the characters which the Dravidian and Australian languages have in common, tend to assimilate them. The existence of the boomerang [7] in the two countries, and some remnants of caste in Australia, help to support the opinion. But the state of extreme misery of the inferior tribes may equally explain some of the physical differences which they present. Woolly hair appears now to be but seldom seen. A few examples have been noticed in the York peninsula and the north-west point, which might be accounted for by the immigration of Papuans from New Guinea, and in the south by the passage over to the other side of Behring's Straits of some Tasmanians to the continent. On the other hand, on studying the Australian skull, we notice tolerably-marked differences of type, and it is certain that the Polynesians landed at some period or other in the north-west, and the Malays in the north-east. Lastly, if the Australians are thorough Hindoos as regards their hair, they are Melanesians, or, if you will, new Hebrideans, new Caledonian Negroes, in every other respect. The question may, therefore, be left. We are still in ignorance as to whether the present Australian race took its origin on the spot, with the characters that we admit as belonging to it, or whether, on the contrary, it was altogether constituted in Asia, or whether it is a cross race, and, in that case, of what elements it is composed. Those which we might consider in India as of the same race are the Bhils, Ghonds, Khonds, Mahairs, Varalis, Mundas; Veddahs, Yanādis, and Maravers of the coast of Coromandel. Among the Todas of the Nilgherries, and, strangely enough, farther on towards the north,

---

[7] *Vide* Oppert, Journal, Madras Literature Society, Vol. XXV. Boomerangs are used by the Tamil Maravars and Kallans when hunting deer. The Madras Museum collection contains three (two ivory, one wooden) from the Tanjore armoury. In the arsenal of the Pudukkóttai Rája a stock of wooden boomerangs is always kept. Their name in Tamil is valai tadi (bent stick). When thrown, a whirling motion is imparted to the weapon, which causes it to return to the place from which it was thrown. The Natives are well acquainted with this peculiar fact.

among certain of the Ainus, two of the fundamental Australian traits are met with; namely, the very projecting superciliary arch, and the abundant hair over the whole body. In the same Nilgherry hills, in the desired conditions for concealing the remnants of ancient races, two tribes, the Irulas and Kurumbas, especially afford matter for reflection." And to these must be added the Paniyans, Kādirs, Sholigas, and other jungle tribes, in the investigation of which I am at present interested. Finally, Topinard points out, as a somewhat important piece of evidence, that, in the west, about Madagascar, and the point of Aden in Africa, there are black tribes with smooth hair, or, at all events, large numbers of individuals who have it, mingled particularly among the Somālis and the Gallas, in the region where M. Broca has an idea that some dark and not Negro race, now extinct, once existed. He also refers, in a sketch of ethnic characters, to the institution of caste, which is regularly established in India, and found in Australia in a rudimentary state, as well as in some parts of the Malay Peninsula.

At the last meeting of the British Association, Mr. W. Crooke gave expression to the view that the Dravidians represent an emigration from the African continent, and discounted the theory that the Aryans drove the 'aboriginal' inhabitants into the jungles with the suggestion that the Aryan invasion was more social than racial, viz., that what India borrowed from the Aryans was manners and customs. According to this view it must have been reforming 'aborigines' who gained the ascendancy in India, rather than new comers; and those of the 'aborigines' who clung to their old ways got left behind in the struggle for existence.

In an article devoted to the Australians, Professor R. Semon writes as follows[8]: "We must, without hesitation, presume that the ancestors of the Australians stood, at the time of their immigration to the continent, on a lower rung of culture than their living representatives of to-day. They must have brought with them their only domestic animal, the Dingo dog, for they could not have found it in Australia, which contains marsupials, but no placental mammals. Whence, and in what manner the immigration took place, it is difficult to determine. In the neighbouring quarter of the globe there lives no race, which is closely related to the Australians. Their nearest neighbours, the Papuans of New

---

[8] Die Natur. No. 20, 17 May, 1896.

Guinea, the Malays of the Sunda Islands, and the Maoris of New Zealand, stand in no close relationship to them. On the other hand, we find further away, among the Dravidian aborigines of India, types which remind us forcibly of the Australians in their anthropological characters. In drawing attention to the resemblance of the hill-tribes of the Deccan to the Australians, Huxley says: ‘An ordinary cooly, such as one can see among the sailors of any newly-arrived East Indian vessel, would, if stripped, pass very well for an Australian, although the skull and lower jaw are generally less coarse.’ Huxley here goes a little too far in his accentuation of the similarity of type. We are, however, undoubtedly confronted with a number of characters—skull formation, features, wavy curled hair—in common between the Australians and Dravidians, which gain in importance from the fact that, by the researches of Norris, Bleek, and Caldwell, a number of points of resemblance between the Australian and Dravidian languages have been discovered, and this despite the fact that the homes of the two races are so far apart, and that a number of races are wedged in between them, whose languages have no relationship whatever to either the Dravidian or Australian.

“There is much that speaks in favour of the view that the Australians and Dravidians sprang from a common main branch of the human race. According to the laborious researches of Paul and Fritz Sarasin, the Veddas of India and Ceylon, whom one might call pre-Dravidians, would represent an off-shoot from this main stem. When they branched off, they stood on a very low rung of development, and seem to have made hardly any progress worth mentioning. The remarkable ainus of Japan, and the ‘Khmers’ and Chams of Cambogia seem to be scattered off-shoots of the Dravidian-Australian main branch.

“The Caucasians have probably sprung from the Dravidians, and we, Europeans, should, therefore, have to look upon the low savages of Australia as relations, very distant it is true, but yet nearer related to us than Negroes, Malays, and Mongols. It has been pointed out by several observers that the features of the Australians, with all their ugliness and coarseness, frequently remind one of low types of the Caucasian features. To those who regard it as a degradation to the human race, when science draws the conclusion that man has sprung from the brute inhabitants of the earth, and stands in close relationship with the ape-family, the reflection will be also unpleasant that, among the human species, the

Caucasians, who, for several thousand years, have progressed so splendidly and so far, have as near relations the nomad savages of Australia, and the Veddahs who are designated monkeys in the Hindu legend. To science the only consideration is whether the conclusions are correct, not whether they are according to the personal taste of the few. It is difficult to understand how there can be anything degrading in belonging to a race, which, from crude beginnings, has worked itself up to the still rather modest level of modern Caucasian civilisation through stages, which are represented by the Veddahs, Australians, and Dravidians. On the other hand, there is something sublime in the conviction that the development of the human race, both bodily and intellectual, is as yet unfinished, and that our present state of civilisation, burthened with innumerable imperfections, will be regarded by our descendants in the far future as a long surpassed one, as derisively as we now look down on the state of civilisation and culture of the Australians and Veddahs."

In dealing with the Australian problem, Mr. A. H. Keane [9] refers to the time when Australia formed almost continuous land with the African continent, and to its accessibility on the north and north-west to primitive migration both from India and Papuasia. "That such migrations," he says, "took place, scarcely admits of a doubt, and the Rev. John Mathew [10] concludes that the continent was first occupied by a homogeneous branch of the Papuan race either from New Guinea or Malaysia, and that these first arrivals, to be regarded as true aborigines, passed into Tasmania, which at that time probably formed continuous land with Australia. Thus the now extinct Tasmanians would represent the primitive type, which, in Australia, became modified, but not effaced, by crossing with later immigrants, chiefly from India. These are identified, as they have been by other ethnologists, with the Dravidians, and the writer remarks that 'although the Australians are still in a state of savagery, and the Dravidians of India have been for many ages a people civilized in a great measure, and possessed of literature, the two peoples are affiliated by deeply-marked characteristics in their social system as shown by the boomerang, which unless locally evolved, must have been introduced from India. But the variations in the physical characters of the Natives appear to be too great to be accounted for by a single graft; hence

---

[9] 'Ethnology,' 1896.
[10] Proc. R. Soc. N. S. Wales, XXIII, part III.

Malays also are introduced from the Eastern Archipelago, which would explain both the straight hair in many districts, and a number of pure Malay words in several of the native languages." Dealing later with the ethnical relations of the Dravidas, Mr. Keane says that "although they preceded the Aryan-speaking Hindûs, they are not the true aborigines of the Deccan, for they were themselves preceded by dark peoples, probably of aberrant Negrito type. They are usually regarded as a Mongoloid people, who entered India from the north-west, leaving on the route the Brahûis of Baluchistan, whose language shows some remote resemblance to Dravidian. But at present the type cannot be called Mongolic; it scarcely differs from the average Hindu, except in some districts, where it has been somewhat modified by contact with the Kolarians and dark aborigines . . . . It would seem that the position of the Indian Dravidas is somewhat analogous to the Caucasic type, and both have accepted Aryan culture, while preserving intact their non-Aryan speech."

Placing the Dravidians with the Negrito and Negrito-Papuan families of the Negrito section of the Indo-Melanesian branch of the Negro or Ethiopian trunk, de Quatrefages [11] lays special stress on the influence of crossing (métissage), while recognising that the Kurumbas, and other jungle tribes, have preserved their purity of blood and ethnological characters more or less completely. Which purity of blood and preservation of characters are unhappily commencing to degenerate as the result of the opening up of the jungles for tea and coffee estates, and the contact with more civilised tribes and races, black and white. "In the Gangetic peninsula," de Quatrefages says, "and the whole of India to the foot of the Himālayas, this crossing is carried out on an immense scale. All the so-called Dravidian population, and many others known by different names, indicate, by their physical characters, the presence of a black ethnological element. Documents of all sorts, photographs, skulls, etc., testify that this element is almost constantly Negrito. The rôle played in this admixture by the three fundamental types is very unequal, and varies according to the country which one examines. But, wherever Dravidians exist, the Blacks constitute the foundation of the half-breed race. Most frequently it is the yellow race, represented by the Thibetans, which has united with them. The white race only ranks in

[11] 'Histoire générale des Races Humaines.'

the third line. The legend of Ráma permits us to allow that the Aryans, on their arrival in Southern India, did not disdain to contract political alliances with these little black people.[12] In India most of the Dravidian tribes appear to owe their characters to an admixture of black and yellow. In the valleys of the Upper Bráhmaputra, and many other localities, the influence of Thibetan races is very marked. The general type has been altered by crossing with Bráhmanical Aryans, and other white races. It is this *ensemble* of half-caste races, all having Negrito blood in common, possibly also some traces of Australian blood, that I propose to designate by the name of Dravidians. In a region invaded a thousand times since the most remote times, many of the peoples cannot but have been profoundly modified from an ethnological point of view, though preserving their languages; while others forgot the language of their fathers, whose essential physical characters they, however, preserved."

Turning now to writers, who have spent a great part of their lives in the Madras Presidency. In the 'Manual of the Administration' of this Presidency, Dr. C. Maclean writes as follows: "The history proper of the south of India may be held to begin with the Hindu dynasties formed by a more or less intimate admixture of the Aryan and Dravidian systems of Government. But, prior to that, three stages of historical knowledge are recognizable; first, as to such aboriginal period as there may have been prior to the Dravidian; secondly, as to the period when the Aryans had begun to impose their religion and customs upon the Dravidians, but the time indicated by the early dynasties had not yet been reached. Geology and natural history alike make it certain that, at a time within the bounds of human knowledge, Southern India did not form part of Asia. A large southern continent, of which this country once formed part, has ever been assumed as necessary to account for the different circumstances. The Sanscrit Pooranic writers, the Ceylon Boodhists, and the local traditions of the West Coast, all indicate a great disturbance of the point of the Peninsula and Ceylon within

---

[12] How great must have been the influence of hybridisation on the population of Southern India, when carried on through ages, is accentuated by reference to the practical outcome of only a few centuries of contact between Europeans and Natives, which has resulted in the creation and establishment of a fertile half-breed race, numbering, according to the Madras Presidency Census return, 1891, 26,648—*vide* Madras Museum Bulletin, Vol. II, No. 2, 1898.

recent times.[13] Investigations in relation to race show it to be by no means impossible that Southern India was once the passage-ground, by which the ancient progenitors of Northern and Mediterranean races proceeded to the parts of the globe which they now inhabit. In this part of the world, as in others, antiquarian remains show the existence of peoples, who used successively implements of unwrought stone, of wrought stone, and of metal fashioned in the most primitive manner.[14] These tribes have also left cairns and stone circles indicating burial places. It has been usual to set these down as earlier than Dravidian. But the hill Coorumbar of the Pulmanair plateau, who are only a detached portion of the oldest known Tamulian population, erect dolmens to this day. The sepulchral urns of Tinnevelly may be earlier than Dravidian, or they may be Dravidian. It has been stated that the wild tribes of Southern India are physiologically of an earlier type than the Dravidian tribes. This position has been found not to be proved, the conclusions being of a negative nature. The evidence of the grammatical structure of language is to be relied on as a clearly distinctive mark of a population, but, from this point of view, it appears that there are more signs of the great lapse of time than of previous populations. The grammar of the south of India is exclusively Dravidian, and bears no trace of ever having been anything else. The hill, forest, and Pariah tribes use the Dravidian forms of grammar and inflection . . . . The Dravidians, a very primeval race,[15] take a by no means low place in the conjectural history of humanity. They have affinities with the Australian aborigines, which would probably connect their earliest origin with that people. But they have emerged

---

[13] "It is evident that, during much of the tertiary period, Ceylon and South India were bounded on the north by a considerable extent of sea, and probably formed part of an extensive southern continent, or great island. The very numerous and remarkable cases of affinity with Malaya require, however, some closer approximation to these islands, which probably occurred at a later period." Wallace, 'Geographical Distribution of Animals.'

[14] *Vide* Breeks' 'Primitive Tribes and Monuments of the Nílgiris'; Phillips 'Tumuli of the Salem district'; Rea, 'Prehistoric Burial Places in Southern India'; and the Madras Museum collection. Mr. R. Bruce Foote has, I am happy to say, in hand the preparation of a catalogue raisonné of his magnificent collection of Indian 'Prehistoric Implements, &c.'

[15] Sir John Evans, in his Presidential address at the meeting of the British Association, 1897, referred to the possibility of Southern India being 'the cradle of the human race.'

from the lower type, and acquired characteristics putting them at no great distance in the physiological scale from the later developed Semitic and Caucasian races. As now known, they are not straight-haired like the Malays and Mongolians, but more or less curly-haired, like both of the last named. The theory that they came to India from without, passing over the north-west boundary, and through Scinde, does not rest on sufficient evidence. If the Dravidians moved into India at all, it may be more reasonably conjectured that they came from the south or the east.

"About 2,000 or 3,000 years B.C., perhaps at the beginning of what has been styled the Kaliyog, or 3101 B.C., the Sanscrit-speaking Aryans came into India from their original home at the sources of the Oxus in the neighbourhood of Bokhara, where they had resided till the period when the Iranic branch of the tribe went to the south-east. The Indic branch of the Aryans advanced down the basins of the Indus and the Ganges to the estuary of both rivers; and then proceeded by different routes into the lower and middle range of the Himālaya, up the valley of Assam, down the Coast of the Bay of Bengal as far as Chicacole in the Ganjám district, across the rivers Nerbudda and Mahanuddy into Central India, and along the West Coast as far south as Goa. Another portion of the same branch went by sea to Ceylon, and laid the foundation of the Singhalese civilization."

Adopting a novel classification, Dr. Maclean, in assuming that there are no living representatives in Southern India of any race of a wholly pre-Dravidian character, sub-divides the Dravidians into pre-Tamulian and Tamulian, to designate two branches of the same family, one older or less civilised than the other.

Bishop Caldwell[16], in summing up the question whether the forest tribes, the lower castes, and the so-called "outcasts" which speak the Dravidian languages, are of the same origin and of the same race as the Dravidians of the higher castes, expresses his opinion that the supposition that the lower castes in the Dravidian provinces belong to a different race from the higher, appears to him untenable. "It seems," he says, "safer to hold that all the indigenous tribes, who were found by the Aryans in Southern India, belonged substantially to one and the same race. It is probable enough that the Dravidians were broken up into tribes before the Aryan

[16] 'Comparative Grammar of the Dravidian Languages.'

immigration, and that the distinctions, not only of richer and poorer, but also of master and slave, had already come into existence among them. Those distinctions may have formed the foundation of the caste system, which their Brahmanical civilisers built up, and which was moulded by degrees into an exact counterpart of the caste system of Northern India."

In his 'Original Inhabitants of Bharatavarsha or India,' Dr. G. Oppert contends that the names of many Dravidian tribes are derived from the Dravidian roots 'mal' and 'ku' both meaning a mountain. He thus traces an ultimate philological identity between the names of tribes and castes scattered throughout India, such as the Málas, Malayális, and Maravars; the Kois, Khonds, Gonds, Koravas, Kurumbas, Kodagus; and very many others. The relation of the existing hill and jungle tribes to the inhabitants of the plains is discussed in the Transactions of the Ethnological Society[17] by Mr. J. Crawfurd, who there challenges the theory which supposes the rude mountaineers to be the sole 'aborigines' of India, while it imagines the civilised inhabitants to be intrusive strangers, who, in a remote antiquity, invaded India, conquered it, and settled in it under the imposed names of Aryans for Northern and Turanian for Southern India. "To suppose," Mr. Crawfurd writes, "so great and fertile a region of the earth, and one consequently so favourable to the promotion of an early civilisation, to have been, within the historical period, destitute of any other original inhabitants than the few rude tribes now confined to its least favourable localities, until it came to be peopled by immigrant strangers from remote countries, is contrary to what is known to be the case, in all other portions of the globe. For my own part, I am satisfied that both the mountaineers and the inhabitants of the open plains and valleys are alike Natives of the soil and of the same race, allowance being made for such varieties of type as are found to exist in other large regions of the earth. . . . It is an opinion very generally entertained by Indian ethnologists that the races which they suppose to be the aborigines of India partake of a Negro character, in contradistinction to the civilised people of the low-lands; but this is a notion, for which I am satisfied there is no ground whatever. Throughout the continent of India no Negro or Negroid race has

---

[17] Vol. VI, 1868—The supposed Aborigines of India as distinguished from its Civilised Inhabitants.

ever been found to exist. Wherever Negritos or Negroid races exist, their presence is unmistakably pronounced, as in the case of the Andaman Islands."

In an article entitled, "Caste and Colour" Mr. C. Johnston (Calcutta Review, 1895) divides the people of India on a simple colour basis into four or five principal types, with a series of intermediate types gradually melting into each other. These principal types are—

1. Fair, almost white. Brāhman.
2. Red. Râjput.
3. Yellow. Purest examples, the Kocch and Santâli in lower Bengal, and the Sâvara in Madras.
4. Black, or nearly black. Dravidian.

"We must," Mr. Johnston says, "content ourselves for the present with saying that it seems fairly certain that there is a great ethnical family in Southern India, distinguished primarily by black or almost black skin; that this ethnical family cannot number less than a hundred million individuals; and that this great ethnical family is not related to any other ethnical family in Asia, but is isolated and distinct; so that we must seek for the ethnical kindred of the black Dravidian, if such kindred exist, outside Asia altogether, in some direction at present undermined. . . . It has for a long time been conceded that the fourth caste of the Brāhmanical polity was drawn from this black race."

Conversion Table.

In.	Cm.	Ft.	In.	Cm.
	2·54	1	0	30·48
2	5·08	1	6	45·72
3	7·62	2	0	60·96
4	10·16	2	6	76·20
5	12·70	3	0	91·44
6	15·24	3	6	106·68
7	17·78	4	0	121·92
8	20·32	4	6	137·16
9	22·86	5	0	152·40
10	25·40	5	6	167·64
11	27·94	6	0	182·88
12	30·48	6	6	198·12

AGENTS FOR THE SALE OF GOVERNMENT PUBLICATIONS.

IN INDIA.

Newman & Co., Calcutta.

Thacker, Spink & Co., Calcutta.

Higginbotham & Co., Mount Road, Madras.

Thacker & Co. (Limited), Bombay.

E. Seymour Hale, Bombay.

IN LONDON.

E. A. Arnold, 37, Bedford Street, Strand, W.C.

Constable & Co., 2, Whitehall Gardens, S.W.

Sampson Low, Marston & Co., St. Dunstan's House, Fetter Lane, E.C.

P. S. King & Son, 9, Bridge Street, Westminster, S.W.

Luzac & Co., 46, Great Russell Street, W.C.

Kegan Paul, Trench, Trübner & Co., Charing Cross Road, W.C.

B. Quaritch, 15, Piccadilly, W.

ON THE CONTINENT.

Friedländer & Sohn, 11, Carlstrasse, Berlin.

Otto Harrassowitz, Leipzig.

Karl W. Hiersemann, Leipzig.

Ernest Leroux, 28, Rue Bonaparte, Paris.

Martinus Nijhoff, The Hague, Holland.